Praise for Martin Newman's *R(*

'A masterclass in success measurement and blueprint for transformational change! A must-read for today's leaders and operators. Martin sets out defining metrics for sustainable growth with true examples of brands who are embracing them and the consequences when you don't measure the right things. Thought-provoking, practical and powerful, this book can really help anyone committed to building a thriving business. A refreshing approach to modern business that works across different sectors from banking to retail to hospitality.'
—**Nadine Neatrour, CMO Gordon Ramsey**

'Insightful, practical and actionable – this book is a must-read for anyone looking to develop deep and lasting consumer relationships.'
—**Fran Minogue, Managing Partner, Clarity**

'*ROI Reimagined* will make you rethink how value is created in business. It goes far beyond the numbers to get to the heart of how meaningful value is created. A must-read for any leader navigating the complexity of today's world.'
—**Debbie Hewitt, Chair, The FA**

'This book is essential reading for retailers who want to stay relevant and thrive. It's a wake-up call you'll be glad you answered.'
—**Dame Anya Hindmarch**

'Fresh, practical and purpose-driven – *ROI Reimagined* redefines how we measure success, moving beyond conventional metrics to focus on what truly drives long-term value. A must-read for leaders who want to put customers and culture at the heart of growth.'
—**Scott Barton, Managing Director, Corporate and institutional banking, Lloyds Banking Group**

'Martin Newman's latest book is a masterclass in customer centricity – a guaranteed return on inquisitiveness for anyone looking to deliver business results.'
—Jeremy Snape, International Coach, Sporting Edge (Former England Cricketer)

'*ROI Reimagined* is a transformative read that challenges your thinking on customer metrics and business success. It brings to life the vital role of the workforce and building trust to truly foster long-term customer relationships. With relatable case studies and actionable insights, this book is essential for anyone looking to create lasting customer value and will prepare you for the future with rapidly changing customer expectations.'
—Joanne Garland, Director, Consumer Engagement (EMEA), The LEGO Group

'Martin has successfully challenged the traditional return on investment metrics and articulated clearly how one should drive and measure success, supported by some great evidence and business examples. The customer has, and always will be, key to the success of any business, and Martin's new 11 ROIs encapsulate this theory, whilst also integrating a blend of strategic wins and long-term gains for each ROI. A great read for beginners through to established retailer leaders!'
—Nigel Oddy, CEO, American Golf

'Turning ROI on its head, Martin offers a novel, customer-focused framework that helps businesses assess whether they're on track to deliver both now and in the future. As expected from Martin, this book is packed with practical advice, along with insightful examples to learn from. A valuable and actionable guide for any business leader.'
—Eve Henrikson, SVP Trips, Booking.com

ROI
REIMAGINED

REDEFINING
BUSINESS SUCCESS

11 BOLD NEW WAYS TO MEASURE
WHAT REALLY MATTERS

MARTIN NEWMAN

First published in 2025 by
Martin Newman, in partnership with Whitefox Publishing Ltd

www.wearewhitefox.com

EU GPSR Authorised Representative
LOGOS EUROPE, 9 rue Nicolas Poussin, 17000, LA ROCHELLE, France
E-mail: Contact@logoseurope.eu

ISBN 978-1-917523-77-6
Also available as an eBook
ISBN 978-1-917523-78-3
Also available as an audiobook
ISBN 978-1-917523-79-0

Edited by Helen Wedgewood
Designed and typeset by seagulls.net
Cover design by Steve Leard

Project management by Whitefox Publishing

CONTENTS

REDEFINING BUSINESS SUCCESS: WHY, HOW AND FOR WHOM

REDEFINING SUCCESS FOR THE FUTURE OF BUSINESS

For decades, businesses have relied on outdated, transactional metrics to define success. Profit, revenue growth, Net Promoter Score (NPS) and traditional Return on Investment (ROI) have been treated as the gold standard of performance measurement.

But here's the reality: these numbers don't tell the full story.

- **Revenue and profit** can be driven by short-term gains at the expense of long-term customer loyalty.
- **NPS measures intent, not behaviour** – customers may say they'll recommend a brand, but do they stay, buy and advocate?
- **Traditional ROI focuses only on financial returns**, ignoring the customer experience, innovation, integrity and cultural impact that truly drive sustainable success.

The companies that will win in the future aren't the ones simply chasing short-term metrics. They're the ones understanding, engaging and inspiring their customers and employees in innovative ways. Amazon and Apple, for instance, have moved beyond conventional measures, prioritising seamless customer experiences, emotional connections and continuous innovation – setting them apart from competitors.

Importantly, this book is as applicable to B2B organisations as it is to consumer-facing businesses. While the examples provided often focus on consumer brands, the principles, strategies and new ROIs explored within these pages hold significant value for B2B companies as well. Whether your customers are individual consumers or other businesses, the core themes of integrity, innovation, inclusion and customer-centricity remain critical. B2B businesses, just like consumer-facing ones, benefit immensely from prioritising long-term relationship building, trust and meaningful customer engagement.

Despite this, most businesses still measure success in outdated ways. This book challenges that status quo.

WHY THIS BOOK MATTERS NOW

You are living through one of the most significant transformations in business history. Customer expectations have shifted dramatically; employee engagement has become crucial and businesses must innovate faster than ever. The traditional focus on short-term, transactional metrics is being replaced by a more holistic, customer-centric approach. Companies unable to adapt face irrelevance, while those embracing this new mindset thrive.

WHO THIS BOOK IS FOR

This book is written specifically for leaders and professionals who want to challenge conventional wisdom and build meaningful, sustainable, customer-focused businesses:

- **Executives, CEOs and senior leaders:** To redefine success beyond traditional financial metrics, embedding innovation, cultural transformation and long-term customer loyalty into their organisations.
- **Operational managers and team leaders:** To apply measurable frameworks that streamline processes, build high-performing teams and drive continuous improvement.
- **Strategy, innovation and transformation teams:** To adopt practical, relevant metrics aligned with evolving customer expectations and to foster innovation.

- **Marketing and sales professionals:** To leverage customer insights to develop impactful campaigns, personalise customer interactions and strengthen brand loyalty.
- **HR and people teams:** To embed a culture of inspiration, inclusion and integrity, ensuring employees become empowered advocates for their brand.
- **Customer experience and service teams:** To enhance customer relationships by providing effortless interactions, building trust and proactively resolving issues.
- **Consultants and board advisors:** To equip them with relevant, impactful tools for guiding businesses toward meaningful success and long-term sustainability.

THE MISSION

This book is a call to action, redefining how businesses measure and drive success. It introduces 11 new Returns on Investment (ROIs), providing deeper, actionable insights into what truly drives sustainable growth and loyalty.

It is time to rethink traditional metrics and take a new approach to measuring success that shifts the focus from simply reporting outcomes to understanding the causes behind them.

Introducing 11 new ROI metrics that emphasise customer engagement, loyalty and experience over raw transaction data. These metrics are:

1. **Return on Inspiration** – How well does your company inspire employees and customers to believe in what you do?
2. **Return on Integrity** – Are you building trust through transparency, ethics and social responsibility?
3. **Return on Inclusion** – Does your business reflect the diversity of your customers and employees?

4. **Return on Image** – Is your brand recognised for authenticity and purpose, not just marketing?
5. **Return on Intervention** – How quickly and effectively do you resolve customer issues?
6. **Return on Interaction** – Are you engaging customers across all touchpoints in meaningful ways?
7. **Return on Improvements** – Are you continuously evolving beyond transactions to provide better service and experiences?
8. **Return on Involvement** – How well do you personalise messaging and deepen customer loyalty?
9. **Return on Insight** – Are you leveraging data and customer feedback to make strategic, experience-driven decisions?
10. **Return on Innovation** – How quickly do you adapt, improve and bring new ideas to market?
11. **Return on Integration** – Is your entire business aligned and working toward a common North Star goal?

This book is not just a guide, it's a movement. It's a call to redefine success and build businesses that customers love, employees are proud of and competitors struggle to keep up with. This book is designed to:

- **Challenge the status quo.** It's time to move beyond vanity metrics and focus on what truly drives business success.
- **Provide a clear, actionable framework.** The 11 new ROIs are designed to be measurable, practical and applicable across industries.
- **Help businesses create meaningful impact.** A company's success should not just be measured in numbers but in its ability to inspire, innovate and integrate.
- **Build the next generation of business leaders.** Leaders who focus on customer value, cultural integrity and long-term sustainability will shape the future.

The companies that adopt these new ROIs today will be the market leaders of tomorrow.

HOW TO GET THE MOST FROM THIS BOOK

Each chapter is designed to help you apply the principles of the different ROIs to your organisation with a clear and consistent format to ensure the ideas are actionable:

- **Introducing the ROI:** Familiarise yourself with the core concept of the ROI and how it can be applied in your organisation.
- **Leveraging the ROI:** Understand the key goals of the chapter and why the ROI is important for your organisation's long-term success.
- **The ROI in action:** Learn from real-life case studies that demonstrate how companies have successfully implemented these ROI strategies.
- **How to measure success within the ROI:** Identify key metrics to track the impact of your efforts and ensure measurable results over time.
- **Implementing the ROI:** Learn how to implement both quick wins and long-term strategies, while engaging all levels of your organisation to embed the ROI into your culture.
- **The lasting impact of the ROI:** Understand the long-term benefits of implementing the ROI, including improved operations, employee engagement and customer relationships.
- **Take action:** Apply the principles of the ROI in your organisation by starting with immediate actions and planning for long-term success to drive measurable impact.

The 11 ROI chapters follow this structured approach to provide a comprehensive understanding of each metric and its strategic importance. The final two chapters take a broader, action-focused approach, equipping you to strategically prioritise and effectively embed these ROIs within your organisation's culture, leadership and long-term vision.

To effectively leverage these insights:

- Start with the biggest gaps in your business. Review the 11 ROIs and prioritise the ones where your organisation is struggling the most.
- Use the measurement frameworks to benchmark progress. Define success metrics early and track improvements over time.
- Leverage cross-functional collaboration. These ROIs are not siloed – apply them across departments to create a unified approach to success.
- Embed these principles into company culture. The real value comes from sustained, long-term adoption, not just quick fixes.

By using this book as a guide, reference tool and strategic playbook, you can drive lasting change that strengthens customer trust, improves employee engagement and creates a business built for the future.

The most successful companies of tomorrow will measure differently. It's time to redefine success metrics and build a resilient, customer-focused business that competitors strive to emulate.

WHY TRADITIONAL METRICS FALL SHORT

I n the world of consumer-facing businesses – whether in retail, automotive, hospitality, travel, entertainment or financial services – success has traditionally been defined by a narrow set of numbers. Companies track and report on the metrics that reveal what has happened: sales, profits, conversion rates, average order values, units per transaction, customer retention rates and the like. These indicators are celebrated and scrutinised in performance reviews, annual reports and strategic meetings. But they represent only the result, leaving out the richer story of what drove these outcomes. They show what was purchased, how many transactions took place and how much revenue was generated. Yet, they tell you almost nothing about why customers bought, or, equally important, why they didn't.

This reliance on traditional metrics limits your understanding of what really drives your business. Many businesses are so focused on counting the results that they miss valuable opportunities to learn about the customer motivations, frustrations and unmet needs that shape those results. What inspired some customers to buy? What barriers stopped others? What caused some to feel loyalty and others to feel indifference? Failing to ask these questions means you often lose sight of what could be improved, what could be eliminated and what could be reimagined to create stronger connections with customers and drive sustainable growth.

OUTCOME FOCUSED METRICS

Traditional metrics such as sales numbers, profit margins and conversion rates offer only a surface-level view of business performance. They focus on outcomes without providing any understanding of the causes behind them. Here are a few key ways in which these metrics fall short:

- **Lack of insight into customer motivations**
  Sales figures show what was bought, but they don't reveal why customers were motivated to buy a particular product

or service or why they weren't. Conversion rates tell you how efficiently you turn browsers into buyers, but they don't help you understand what prevents others from completing a transaction. Did potential customers abandon their carts because the checkout process was too complex? Did they leave the store because of long lines or lack of assistance? Without these insights, businesses are left in the dark about the potential friction points that could be improved.

- **Blind spots in customer experience**
  Metrics such as average order values or units per transaction show patterns of purchasing behaviour but ignore the experience that accompanied those purchases. Did customers enjoy a seamless, supportive and engaging experience, or did they encounter frustrations? Did they leave feeling valued or overlooked? Metrics focused on transactions alone don't capture the nuances of customer experience, which is a key driver of repeat business and brand loyalty.

- **Failure to account for missed opportunities**
  Traditional metrics measure only completed transactions, meaning they ignore the impact of missed opportunities. For instance, a high number of website visits or store entries may look promising, but without knowing why many of those visitors left without buying, you miss crucial insights into areas for improvement. What concerns or obstacles might have led these potential customers to abandon their purchase? What changes might have converted them into buyers? By focusing solely on completed transactions, you miss the chance to learn from, and address, missed opportunities.

- **A rearview mirror perspective**
  Traditional metrics look backward; they show what has already happened, providing a historical view without any forward-looking insight. As a result, companies are often reactive rather than proactive, adjusting their strategies based on past performance rather than anticipating future needs. This backward focus limits a company's ability to adapt quickly and leaves it vulnerable to competitive shifts, changes in consumer preferences and new market trends.

THE RISKS AND IMPACT OF ARBITRARY COST-CUTTING

When traditional metrics indicate a decline in sales or profits, many companies reflexively turn to cost-cutting measures to stabilise financial performance. This often involves reducing headcount, limiting store hours, downsizing digital or customer service teams or delaying investments in technology and innovation. But these decisions, frequently made with a narrow focus on immediate savings, overlook the longer-term impact on the customer experience and fail to consider the full cause-and-effect implications:

- **Reduced in-store staff and customer frustration**
  When a retail business, bank, car dealer, restaurant or other consumer-facing business reduces staff numbers to cut costs, it may initially appear to be a smart way to trim overheads. However, with fewer employees available to greet, assist and serve customers, the quality of the in-store experience quickly deteriorates. Customers encounter longer wait times, less personalised assistance and potentially a more chaotic environment as fewer employees struggle to manage a high volume of tasks. This creates frustration, often resulting in lost

sales as customers decide to take their business elsewhere. The short-term savings achieved by reducing headcount ultimately backfire, as lower service levels drive away customers and erode brand loyalty, costing the business far more than it saved.

- **Digital resource reduction and conversion loss**
  In an era when online interactions are often a customer's first and primary contact with a brand, reducing resources for digital teams can have severe consequences. For instance, a decision to downsize the digital support team might lead to slower response times, diminished website functionality, or reduced ability to provide timely and helpful answers to customer questions. Customers who experience delays, confusing navigation or lack of assistance are far more likely to abandon their purchase. In this way, a seemingly simple cost-saving decision results in significant losses in conversion rates, customer satisfaction and brand reputation – consequences that far outweigh the original savings.

- **Understaffed customer service teams and erosion of trust**
  In customer service, a reduction in staffing or resources can translate directly to a decline in service quality. Fewer resources mean longer wait times, less personalised responses and a reduced ability to solve complex issues efficiently. Customers left waiting or receiving inadequate support may not only abandon their current transaction but also lose trust in the brand. In today's marketplace, where word of mouth spreads quickly through reviews and social media, the impact of poor service is amplified. What started as a short-term cost-cutting measure can lead to a long-term erosion of trust, driving away loyal customers and making it harder to attract new ones.

- **Delaying innovation and loss of competitive edge**
  In the name of cost-cutting, many businesses delay investments in new technology, data capabilities, or other innovations. This can leave companies lagging behind competitors who are better equipped to deliver a modern, seamless customer experience. For example, a retailer that delays updating its website to include personalisation features may find it is losing customers to competitors with a more tailored online experience. The short-term savings of delaying innovation may lead to long-term losses as competitors capture market share by offering a more relevant and responsive customer experience.

WHY NPS ALONE IS NOT ENOUGH

For decades, Net Promoter Score (NPS) has been the go-to metric for measuring customer satisfaction and loyalty. Companies across industries – from retail and financial services to automotive, travel and hospitality – have embedded it into boardroom discussions, executive dashboards and performance reviews.

At first glance, NPS seems intuitive: ask customers a single question, 'How likely are you to recommend us to a friend or colleague?' and assign a score that categorises them as promoters, passives or detractors. It's simple, scalable and easy to track.

However, while NPS remains a useful indicator of customer advocacy, relying on it alone offers an incomplete picture. To truly understand and enhance customer loyalty, businesses must look beyond NPS and embrace a more comprehensive set of metrics.

NPS measures intent, not action
NPS captures stated intentions, but these don't always translate into actual behaviours. Customers who indicate they would recommend a company

may not actively refer others, leave positive reviews or increase their spending. Meanwhile, some valuable customers – who might not rate a perfect 10 – quietly continue to make repeat purchases and significantly contribute to revenue.

NPS lacks context and depth

A single numerical score does not fully explain why a customer feels positively or negatively about a company. Did they have an exceptional service experience, find the perfect product or remain satisfied despite challenges because alternatives were limited? Businesses that rely solely on NPS may miss critical qualitative insights, making it difficult to pinpoint exactly what to improve.

Potential for manipulation

NPS can sometimes be influenced by internal practices aimed at artificially boosting scores, such as selectively surveying only satisfied customers or pressuring employees to encourage positive ratings. This can transform NPS from a valuable metric into a vanity score, obscuring real customer sentiment.

NPS doesn't capture all loyalty drivers

Customer loyalty is complex and involves more than just recommendations. Factors such as emotional connection, ease of doing business and customer effort play significant roles in driving loyalty. Traditional NPS does not measure these important dimensions, which can significantly influence customer retention and advocacy.

NPS alone doesn't guarantee growth

Despite its popularity, an increase in NPS does not always correlate directly with revenue growth. High NPS scores can coexist with financial struggles, while some companies with modest NPS scores achieve substantial success by excelling in areas like operational efficiency, product quality and consistent service delivery.

Consider Amazon – one of the world's most customer-centric companies. Many customers might hesitate to recommend Amazon because they view the relationship as transactional, yet they consistently purchase from and engage with the brand due to its frictionless and convenient experience.

EMBRACING A MORE HOLISTIC APPROACH

While NPS provides valuable insights into customer advocacy, it should be part of a broader, more holistic approach. This book introduces 11 new ROIs (Returns on Investment), which together offer a more complete, actionable and business-relevant way to measure success. These metrics allow businesses to make informed decisions to enhance customer experiences, drive genuine loyalty and promote sustainable growth.

The businesses poised to win in the future won't rely solely on NPS. They'll integrate multiple, complementary measures to deeply understand and continuously improve the customer journey. NPS is valuable, but it's just the beginning.

It's time to redefine how you measure success.

Understanding the cause and effect of decisions

Using these new metrics enables companies to understand the cause-and-effect dynamics of their business decisions. By tracking Return on Interaction, a company can understand that investing in customer service leads to better customer satisfaction and higher retention, far outweighing the cost of additional resources. Similarly, by measuring Return on Involvement, a company can see that by empowering employees to make customer-centred decisions, they drive loyalty and advocacy, creating a positive feedback loop for the brand.

Redefining success in a customer-centric world

Ultimately, this book challenges businesses to rethink their definition of success. By focusing on *why* customers buy – or don't buy – companies can gain richer insights into the real drivers of performance. It's time to look beyond immediate cost savings and short-term metrics, toward a customer-centred approach that prioritises sustainable growth and brand loyalty.

This shift in focus allows you to identify areas where investment can drive genuine impact, rather than relying on cost-cutting measures that erode value. Embracing a *why*-driven approach helps businesses build stronger, more resilient brands that stand the test of time. The future of growth lies in understanding customers, making strategic investments in their experience and ultimately redefining success as the ability to create meaningful, lasting relationships.

MEASURING WHAT TRULY MATTERS

Consumer-facing businesses operate in an ever-changing landscape – marked by rapid technological advancements, shifting consumer behaviours and heightened competition. Despite these challenges, some brands manage to thrive, while others falter and fade into irrelevance.

The difference often lies in how well businesses understand, engage and inspire their customers – and whether they measure success through the right metrics. Traditional business KPIs like revenue, market share and Net Promoter Score (NPS) often create a false sense of security, making leaders believe they are on the right track while their customers move on to better alternatives.

In contrast, the companies that succeed today are those that embrace new ways of measuring success, using metrics like the 11 ROIs in this book to track customer engagement, brand integrity, innovation and internal alignment – all of which are critical in a world where consumer expectations evolve faster than ever before.

The consequences of measuring the wrong things

BLOCKBUSTER: FAILURE TO MEASURE RETURN ON INNOVATION

Blockbuster's demise is one of the most infamous examples of corporate complacency. The brand dominated the home entertainment industry in the 1990s, with thousands of stores worldwide. However, its failure was not just about technology – it was about failing to measure innovation and consumer behaviour correctly.

What went wrong?

- **Failure to track Return on Innovation** ➜ Blockbuster had multiple opportunities to pivot to streaming and even passed on a chance to buy Netflix in 2000 for $50 million, dismissing it as a niche market (Fortune, 2023).
- **Ignoring Return on Interaction** ➜ Customers wanted a more convenient way to rent films, but Blockbuster clung to its in-store model, known for late fees and limited accessibility.
- **Weak Return on Integration** ➜ Rather than integrating physical and digital services, it remained focused on revenue from brick-and-mortar stores.

Meanwhile, Netflix measured success differently. It prioritised Return on Innovation by focusing on streaming technology and data-driven personalisation, making it effortless for customers to discover and consume content on demand (Hastings & Meyer, 2020). Netflix also tracked Return on Interaction, ensuring a frictionless, digital-first experience.

The result? Netflix became a household name while Blockbuster filed for bankruptcy in 2010 (New York Times, 2010).

TOYS 'R' US: FAILURE TO MEASURE RETURN ON INTERACTION AND INTEGRATION

Toys 'R' Us was once the undisputed leader in toy retail, yet by 2017, it had collapsed into bankruptcy (BBC News, 2017). The root cause wasn't just e-commerce – it was a failure to evolve with consumer expectations.

What went wrong?

- **Failure to measure Return on Interaction** ➜ As consumers moved towards seamless online shopping experiences, Toys 'R' Us failed to create engaging digital touchpoints for customers.
- **Poor Return on Integration** ➜ Rather than developing its own e-commerce presence, Toys 'R' Us outsourced its online operations to Amazon in 2000, losing valuable data and customer insights in the process (CNN Money, 2000).
- **Lack of Return on Involvement** ➜ The brand did little to foster customer loyalty or engagement, failing to create personalised shopping experiences for parents and children.

Despite this, the brand is making a comeback in the US and UK with multiple store openings.

In contrast, Amazon dominated by investing in Return on Interaction (frictionless digital experiences), Return on Inclusion (broad product selection across demographics) and Return on Insight (customer-driven personalisation powered by AI and data analytics).

The result? Amazon became the ultimate toy store, and Toys 'R' Us disappeared.

BRITISH AIRWAYS VS. EMIRATES: A CASE OF RETURN ON INSPIRATION AND INTEGRITY

British Airways, once seen as the gold standard of air travel, has suffered in recent years due to cost-cutting, service downgrades and loss of consumer trust (LBC, 2024). In contrast, Emirates continues to thrive by focusing on:

- **Return on Inspiration** ➜ Creating an aspirational brand experience that travellers admire.
- **Return on Integrity** ➜ Maintaining high service levels even during challenging economic conditions.
- **Return on Interaction** ➜ Personalised experiences, strong loyalty programmes and premium service touchpoints.

The result? Emirates continues to be one of the most preferred airlines in the world (Emirates, 2024), while British Airways has seen declining customer sentiment (Which, 2025).

SEARS VS. TARGET: A CASE OF RETURN ON INNOVATION AND RETURN ON IMAGE

Sears, once the largest retailer in the US, failed to evolve, focusing solely on cost-cutting and store maintenance while ignoring customer experience (Castus Global, 2021). Meanwhile, Target flourished by investing in:

- **Return on Innovation ➜** Building a strong digital presence and seamlessly integrating online and in-store shopping.
- **Return on Image ➜** Establishing a modern, stylish brand identity with curated products and marketing aimed at younger demographics.

The result? Sears shut down stores nationwide, while Target continues to grow, especially in digital commerce (Target, 2025).

The businesses that succeed are measuring the right things

APPLE: RETURN ON INSPIRATION AND RETURN ON INTERACTION

Apple's continued success is not just about product innovation – it's about how customers interact with the brand at every touchpoint (Retently, 2024).

The Apple Store is not just a store, it's an experience.

- **Return on Inspiration ➜** Fuels its fanatical brand loyalty.
- **Return on Interaction ➜** Ensures that its products, ecosystem and customer service feel seamless.

STARBUCKS: RETURN ON INVOLVEMENT AND RETURN ON IMPROVEMENTS

Starbucks understands that customer experience is not just about coffee – it's about personalisation, connection and engagement (Brand Vision Marketing, 2025).

- **Return on Involvement** ➜ A best-in-class loyalty programme that keeps customers engaged.
- **Return on Improvements** ➜ Constant menu innovations and digital enhancements to stay ahead of consumer trends.

PATAGONIA: RETURN ON INTEGRITY AND RETURN ON IMAGE

Patagonia doesn't just sell outdoor gear, it builds trust and loyalty through purpose-driven leadership (Humans of Globe, 2024).

- **Return on Integrity** ➜ Pioneering environmental sustainability efforts.
- **Return on Image** ➜ Customers see Patagonia as an ethical brand with strong values.

The real reason consumer businesses fail

Blockbuster, Toys 'R' Us, Sears and many others didn't fail because of technology or market changes alone. They failed because they measured success in the wrong way.

The companies that continue to thrive – Amazon, Apple, Starbucks, Patagonia, Emirates – are measuring beyond profit and NPS. They are tracking the real drivers of sustainable success:

- **Return on Inspiration** ➜ How much belief do customers and employees have in your brand?
- **Return on Interaction** ➜ How seamlessly do customers engage with your business across touchpoints?
- **Return on Integrity** ➜ Do consumers trust you and align with your brand's values?

- **Return on Innovation** ➜ How quickly do you evolve and adapt to changing demands?

The message is clear: businesses that continue to measure success with outdated metrics risk becoming the next Blockbuster.

THE NEW WAYS OF MEASURING SUCCESS

Traditional metrics like revenue growth, profit margins and market share have long been the barometers of business success. While these financial metrics are essential, they do not provide a comprehensive picture of what drives long-term sustainability. In today's consumer-centric world, businesses must look beyond these conventional measures to include metrics that focus on Customer Lifetime Value (CLV), employee engagement, trust and brand loyalty.

CLV has emerged as a critical measure of business success. Unlike one-off sales, CLV looks at the total worth of a customer over their entire relationship with a brand. Companies that excel in nurturing this long-term relationship understand that success is about more than immediate revenue – it's about consistent engagement, repeat business and advocacy.

This book introduces a groundbreaking framework based on 11 new ROIs that redefine success by focusing on what truly matters: inspiring employees, building trust, ensuring inclusivity and more. These new ways of measuring success emphasise the importance of fostering strong, long-term relationships with customers and employees. When integrated into the strategic core of a company, these ROIs can guide organisations in building a sustainable, resilient future.

It's time for a new way of measuring success. It's time for the 11 ROIs.

BUSINESS OUTCOMES YOU CAN EXPECT

By applying the insights and strategies in this book, you can expect to:

- **Embed customer-centricity:** Build lasting customer relationships, driving sustainable growth.
- **Implement actionable strategies:** Integrate these 11 ROIs effectively across your organisation.
- **Measure and track success:** Adopt metrics capturing real impact on customer satisfaction, employee engagement and long-term success.
- **Cultivate innovation:** Foster a culture that continuously evolves to exceed customer expectations.
- **Achieve long-term competitive advantage:** Develop resilient strategies and an organisational culture which competitors admire and customers value.

Implementation roadmap for new ROI metrics

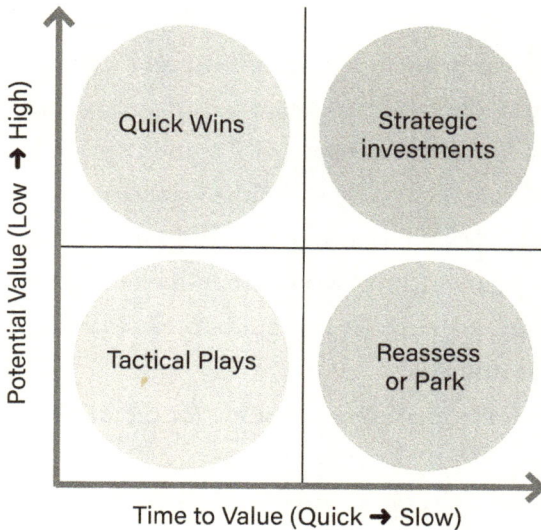

Quick Wins

Strategic investments

Tactical Plays

Reassess or Park

Potential Value (Low → High)

Time to Value (Quick → Slow)

There is always low-hanging fruit and quick wins that businesses can pursue. The diagram above is a quick route to plotting where different opportunities sit in relation to their potential impact, as well as how easy or challenging they might be to implement.

THE NEW ROI FRAMEWORK: A BLUEPRINT FOR LONG-TERM, SUSTAINABLE SUCCESS

The new ROI framework provides businesses with practical tools and clear strategies for redefining success beyond traditional metrics. This framework equips organisations with metrics that track meaningful outcomes, ensuring a balanced approach that values both short-term performance and long-term sustainability.

Throughout this book, you will explore real-world examples and case studies demonstrating how industry-leading companies are effectively using the new ROI framework. These examples highlight the tangible benefits of prioritising inspiration, integrity, inclusion and other key dimensions of ROI. Companies adopting this holistic approach are better equipped to navigate challenges, adapt quickly and achieve lasting success.

The new ROI framework provides a clear blueprint to help organisations become more resilient, adaptable and aligned with societal values. By expanding the concept of ROI, businesses can make informed decisions benefiting all stakeholders, creating value beyond financial returns alone.

This book invites business leaders, managers and stakeholders to rethink their approach to success, recognising profit as just one component of a larger, purpose-driven equation. By adopting these new ROIs, organisations can foster greater customer loyalty, employee engagement and sustainable growth, positioning themselves as leaders in a future where purpose, responsibility and meaningful impact define market success.

Ultimately, this book serves as a strategic guide, empowering businesses to transform their approach and emerge as resilient, innovative and purpose-driven organisations prepared for the future.

Let's get started!

REFERENCES

BBC News (2017) 'Toys "R" Us files for bankruptcy protection in US', BBC News, 19 September. Available at: www.bbc.co.uk/news/business-41316205 (Accessed: 25 April 2025).

Brand Vision Marketing (2025) 'Starbucks Marketing Strategy: Creating A Global Brand'. Available at: www.brandvm.com/post/starbucks-marketing (Accessed: 25 April 2025).

Castus Global (2021) 'The downfall of Sears: 5 key reasons why the retail giant went under', Castus Global, 9 November. Available at: www.castusglobal.com/insights/the-down fall-of-sears-5-key-reasons-why-the-retail-giant-went-under (Accessed: 25 April 2025).

CNN Money (2000) 'Amazon, Toysrus.com team up', CNN, 10 August. Available at: www.money.cnn.com/2000/08/10/technology/amazon/index.htm (Accessed: 25 April 2025).

Emirates (2024) 'Emirates flying high with title of "World's Best Airline" from new comprehensive study', Emirates Media Centre, 18 October. Available at: www.emirates.com/media-centre/emirates-flying-high-with-title-of-worlds-best-airline-from-new-comprehensive-study/ (Accessed: 25 April 2025).

Hastings, R. and Meyer, E. (2020) *No Rules: Netflix and the Culture of Reinvention*. New York: Penguin Random House.

Humans of Globe (2024) 'Patagonia's leadership in environmental and social responsibility', Humans of Globe, 29 January. Available at: www.humansofglobe.com/patagonia-leadership-in-environmental-and-social-responsibility/ (Accessed: 25 April 2025).

Fortune (2023) 'Netflix cofounder recalls Blockbuster rejecting chance to pay $50M', Fortune, 14 April. Available at: www.fortune.com/2023/04/14/netflix-cofounder-marc-randolph-recalls-blockbuster-rejecting-chance-to-buy-it/ (Accessed: 25 April 2025).

LBC (2024) 'British Airways leaves seasoned flyers fuming after scrapping three-course in-flight meals in "cost-cutting" move', LBC, 29 October. Available at: www.lbc.co.uk/news/british-airways-scraps-three-course-flight-meals-seasoned-flyers-fuming/ (Accessed: 25 April 2025).

Which? (2025) 'British Airways finishes bottom of Which? long-haul flights survey and rivals Ryanair for poor customer service'. Which? Feb. 2025. Available at: https://www.which.co.uk/policy-and-insight/article/british-airways-finishes-bottom-of-which-long-haul-flights-survey-and-rivals-ryanair-for-poor-customer-service-avXK49v3VAv0 [Accessed 21 August 2025].

Retently (2024) 'The reasons behind Apple's customer loyalty and high NPS', Retently. Available at: www.retently.com/blog/apple-nps/ (Accessed: 25 April 2025).

Target (2025) 'Target announces strategic plans to drive more than $15 billion in sales growth by 2030', Target Corporate, 4 March. Available at: www.corporate.target. com/press/release/2025/03/target-announces-strategic-plans-to-drive-more-than-$15-billion-in-sales-growth-by-2030 (Accessed: 25 April 2025).

The New York Times (2010) 'Blockbuster, hoping to reinvent itself, files for bankruptcy', *The New York Times*, 24 September. Available at: www.nytimes.com/2010/09/24/business/24blockbuster.html (Accessed: 25 April 2025).

Which?. (2025) *British Airways finishes bottom of Which? long-haul flights survey and rivals Ryanair for poor customer service.* Which? Feb. 2025. Available at: https://www.which.co.uk/policy-and-insight/article/british-airways-finishes-bottom-of-which-long-haul-flights-survey-and-rivals-ryanair-for-poor-customer-service-avXK49v3VAv0 [Accessed 21 August 2025].

CHAPTER 1
RETURN ON INSPIRATION – SETTING YOUR COLLEAGUES UP FOR SUCCESS

INTRODUCING RETURN ON INSPIRATION

In today's complex and competitive global marketplace, the ability of a business to foster loyalty, drive innovation and maintain a resilient workforce has become increasingly central to long-term success. However, many organisations still rely on traditional performance metrics, such as revenue growth and profit margins, to gauge success. While these metrics are important, they fail to capture the holistic impact of employee engagement and satisfaction on a company's overall performance and brand loyalty. All too often brands look at their people as a cost centre rather than a profit centre.

Return on Inspiration is a forward-thinking approach that acknowledges the vital role of an engaged and motivated workforce in building a competitive advantage, enhancing the customer experience and creating a sustainable growth trajectory. Rather than viewing employees as resources to be managed, ROI recognises them as strategic assets whose dedication, creativity and motivation can profoundly influence an organisation's success.

An inspired employee does more than simply fulfil daily responsibilities; they become advocates for the company, driving innovation, improving processes and better serving customers. When employees feel inspired, aligned with the company's mission and supported by leadership, they contribute far more than just their labour. They bring their best ideas, passion and commitment, which directly enhances customer satisfaction, fosters brand loyalty and differentiates the company in a crowded market.

Consider Gallup's insights on employee engagement, which found that organisations with highly-engaged employees experience a 21% increase in profitability, 41% lower absenteeism and 24% less staff turnover than their less-engaged counterparts (Gallup, 2023). Deloitte's Gen Z and Millennial survey also reveals that employees who feel connected to their company's mission are 75% more committed to their work and 89% more likely to recommend their employer to others (Deloitte, 2024). These statistics underscore the growing recognition that an engaged workforce is not only more productive and innovative, but also better equipped to deliver superior customer experiences.

In contrast, companies that neglect employee inspiration risk facing issues, such as low morale, high turnover and declining productivity. Disengaged employees are more likely to underperform, disengage and ultimately leave the company, leading to recruitment and training costs, as well as disruptions in customer service, lower satisfaction levels and weakened brand loyalty (HRZone, 2024).

By investing in a culture of inspiration, companies can empower employees to take ownership of their work, collaborate effectively and align their efforts with the organisation's overarching mission. This chapter explores the concept of Return on Inspiration as a strategic imperative and offers actionable insights and tools for cultivating an environment where employees feel motivated, valued and empowered. We will examine how organisations across industries can harness the power of inspiration to enhance employee engagement and drive long-term business growth.

To move from theory to practice, this chapter breaks down how to apply Return on Inspiration in real-world settings – across leadership, culture and employee experience.

LEVERAGING RETURN ON INSPIRATION

By the end of this chapter, you will have a clear understanding of how to implement and sustain Return on Inspiration within your organisation, regardless of size or sector. You'll gain practical tools and strategic insight to help cultivate a workforce that feels valued, motivated and meaningfully connected to your company's mission. This chapter will equip you to:

- **Maximise the strategic value of inspiration**
  Understand how inspiration fuels employee engagement, drives innovation, enhances customer experience and strengthens

brand loyalty. An inspired workforce delivers improved performance, greater resilience and sustained competitive advantage in today's customer-focused business environment.

- **Build the core elements of an inspiring workplace**
  Explore the key ingredients of an inspiring culture, including autonomy, growth opportunities, recognition, transparent communication and purpose-driven leadership. These elements form the foundation for stronger engagement, higher retention and improved organisational outcomes.

- **Empower employees to take ownership and shape the future**
  Discover how to create a workplace where employees feel empowered to contribute ideas, take initiative and actively shape the direction of the business. A culture of ownership deepens commitment, unlocks innovation and aligns individual purpose with organisational goals.

- **Implement best practices from leading organisations**
  Through case studies from innovative companies across sectors, such as technology, retail, hospitality and food service, learn how industry leaders are putting Return on Inspiration into action. These real-world examples demonstrate how purpose, culture and leadership combine to deliver meaningful results.

- **Measure success using meaningful metrics**
  Gain insight into how to evaluate the impact of inspiration-focused initiatives using both qualitative and quantitative methods. Learn how to apply key performance indicators (KPIs) – including employee satisfaction, productivity, customer experience and retention – to continuously improve and refine your approach.

- **Apply practical strategies for short- and long-term impact**
  Explore a blend of quick wins and long-term strategies that
  embed inspiration across your business. From recognition
  programmes and communication improvements to leadership
  development and culture-building efforts, these initiatives help
  foster motivation and momentum over time.

- **Prioritise and align inspiration initiatives for maximum value**
  With limited time and resources, it's essential to focus efforts
  where they'll deliver the greatest impact. Learn how to prioritise
  and align inspiration-driven initiatives with your broader
  business strategy to create meaningful, measurable change at
  every level of the organisation.

Now let's bring Return on Inspiration to life.

RETURN ON INSPIRATION IN ACTION

To better understand how these principles can be applied in real-world
scenarios, let's explore several case studies that highlight the practical
impact of fostering a culture of inspiration, customer engagement and
continuous improvement.

GOOGLE – CULTIVATING INSPIRATION
THROUGH AUTONOMY AND GROWTH OPPORTUNITIES

Google's reputation as an inspiration powerhouse is not only due
to its cutting-edge technology but also its commitment to fostering
a workplace where employees feel inspired and empowered. A key
component of this approach is Google's '20% time' policy, which allows
employees to spend one-fifth of their working hours on personal projects

beyond their core responsibilities. This policy enables employees to explore ideas, take risks and contribute to projects that genuinely interest them. Over the years, iconic products such as Gmail, Google News and AdSense have emerged from employee-driven projects initiated during 20% time (Conversational Leadership, 2015).

In addition to autonomy, Google offers comprehensive development resources, including workshops, online courses, mentorship programmes and lectures from industry leaders. These resources not only improve employees' technical skills but also inspire a sense of purpose and growth, aligning personal ambitions with the company's mission of organising the world's information. According to Team Tactics (2023), Google's strong emphasis on employee autonomy and alignment with the company's mission inspires a highly motivated workforce, which in turn drives customer-centric innovation and sustained business success.

Key takeaway: Providing autonomy and growth opportunities fosters a culture of inspiration and employee satisfaction, benefiting customer loyalty. For operational managers, this might involve granting flexibility in task management, while executives can focus on building a culture that values development.

ZAPPOS - CRAFTING A CUSTOMER-CENTRIC CULTURE THROUGH CORE VALUES

Zappos, a US-based leader in online retail of footwear, exemplifies how a strong culture rooted in customer-centric values can inspire employees to deliver exceptional service. Each new hire at Zappos undergoes a unique cultural onboarding programme that emphasises the company's customer-first philosophy and core values. This onboarding process is crucial in creating a workplace where employees feel empowered to make decisions that benefit the customer. At the end of this programme, new hires are offered $2,000 to leave if they do not feel aligned with the company's values. This 'Pay to Quit' programme ensures that only those committed to Zappos' mission remain (HBR, 2008).

The results of this approach are evident in Zappos' high Net Promoter Scores (NPS) and strong customer loyalty metrics. According to Zappos' internal surveys reported in company case studies, approximately 92% of employees feel motivated by the company's culture to prioritise the customer experience (Zappos Insights, 2025).

This culture-first approach creates a direct link between employee inspiration and customer satisfaction, showing that when employees are genuinely committed to the company's values, they deliver service that keeps customers coming back.

Key takeaway: A culture rooted in customer-centric values inspires employees to exceed expectations. For executives, aligning values with customer goals can reinforce this culture, while operational leaders can focus on embedding these values in training and day-to-day operations.

PATAGONIA - DRIVING PURPOSE THROUGH ENVIRONMENTAL RESPONSIBILITY

Patagonia's mission-driven approach to business, centred on environmental conservation, aligns deeply with the values of its employees and customers. The company actively encourages employees to engage in volunteer work for environmental causes by offering paid time off and supporting employee-led initiatives (Patagonia, 2025). Patagonia's corporate mission, 'We're in business to save our home planet', inspires employees to go beyond profit-driven goals and contribute to a purpose that resonates on a personal level (Strategic Leadership, 2024).

The impact of this purpose-driven approach is evident in both employee engagement and customer loyalty. According to a Deloitte study, 80% of employees at purpose-driven organisations report increased job satisfaction and stronger alignment with their company's mission (Deloitte, 2022). Patagonia's alignment of its mission with employees' personal values has created a workforce that is not only highly engaged but also deeply loyal to the brand. Customers who resonate with

Patagonia's environmental ethos are more likely to remain loyal, viewing their purchases as support for a greater cause (Forbes, 2024).

Key takeaway: Purpose-driven missions that resonate with employees and customers build loyalty and engagement. For executives, defining and clearly communicating a meaningful mission can foster a culture of purpose, enhancing both employee and customer loyalty.

MOD PIZZA – SUPPORTING EMPLOYEE WELL-BEING FOR CUSTOMER-CENTRIC SERVICE

MOD Pizza's people-first culture emphasises creating a supportive environment where employees in customer-facing roles feel valued and empowered. The company offers fair wages, career growth opportunities and a team-oriented workplace culture that promotes respect and inclusion. This emphasis on well-being has led to high employee satisfaction, which translates directly into positive customer interactions (Forbes 2018). MOD Pizza's focus on employee engagement and inclusive culture has led to a more motivated workforce that delivers superior customer experiences, supporting customer loyalty and business growth (SAP, 2022).

Key Takeaway: Supporting employee well-being in frontline roles can enhance customer experience and build brand loyalty. For executives, this might mean prioritising competitive compensation and growth opportunities, while operational leaders focus on creating a culture that values and respects each employee.

CAFÉ GRATITUDE (LA) – FOSTERING COMMUNITY AND MINDFULNESS IN DAILY OPERATIONS

Café Gratitude, a small but well-loved chain of organic cafés, integrates mindfulness into its daily operations, creating a culture of gratitude and positivity that extends to both employees and customers. Employees at Café Gratitude participate in daily gratitude exercises, such as answering a 'question of the day' to encourage self-reflection and community spirit. This practice not only strengthens team cohesion but also creates a welcoming environment which customers feel as soon as they walk through the door. Café Gratitude's commitment to mindfulness demonstrates that even smaller businesses can leverage Return on Inspiration to build a loyal customer base through a community-focused approach (Café Gratitude, 2023).

Key Takeaway: Mindfulness practices that promote positivity and gratitude improve both employee morale and customer experience, especially for small businesses that want to foster a community-driven brand. Operational leaders can incorporate similar practices to reinforce a positive workplace culture, while executives can support these initiatives with company-wide policies that reflect the same values.

THE CONTAINER STORE – ELEVATING CUSTOMER SERVICE THROUGH EXTENSIVE TRAINING

The Container Store is a specialty retail chain in the United States that focuses on storage and organisation solutions for homes and businesses. Founded in 1978 in Dallas, Texas, the company has built a strong reputation for offering:

- **Storage products** (closet systems, bins, boxes, shelving)
- **Custom closets and design services** (including its premium Elfa, Avera, and Preston closet lines)
- **Home organisation solutions** across every room, from kitchens to garages

The Container Store's commitment to comprehensive training programmes is a cornerstone of its workplace culture, designed to empower employees to deliver exceptional customer service. New full-time employees receive nearly 300 hours of training in their first year, covering product knowledge, customer service techniques and alignment with company values. This substantial investment in employee training led to a 15% improvement in customer satisfaction and a 20% reduction in employee turnover, underscoring the link between an empowered workforce and high-quality customer service (Brand Autopsy, 2014).

Key Takeaway: Investing in thorough training programmes builds an empowered workforce that positively impacts customer experience. For operational leaders, ongoing training improves team performance, while executives should view training as a strategic investment that benefits both employee retention and customer satisfaction.

HOW TO MEASURE SUCCESS WITHIN RETURN ON INSPIRATION

Measuring the success of inspiration-focused initiatives requires a multifaceted approach that considers both quantitative and qualitative indicators. Below is an extended list of KPIs and evaluation techniques to assess the impact of Return on Inspiration on employee engagement, customer satisfaction and organisational performance.

Employee engagement and satisfaction scores

One of the most direct ways to measure Return on Inspiration is through employee engagement surveys, such as Gallup's Q12 or customised internal surveys. These tools capture critical engagement dimensions, such as job satisfaction, alignment with company values and motivation levels. By conducting these surveys on a regular basis, companies can track engagement trends over time and assess how inspiration-focused initiatives are affecting employee morale.

- **How to measure**: Use consistent employee engagement surveys across departments or time periods. Capture both quantitative scores and open-ended responses to provide a full view of sentiment and shifts in morale.
- **Qualitative insight**: In addition to numerical scores, anonymous feedback sections within these surveys provide valuable insights. Employees can voice specific suggestions for improvement, share their experiences and highlight any

obstacles that might hinder their motivation. Analysing these insights helps leaders identify underlying factors affecting engagement and make data-informed adjustments. You might think of this as the 'Voice of the Colleague' – which is as important as listening to the 'Voice of the Customer'.

Productivity and innovation metrics

Tracking productivity and innovation is essential for assessing the tangible impact of an inspired workforce. Metrics to consider include the number of new product ideas generated by employees, efficiency improvements or customer service innovations introduced by staff. For example, measuring the frequency and impact of employee-driven initiatives offers a clear picture of how autonomy and empowerment are contributing to overall business performance.

- **How to measure:** Monitor the volume of employee-submitted ideas, implemented innovations and process changes through internal platforms or team reports.
- **Long-term tracking:** To gauge innovation over time, leaders can monitor the development and success rates of employee-generated projects or ideas. Recognising employees whose contributions lead to improved products or services reinforces a culture of innovation and motivates others to contribute proactively.

Customer Satisfaction (CSAT) and Net Promoter Score (NPS)

Customer satisfaction and NPS scores are key indicators of how employee engagement influences customer experience. Engaged employees are often more attentive, proactive and solution-focused, which translates into a higher level of customer service. By regularly analysing CSAT and NPS scores, companies can identify whether improvements in employee engagement are positively impacting customer loyalty and satisfaction.

- **How to measure:** Use post-interaction CSAT surveys and regular NPS checks, ideally after meaningful service delivery moments or campaign launches. Compare scores across time and different initiatives.
- **Segmented analysis:** For a more comprehensive understanding, companies can break down customer satisfaction data by department or service area. This approach allows leaders to pinpoint specific teams or regions where employee inspiration has the most significant impact on customer experience, helping focus efforts where they are needed most.

Employee retention and turnover rates

High retention rates often reflect a positive, inspiring work environment, while high turnover can indicate disengagement. Monitoring employee turnover rates over time is essential for evaluating the effectiveness of inspiration-focused initiatives. Low turnover rates reduce recruitment and training costs, ensuring service consistency and contributing to a stable, experienced workforce.

- **How to measure:** Track voluntary turnover rates, average tenure by department and reasons for exit over consistent timeframes.
- **Exit and stay interviews:** Exit interviews provide insights into why employees may choose to leave, while stay interviews – conducted with current employees – help understand why employees remain with the company. Together, these interviews offer valuable information that can guide retention-focused strategies and identify areas for improvement in the work environment.

Internal promotion and career progression rates

Tracking internal promotions and career advancement rates is another valuable indicator of how well the company is supporting employee growth and development. High rates of promotion signal that employees feel valued, supported in their career goals and motivated to contribute to the company's success. This metric also highlights the organisation's commitment to nurturing talent, which strengthens employee loyalty and engagement.

- **How to measure:** Monitor internal mobility rates, average time to promotion and proportion of leadership roles filled internally.
- **Skill development tracking:** Companies can use skill development tracking systems to monitor employees' progress in their training programmes. By correlating training data with performance and promotion outcomes, leaders can identify which development programmes are most effective in fostering employee growth, engagement and inspiration.

Measuring Return on Inspiration requires a holistic approach that blends hard metrics with human insight. By combining quantitative KPIs – such as engagement scores, innovation outputs and customer satisfaction – with qualitative feedback and career progression data, companies gain a clear understanding of how inspiration is shaping employee experience and organisational performance. This comprehensive approach not only identifies areas for improvement but also validates the role of inspiration as a strategic driver of motivation, innovation and long-term success.

IMPLEMENTING RETURN ON INSPIRATION

Inspiring a workforce requires a blend of immediate actions that build momentum and long-term strategies that embed purpose into the company's culture. Quick wins offer tangible, morale-boosting changes that reinforce a sense of value and connection, while sustained efforts help create a more empowered, purpose-driven organisation. For Return on

Inspiration to take root, it must be reinforced across every level of the business, from leadership and HR to operations and customer-facing teams. When everyone plays a role in fostering motivation, trust and alignment, inspiration becomes a driving force for performance and long-term success.

Quick wins

1. **Establish a recognition programme**
   Recognition programmes are a quick and effective way to boost morale and highlight the accomplishments of employees. By establishing initiatives that celebrate individual and team achievements, such as monthly awards or peer-nominated recognition, companies can create a positive feedback loop that reinforces employee contributions. Leaders can make these initiatives more impactful by tying them to company values or customer feedback, fostering a culture of appreciation that aligns with organisational goals.

2. **Enhance communication channels**
   Open and transparent communication builds trust within the organisation. Implementing town halls, regular team check-ins and Q&A sessions with leadership allows employees to feel more connected to the company's mission. Leaders can also use digital tools like Slack, Microsoft Teams or dedicated forums to facilitate open communication and real-time feedback. By promoting a culture of openness, employees are encouraged to voice their ideas and concerns, which fosters collaboration and strengthens team cohesion.

3. **Empower frontline employees with decision-making power**
   Empowering employees, especially those in customer-facing roles, to make on-the-spot decisions enhances their confidence

and engagement. When employees have the autonomy to address customer issues directly, they are more likely to take ownership of their roles and exceed customer expectations. Leaders can set clear guidelines for decision-making while giving employees the flexibility to make judgement calls. This empowerment not only improves customer satisfaction but also builds trust between employees and management.

4. **Offer skill development opportunities**

Providing access to skill development workshops, certifications and online courses signals to employees that their growth is a priority. Companies can offer a range of options, such as technical training, leadership development and customer service excellence, to support employees in expanding their expertise. Even a small investment in professional growth contributes to a motivated workforce that is well-equipped to adapt to new challenges and take on greater responsibilities.

Long-term strategies

1. **Align company mission with employee values**

Aligning the company's mission with employee values requires a sustained commitment to purpose-driven initiatives. Leaders can host mission-driven events, like volunteer days or community projects, where employees can see the impact of their work firsthand. Providing platforms for employees to share stories about how their work contributes to the mission fosters a sense of shared purpose, enhancing engagement and strengthening the organisation's culture.

2. **Develop robust training programmes**

A comprehensive training programme that includes both technical skills and soft skills, like customer engagement and problem-solving, empowers employees to excel in their roles. Leaders can develop modular training programmes that allow employees to build competencies over time. Regular training not only equips employees with the tools they need to perform effectively but also demonstrates the organisation's commitment to their professional growth, which is key for long-term engagement.

3. **Support work-life balance initiatives**

   Supporting the work-life balance of employees is critical for creating a sustainable and inspiring work environment. Leaders can promote work-life balance by implementing flexible work arrangements, providing wellness programmes and setting realistic performance expectations. When employees feel supported in balancing work and personal life, they are more motivated, productive and loyal. Work-life balance initiatives are particularly important for retention, as employees who feel burned out are more likely to disengage or leave the organisation.

4. **Foster purpose-driven leadership**

   Purpose-driven leadership emphasises the position of leaders as role models who embody the organisation's values. Training leaders to practice empathy, actively listen and set an example of integrity and commitment creates a trickle-down effect that inspires employees. Leaders can create mentorship programmes where senior staff work directly with junior employees, providing guidance and fostering an environment of support and shared vision. Purpose-driven leadership helps create a strong foundation of trust, where employees feel genuinely valued and inspired to contribute their best.

Driving engagement at every level

For executives and senior leadership:

- **Make inspiration a strategic priority:** An engaged and motivated workforce drives higher productivity, better customer experiences and long-term business success.
- **Lead with vision and purpose:** Employees are most inspired when they feel connected to a company's mission – leaders must communicate and embody this purpose consistently.
- **Invest in employee growth and well-being:** Providing learning opportunities, career development and a supportive work environment enhances job satisfaction and commitment.

For operational managers:

- **Foster a culture of empowerment:** Employees perform best when they are trusted to make decisions, contribute ideas and take ownership of their roles.
- **Recognise and reward contributions:** Acknowledging employee achievements – big or small – creates a sense of value and encourages continued motivation.
- **Create open channels for feedback:** Encouraging regular dialogue between teams and leadership ensures that employees feel heard and engaged.

For HR and people teams:

- **Embed inspiration into hiring and training:** Recruitment should prioritise candidates who align with company values, while ongoing training helps employees develop and stay engaged.
- **Support a positive and inclusive workplace culture:** Employees are most inspired when they feel valued, respected and included, regardless of their role or background.

- **Provide clear career progression opportunities:** Structuring pathways for growth within the organisation boosts motivation and long-term retention.

For customer-facing teams:

- **Bring passion and energy to customer interactions:** Inspired employees create better customer experiences by demonstrating enthusiasm, care and commitment to service excellence.
- **Advocate for customer needs internally:** Employees who feel empowered will proactively suggest ways to improve products, services and experiences for customers.
- **Align daily work with the company mission:** Understanding how their role contributes to the bigger picture helps employees find greater purpose and satisfaction in their work.

By embedding inspiration across leadership, operations, HR and customer experience, businesses can cultivate a high-performing workforce that is engaged, motivated and committed to delivering exceptional results.

THE LASTING IMPACT OF RETURN ON INSPIRATION

Return on Inspiration is not merely an employee engagement initiative; it's a transformative approach that shapes every aspect of an organisation's operations, customer interactions and long-term sustainability. By fostering a culture where employees feel inspired, valued and aligned with the company's mission, organisations can build a foundation for success that goes beyond traditional metrics. An inspired workforce drives innovation, enhances customer satisfaction, strengthens brand loyalty and fosters resilience – qualities that position companies for sustained growth in an increasingly competitive market.

The case studies explored in this chapter demonstrate the profound impact of a Return on Inspiration approach. These companies have cultivated workplace cultures that prioritise employee autonomy, personal growth and purpose-driven leadership, resulting in higher engagement, stronger customer relationships and enhanced profitability. A compelling piece of research by Oxford and Harvard academics, covering over 1,600 publicly traded U.S. companies, revealed something we've long suspected but can now evidence: when people feel inspired, the business performs better. The study connected higher levels of employee well-being – defined by indicators such as fulfilment, happiness, and a sense of purpose – with stronger financial outcomes across the board, including profitability, market valuation, and share price performance (Nilsson, 2024).

Take Nvidia, for example. A brand often applauded for its innovative culture and progressive approach to employee experience, it stands as a living case study for what happens when businesses actively support their people. The results aren't just felt internally – they're seen in the numbers. Investing in well-being, it turns out, doesn't just create a better place to work. It creates a better-performing business. That's Return on Inspiration in action.

By adopting a similar approach, leaders can create environments where employees are motivated to excel, advocate for the brand and contribute to exceptional customer experiences.

Implementing Return on Inspiration requires a balance of quick wins, such as recognition programmes and open communication, and long-term strategies, like purpose-driven leadership and comprehensive training. These efforts enable companies to build an inspiring culture that resonates across all levels of the organisation. For leaders who prioritise ROI, the benefits are clear: lower turnover, stronger brand loyalty, increased profitability and a workforce that thrives in a dynamic market.

In conclusion, Return on Inspiration represents a new paradigm for measuring success – one that encompasses employee engagement, customer satisfaction and long-term brand loyalty, beyond traditional financial metrics. By embedding inspiration into the organisation's culture, leaders can cultivate a resilient and adaptable workforce committed to delivering outstanding customer experiences. For companies seeking to build a loyal customer base and achieve sustainable growth, Return on Inspiration is not just an aspiration, it is an essential investment in the future.

TAKE ACTION

Now that you understand the power of Return on Inspiration, it's time to act. Start by identifying one area within your organisation where employee engagement can be immediately improved. Whether it's through a small recognition programme, a quick conversation with your team about the company mission or empowering your employees to make decisions on the spot – every step counts. Remember, the most inspired teams are those that feel valued, connected to the mission and empowered to make a difference. Take the first step today and watch how inspiration transforms your organisation from the inside out.

REFERENCES

Brand Autopsy (2014) 'The Container Store training philosophy', Brand Autopsy, 14 October. Available at: www.brandautopsy.com/2014/10/container-store-training-philosophy.html (Accessed: 25 April 2025).

Café Gratitude (2023) 'Practicing Gratitude', Café Gratitude Blog. Available at: www.cafegratitude.com/blogs/news/terces (Accessed: 25 April 2025).

Conversational Leadership (2015) 'The Google 20% free time policy', Conversational Leadership, 2 March. Available at: www.conversational-leadership.net/google-free-time-policy/ (Accessed: 25 April 2025).

Deloitte (2022) 'Mind the purpose gap', Deloitte Insights, 20 September. Available at: www2.deloitte.com/us/en/insights/topics/strategy/mind-the-purpose-gap.html (Accessed: 25 April 2025).

Deloitte (2024) '2024 Gen Z and Millennial Survey: Living and working with purpose', Deloitte. Available at: www2.deloitte.com/content/dam/Deloitte/ec/Documents/about-deloitte/deloitte-2024-genz-millennial-survey.pdf (Accessed: 25 April 2025).

Forbes (2018) 'How MOD Pizza's culture drives growth and impact', Forbes, 31 October. Available at: www.forbes.com/sites/simonmainwaring/2018/10/31/how-mod-pizzas-culture-drives-growth-and-impact/ (Accessed: 25 April 2025).

Forbes. (2024) 'The brand promise: Your key to customer loyalty and employee purpose', Forbes, 26 April. Available at: www.forbes.com/councils/forbesbusinesscouncil/2024/04/26/the-brand-promise-your-key-to-customer-loyalty-and-employee-purpose/ (Accessed: 25 April 2025).

Gallup (2023) 'The Benefits of Employee Engagement', Gallup.com. Available at: www.gallup.com/workplace/236927/employee-engagement-drives-growth.aspx (Accessed: 25 April 2025).

HRZone (2024) 'The impact of employee disengagement', HRZone. Available at: www.hrzone.com/blog/the-impact-of-employee-disengagement/ (Accessed: 25 April 2025).

HBR. (2008) 'Why Zappos pays new employees to quit – and you should too', Harvard Business Review, 19 May. Available at: www.hbr.org/2008/05/why-zappos-pays-new-employees-to-quit-and-you-should-too (Accessed: 25 April 2025).

Patagonia (2025) 'What we offer'. Available at: www.eu.patagonia.com/gb/en/what-we-offer/ (Accessed: 25 April 2025).

SAP (2022) 'MOD Pizza: Breaking down barriers to equitable job opportunities and creating a culture of opportunity', SAP Customer Success Stories, 24 August. Available at: www.sap.com/asset/dynamic/2022/8/ed4692e7-32d5-49e9-9240-a0a2dc2f8909.html (Accessed: 25 April 2025).

Strategic Leadership (2024) 'How Patagonia aligns strategy execution with environmental and social responsibility', Strategic Leadership, 21 September. Available at: www.strategicleaders.com/patagonia-aligns-strategy-environmental-social-responsibility/ (Accessed: 25 April 2025).

Team Tactics (2023) 'How does Google motivate their staff?', Team Tactics, 9 January. Available at: www.teamtactics.co.uk/blog/google-motivate-staff/ (Accessed: 25 April 2025).

Zappos Insights (2025) 'About Zappos culture and values'. Available at: www.zappos.com/c/zappos-insights (Accessed: 25 April 2025).

Nilsson, P. (2024) Companies that keep staff happy perform better, study finds. Financial Times, 1 April. Available at: https://www.ft.com/content/044fc5f3-e4b4-4b0d-9849-939d8c4f73da

CHAPTER 2
RETURN ON INTEGRITY – BUILDING TRUST WITH YOUR CUSTOMERS

INTRODUCING RETURN ON INTEGRITY

Integrity is the foundation of trust in today's business landscape, shaping how companies differentiate themselves and build lasting relationships with customers. As consumers become more discerning and informed, they seek brands that not only offer quality products and services but also align with their values, demonstrate transparency and act with accountability. In an era of heightened scrutiny and rapid digital transformation, trust has become a defining factor in brand loyalty and business success. However, earning and sustaining trust requires more than just good intentions – it demands an unwavering commitment to integrity at every touchpoint, from marketing and customer service to supply chain decisions and executive leadership.

Return on Integrity isn't just an ethical stance, it's a measurable business strategy that fosters trust, customer loyalty and long-term resilience. Unlike traditional success metrics, such as profit margins or revenue growth, Return on Integrity is rooted in intangible yet powerful drivers: transparency, ethical decision-making and corporate responsibility.

As consumers increasingly align their purchasing decisions with companies that reflect their values, integrity has emerged as a core differentiator in today's marketplace. According to the Edelman Trust Barometer (2021), over 80% of consumers consider trust a crucial factor in deciding whether to support a brand. This trend is particularly pronounced among younger demographics, who actively seek out companies that demonstrate ethical leadership and social responsibility (CMSWire, 2023).

Integrity-driven businesses understand that trust must be consistently reinforced. Transparency in product sourcing, ethical labour practices and environmental sustainability efforts not only differentiate brands but also cultivate deep, long-term customer loyalty. Moreover, companies that embed integrity into their culture are better equipped to navigate crises and maintain trust even when challenges arise. Research from PwC's Global Consumer Insights Survey (2020) highlights that millennial consumers are particularly likely to support companies that demonstrate transparency and openly communicate their ethical practices, especially during challenging times.

In this chapter, you will explore the pivotal role of Return on Integrity in fostering customer trust and business sustainability. By examining real-world examples from Patagonia, Unilever, REI, The Body Shop, Toyota and Ben & Jerry's, you'll uncover how integrity translates into measurable business advantages – enhancing trust, strengthening customer loyalty and driving long-term sustainability. You will also explore the key metrics that businesses can use to track and quantify the impact of integrity-driven initiatives, from Customer Trust Index (CTI) scores and Net Promoter Scores (NPS) to employee engagement and brand sentiment analysis.

Ultimately, Return on Integrity is not just about ethical behaviour, it's about creating a business culture that resonates deeply with customers, employees and stakeholders. Companies that embed integrity into their DNA are not only building better businesses but are also positioning themselves for sustainable growth and a lasting competitive advantage.

To bring Return on Integrity to life, this chapter explores how businesses can embed ethical leadership and transparency across all functions – turning values into action and trust into a measurable advantage.

LEVERAGING RETURN ON INTEGRITY

By the end of this chapter, you will have a comprehensive understanding of how to implement and prioritise Return on Integrity within your organisation, regardless of industry or size. You'll gain both strategic insight and practical tools, empowering you to build a values-led business that earns trust, deepens customer loyalty and supports long-term growth. This chapter will equip you to:

- **Leverage the strategic importance of integrity**
  Understand how integrity acts as a foundational driver of customer trust, retention and brand reputation. As expectations for transparency and accountability grow, businesses that lead with integrity will strengthen their credibility, differentiate their brand and build lasting customer relationships.

- **Build the core components of a culture of integrity**
  Explore the essential elements required to create a culture rooted in integrity, including ethical sourcing, transparent communication, responsible leadership and values-based decision-making. These components are critical for embedding integrity across your organisation and driving consistent behaviour at every level.

- **Implement best practices from leading organisations**
  Learn from real-world case studies featuring companies such as Patagonia, Unilever, REI, The Body Shop, Toyota and Ben & Jerry's. These examples showcase how leading brands have translated integrity into action – whether through crisis response, purpose-led campaigns or ethical operations – and offer lessons that can be applied to your own context.

- **Measure success using key integrity metrics**
  Gain practical tools to evaluate the success of your integrity-driven strategies using both qualitative and quantitative measures. Learn how to track and analyse key indicators such as the Customer Trust Index (CTI), Net Promoter Score (NPS), customer satisfaction, brand sentiment, and employee engagement.

- **Implement practical strategies for short- and long-term impact**
  Discover a blend of immediate actions and long-term commitments that can embed integrity into daily operations and strategic planning. From enhancing transparency to scaling Corporate Social Responsibility (CSR) initiatives, these strategies help align your internal culture with external expectations.

- **Prioritise and align integrity initiatives for maximum value**
  Recognise where integrity efforts will create the greatest impact and how to align them with broader business goals. Develop a clear approach to prioritising initiatives, managing resources effectively and sustaining progress across the organisation.

Now let's bring Return on Integrity to life.

Consumer trust and integrity model

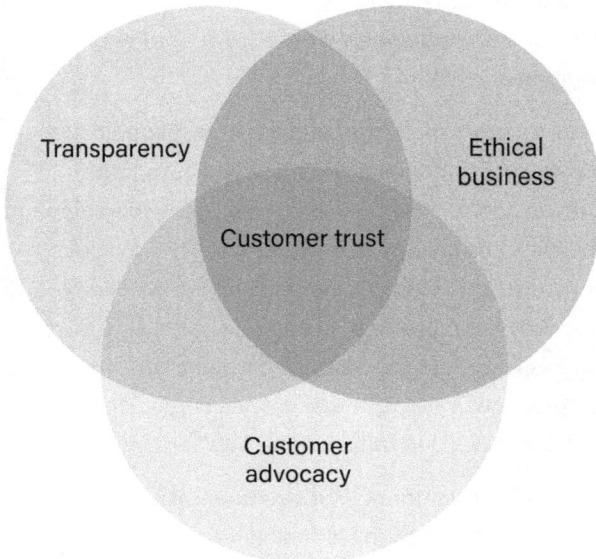

Transparency

Ethical business

Customer trust

Customer advocacy

RETURN ON INTEGRITY IN ACTION

The following case studies offer a practical look at how industry-leading brands have successfully integrated Return on Integrity into their business models. These examples provide valuable insights into the diverse ways in which integrity can be operationalised, offering a blueprint for other companies seeking to enhance customer trust, loyalty and brand resilience.

PATAGONIA - BUILDING BRAND LOYALTY THROUGH ENVIRONMENTAL RESPONSIBILITY

Patagonia has set itself apart as a brand committed to environmental responsibility, consistently aligning its business practices with its mission of 'saving our home planet.' In 2011, the company launched the groundbreaking 'Don't Buy This Jacket' campaign, which encouraged customers to consider the environmental impact of their purchases rather than simply buying more products. This anti-consumerist message was unconventional and risky, but it resonated with Patagonia's customer base, who valued the brand's integrity and commitment to sustainability. The campaign sparked global conversations about conscious consumerism and positioned Patagonia as a brand willing to prioritise ethics over profit (Patagonia, 2011).

Patagonia's Worn Wear programme further underscores its dedication to environmental stewardship (Patagonia, 2025). By encouraging customers to repair, reuse and recycle their Patagonia gear, the company reduces waste and builds a community of environmentally conscious advocates. According to the 2017 Cone Communications CSR Study, 88% of consumers say they are more loyal to companies that support social or environmental issues. Patagonia's example illustrates that when companies align their practices with customer values, they foster deep loyalty and trust that extends beyond transactional relationships.

Key takeaway: Patagonia's commitment to environmental responsibility has helped it cultivate a loyal customer base that values integrity. The brand's example demonstrates that aligning business practices with customer values is a powerful way to build lasting trust and stand apart in a crowded marketplace.

UNILEVER – A RELENTLESS FOCUS ON RESPONSIBLE BUSINESS PRACTICES

Unilever has long been at the forefront of ethical sourcing and responsible business practices, largely through its Sustainable Living Plan. This initiative commits Unilever to reducing environmental impact, promoting health and well-being and improving livelihoods across its value chain (Unilever, 2010).

One of Unilever's best-known brands, Dove, exemplifies this commitment through its Real Beauty campaign, which promotes body positivity and challenges conventional beauty standards. The campaign initially ran in 2004 and has resonated globally, earning trust from customers who value authenticity and inclusivity in advertising (Kantar, 2024). According to Prophet, Dove's brand value grew from approximately $200 million in the 1990s to nearly $4 billion by 2013 (Prophet, 2013), highlighting the power of purpose-led marketing and consistent integrity in brand building.

Unilever's focus on ethical sourcing is central to its integrity-driven approach. Through its Responsible Sourcing Policy and partnerships with suppliers, the company ensures high social and environmental standards across its supply chain (Unilever, 2017). Unilever's commitment to transparency and ethical practices has helped build consumer trust and loyalty, demonstrating how aligning corporate values with customer expectations can drive long-term brand strength (Unilever, 2021).

Key takeaway: Unilever demonstrates that ethical sourcing and transparency in operations are essential for building trust and loyalty among consumers.
This approach not only attracts customers but also strengthens brand equity over the long term.

REI - REINFORCING BRAND VALUES THROUGH MISSION-DRIVEN CAMPAIGNS

REI, a cooperative for outdoor recreational equipment, has created a unique brand identity through its #OptOutside campaign. Launched in 2015, the initiative saw REI close all its retail stores on Black Friday – a major shopping day – to encourage employees and customers to spend time outdoors instead of shopping. The campaign's bold message resonated strongly with REI's community, reinforcing the company's commitment to environmental stewardship and well-being. Opt Outside has since become an annual tradition and a cornerstone of REI's brand identity, demonstrating its values in action (REI, 2017).

This initiative led to a 36% increase in membership applications and more than 1.4 million people pledging to #OptOutside in its first year alone (Marketing Maverick, 2025). The strength of the campaign lies in its authenticity and alignment with REI's cooperative values. By staying true to its mission and inviting customers to share in those values, REI has cultivated a loyal community grounded in shared purpose.

Key takeaway: REI's #OptOutside campaign shows that mission-driven initiatives can strengthen customer relationships and create a loyal community of supporters. When brands lead with integrity and align their actions with customer values, they foster deep trust and connection.

MARKS & SPENCER - SAFEGUARDING CUSTOMER TRUST THROUGH TRANSPARENT CRISIS

Marks & Spencer (M&S), one of the UK's most trusted retail brands, faced a critical test of its customer relationships during its recent cyber security incident. When a potential data breach impacted customer accounts, M&S responded swiftly with a commitment to transparency and customer-first communication.

The company immediately notified affected customers, proactively locked accounts to prevent further risk, and provided clear guidance on how to reset credentials securely (M&S Press Office, 2025). Rather than downplaying the issue, M&S prioritised open updates across its website, email, and social channels, reflecting its long-standing ethos of integrity and customer care.

This approach reinforced M&S's reputation for reliability in an era when cyber threats are increasingly common. Research shows that 72% of UK consumers trust brands more when they communicate openly during a crisis (Edelman Trust Barometer, 2025), a principle M&S exemplified by treating its customers as partners in resolving the issue.

Key takeaway: The M&S example highlights how transparent, empathetic crisis management can protect and even strengthen customer trust. In highly competitive retail markets, a brand's ability to handle security challenges with honesty and speed is a critical pillar of long-term loyalty.

TOYOTA – REGAINING TRUST THROUGH INTEGRITY IN CRISIS MANAGEMENT

In 2009, Toyota faced a significant reputational challenge when millions of vehicles were recalled due to safety issues involving unintended acceleration. Rather than evading responsibility, Toyota responded with transparency and accountability – issuing global recalls, providing regular public updates and addressing customer concerns directly. This response demonstrated the company's commitment to integrity and safety in the face of intense scrutiny (Hyde Street Journal, 2014).

Although the crisis initially damaged Toyota's reputation, the company's swift and responsible response played a key role in rebuilding customer trust. Industry observers have highlighted Toyota's long-term recovery as a case study in crisis management, noting that transparency and clear communication helped the brand preserve loyalty despite serious operational setbacks.

Key takeaway: Toyota's response to its crisis shows that prioritising integrity and accountability in crisis management is essential for preserving customer trust. Transparent and responsive crisis strategies can mitigate reputational damage and reinforce long-term loyalty.

BEN & JERRY'S - ADVOCACY AND ACTIVISM AS A CORE BRAND VALUE

Ben & Jerry's is renowned for its commitment to activism and social justice, consistently using its platform to champion causes such as climate justice, racial equality and fair trade. This unwavering advocacy is deeply embedded in the company's mission and marketing, shaping how it engages with consumers and the wider world. From launching educational campaigns on racial justice to supporting progressive environmental policies, the brand has made activism a defining characteristic of its identity (Ben & Jerry's, 2025).

Rather than appealing to mass-market neutrality, Ben & Jerry's has embraced the risks of taking bold stances, and in doing so, has cultivated a loyal customer base of ethically-minded consumers. According to the company's Social & Environmental Assessment Report, these values are a core reason customers feel aligned with the brand (Ben & Jerry's, 2021). Its integrity-driven activism has helped build a brand that feels authentic, mission-led and trusted.

Key takeaway: The Ben & Jerry's example illustrates that integrity-driven activism can attract and retain customers who share the brand's values. By aligning its mission with its advocacy, Ben & Jerry's has built a deeply loyal customer base and set itself apart in the marketplace.

HOW TO MEASURE SUCCESS WITHIN RETURN ON INTEGRITY

Integrity is not just a value – it's a strategic driver of trust, loyalty and long-term business performance. To measure Return on Integrity effectively, organisations must evaluate both internal and external perceptions of ethical consistency. This includes how trust is earned, maintained and reflected in customer loyalty, employee engagement, public sentiment and operational outcomes. The following metrics offer a comprehensive approach to measuring the tangible impact of integrity across the business.

Customer Trust Index (CTI)

The CTI is a direct reflection of how customers perceive the company's transparency, honesty and ethical consistency. As a custom metric, it offers a clear way to quantify the impact of integrity on brand credibility and long-term customer relationships.

- **How to measure**: Design and deploy surveys with targeted questions around transparency, reliability and communication ethics. Use a standardised scoring system for longitudinal tracking and benchmarking.
- **Segmentation strategy**: Break down trust levels by customer demographics and product lines to see where integrity is perceived most strongly, or needs work.
- **Benchmark**: Compare scores before and after campaigns or policy changes, and against industry trust benchmarks to contextualise results.

Net Promoter Score (NPS)

NPS is more than a loyalty score – it's a reflection of customer trust. When customers recommend a brand, they're often endorsing its values, ethics and transparency. This makes NPS a powerful indirect measure of perceived integrity.

- **How to measure**: Ask the standard NPS questions and calculate the score by subtracting detractors (0–6) from promoters (9–10). Follow up with open-ended questions focused on integrity-driven reasoning.
- **Tip**: Track how NPS shifts after public-facing, trust-building initiatives, such as increased transparency in sourcing or customer policies.

- **Segmentation strategy**: Analyse NPS by engagement levels, purchase history or customer type for deeper insight into trust-based loyalty.

Customer Satisfaction (CSAT) surveys

CSAT surveys provide a direct line to how customers feel during individual touchpoints, including whether they believe they're being treated fairly, honestly and ethically.

- **How to measure**: Add integrity-based questions to standard CSAT surveys (e.g. 'Do you feel the company provides honest information?'). Use a Likert scale to quantify answers across touchpoints.
- **Tip**: Compare CSAT responses across departments and channels to identify where customer perceptions of integrity vary most.
- **Tracking opportunity**: Monitor CSAT shifts before and after launching policies related to ethical advertising or returns.

Brand sentiment analysis

Brand sentiment gives you a real-time view of how the public perceives your ethical stance. Positive sentiment around values like honesty, transparency and fairness reflects a strong Return on Integrity at the brand level.

- **How to measure**: Use tools like Brandwatch or Hootsuite to track online mentions of your brand alongside keywords, such as trustworthy, honest, or ethical.
- **Tool**: Use sentiment scoring to monitor positive/neutral/negative commentary and tie changes to external campaigns or press releases.
- **Tracking tip**: Map sentiment shifts against public announcements, product recalls or value-led campaigns.

Employee engagement and feedback

Integrity isn't just external, it must be felt internally by employees. When team members trust their organisation's ethics, they are more engaged, loyal and effective in serving customers.

- **How to measure**: Use anonymous employee surveys with questions focused on ethics, transparency and trust in leadership.
- **Additional insight**: Monitor participation in ethics training and analyse stay/exit interview data for recurring trust-related themes and patterns.
- **Metric tip**: Track changes in engagement scores pre- and post-ethics initiatives to assess internal impact.

Customer retention and churn rates

Trust drives loyalty, and when it breaks, customer churn follows. Retention metrics reveal how well integrity is contributing to long-term customer relationships.

- **How to measure**: Track retention following campaigns or policy updates tied to integrity (e.g. sustainable sourcing, policy clarity).
- **Segmentation strategy**: Analyse churn rates across customer types or demographics to understand which groups are most sensitive to integrity-driven changes.
- **Insight**: Pair churn data with NPS and CSAT to reveal root causes of loyalty or loss.

Compliance and audit reports

Compliance metrics provide a structured, third-party view of whether the organisation's practices align with legal and ethical standards, reinforcing credibility and trustworthiness.

- **How to measure**: Schedule internal audits and external reviews. Use transparent tracking systems for breaches, resolutions and certifications.
- **Tip**: Report compliance scores and outcomes publicly to build external trust and internal accountability.
- **Benchmark**: Use third-party ethics audits and regulatory feedback as external validation.

Incident reporting and resolution metrics

How you respond to integrity breaches is just as important as how you prevent them. Incident reporting data reflects your transparency, responsiveness and commitment to ethical accountability.

- **How to measure**: Use an accessible, transparent reporting system. Track resolution speed, satisfaction and recurrence of similar complaints.
- **Tracking tip**: Look at resolution time trends and repeat incident types to identify weak spots in policies or training.
- **Tool**: Consider using a centralised dashboard to track and report on resolution metrics.

Stakeholder interviews and focus groups

Perceptions of integrity aren't always captured in surveys. Engaging directly with stakeholders, both internal and external, provides depth, nuance and insight into how your values are being experienced.

- **How to measure**: Conduct regular sessions to gather honest feedback on how the brand's values are perceived.
- **Qualitative insight**: Use insights to refine strategies, language and communications around integrity initiatives.
- **Tracking**: Document common themes and measure shifts in perception over time, especially after major value-led efforts.

Awards and public recognition

Recognition from external bodies affirms your integrity with stakeholders and demonstrates that ethical excellence is visible, credible and appreciated.

- **How to measure:** Track awards won in ethical leadership, CSR or governance. Monitor related media mentions and industry recognitions.
- **Benchmark:** Compare award wins and press mentions year-over-year as an indicator of your brand's ethical momentum.
- **Tip:** Leverage public recognition in marketing and PR to reinforce your values in the eyes of customers.

Measuring success in Return on Integrity requires a holistic approach that incorporates both quantitative and qualitative metrics. From customer surveys and brand sentiment analysis to employee feedback and audit reports, these tools collectively paint a detailed picture of a company's ethical standing and its impact on long-term business outcomes. By tracking these metrics, businesses can identify areas for improvement, reinforce their commitment to transparency and build stronger relationships with customers and employees alike. This comprehensive approach ensures that integrity becomes a strategic pillar for sustainable growth and brand loyalty.

IMPLEMENTING RETURN ON INTEGRITY

Creating a values-led brand requires both immediate action and sustained commitment. Quick wins help establish credibility and build trust through clear, visible behaviours, while long-term strategies embed integrity into the organisation's culture, leadership and operations. For these efforts to succeed, they must be reinforced at every level – from executives and HR to operational teams, supply chain and customer service. When every function upholds integrity through decisions, actions and communication, businesses not only protect their reputation, they build a foundation for lasting loyalty, internal trust and long-term success.

Quick wins

1. **Increase transparency in customer communication**
   Customers want transparency, especially regarding product information, sourcing and company policies. Start by making clear information available on your website, social media channels and marketing materials. For example, share details about your company's production process or the source of materials used in your products. Transparent communication builds trust and shows customers that the company is committed to openness.

2. **Implement ethical sourcing standards**
   Review and update your sourcing practices to align with ethical standards, focusing on sustainability, fair labour and environmentally friendly production methods. Small actions, like choosing certified suppliers or reducing the use of single-use plastics, send a strong message to consumers. Implementing ethical sourcing standards can lead to immediate positive feedback from customers who are increasingly concerned about the impact of their purchases.

3. **Develop accessible customer feedback channels**
   Empower your customers to provide feedback by creating accessible channels such as online reviews, social media or direct customer service lines. When customers feel their voices are heard, they are more likely to develop a sense of trust and loyalty toward the brand. Make it clear that feedback is valued by responding promptly and taking actionable steps based on customer input.

4. **Highlight CSR initiatives in marketing efforts**

   Customers appreciate knowing that their chosen brands are making a difference in the community. Use your marketing channels to showcase CSR initiatives in an authentic, non-promotional way. For instance, include customer stories about how their purchases support causes like environmental conservation or fair trade. This not only reinforces the brand's integrity but also encourages customers to see their purchases as contributing to a greater purpose.

Long-term strategies

1. **Foster a culture of integrity across the organisation**

   Integrity should be a part of the company's DNA, embedded in every aspect of its operations. Leaders can foster this culture by modelling ethical behaviour, establishing clear integrity standards and making integrity a core value in the company's mission. For example, build training programmes focused on ethical decision-making and ensure that integrity is part of the criteria for evaluating employee performance. A culture of integrity becomes a self-reinforcing mechanism when employees understand its value and see it consistently practised by leadership.

2. **Develop a comprehensive and aligned CSR strategy**

   Rather than focusing on sporadic charitable activities, develop a comprehensive CSR strategy that aligns with the company's core values. Take time to assess which social and environmental issues resonate with both the brand's mission and the interests of its target audience. By prioritising meaningful CSR programmes, companies can build a long-lasting positive reputation, attract ethically-minded customers and create a shared sense of purpose among employees.

3. **Emphasise accountability and transparency at leadership level**

   Integrity in leadership is crucial for setting the tone across an organisation. Encourage leaders to be transparent in their decision-making processes, take responsibility for mistakes and demonstrate accountability when challenges arise. Leaders who embody integrity foster a ripple effect, creating a workplace where employees feel aligned with the company's values and empowered to act with integrity in their own roles.

4. **Create crisis management plans focused on integrity and transparency**

   Crises are inevitable, and companies must be prepared to respond with integrity. Develop crisis management plans that prioritise honest communication, accountability and customer reassurance. For example, in the event of a product recall or public relations issue, quickly address the issue with customers, apologise if necessary and offer clear explanations of the steps being taken to resolve the problem. This approach minimises long-term reputational damage and preserves customer trust.

Driving engagement at every level

For executives and senior leadership:

- **Make integrity a strategic priority:** Long-term business success depends on trust – embedding ethical leadership and transparency at the highest levels ensures credibility with customers, employees and stakeholders.
- **Align business objectives with ethical decision-making:** Short-term gains should never come at the expense of integrity.

Leaders must balance profitability with purpose to maintain trust and reputation.

- **Lead by example:** Employees and customers take cues from leadership behaviour. Senior executives must consistently uphold and model the company's values in their decision-making and communication.

- **Build a foundation of trust as a strategic imperative:** Trust drives brand loyalty, encourages customer advocacy and can provide a competitive edge when competitors fall short in transparency or ethical behaviour. Stakeholders who prioritise integrity are positioning the brand not just for short-term gains but for long-term, sustainable growth.

For operational managers:

- **Ensure policies and practices reflect company values:** Integrity must be embedded in daily operations, from fair employee treatment to transparent pricing and responsible sourcing.

- **Foster a culture of accountability:** Encouraging employees to speak up about ethical concerns without fear of repercussions strengthens their trust in the company and builds organisational resilience.

- **Build trust through consistent communication:** Employees, suppliers and customers should have clear visibility into how integrity drives decision-making across all business functions.

- **Ensure consistency across all customer touchpoints:** Integrity must be applied across every aspect of the business – from marketing messages and product quality to customer service and post-sale follow-ups. Operational managers play a crucial role in upholding these standards.

For HR and people teams:

- **Embed integrity into hiring and training:** Recruitment should prioritise cultural fit and ethical decision-making, while ongoing training reinforces the importance of integrity in daily roles.
- **Establish clear guidelines for ethical behaviour:** Codes of conduct, whistleblowing policies and leadership training ensure employees understand and uphold company values.
- **Support a diverse and inclusive workplace:** Integrity is demonstrated through fairness, respect and equal opportunities – ensuring that all employees feel valued and heard.
- **Align CSR with core brand values:** CSR efforts must reflect the brand's authentic mission. Endeavours that resonate with both employees and customers help reinforce the organisation's commitment to doing good – and doing it consistently.

For customer-facing teams:

- **Be transparent in customer interactions:** Trust is built when frontline employees provide honest, clear and ethical communication regarding products, services and policies.
- **Handle customer concerns with integrity:** Resolving issues fairly and openly, without hiding behind policies, enhances brand reputation and customer loyalty.
- **Champion ethical brand advocacy:** Employees should actively communicate the company's values to customers, reinforcing trust and differentiation in the marketplace.
- **Apply transparency and accountability during crises:** In times of challenge, customers look to frontline teams for reassurance. Ensuring customer-facing employees have tools and training to respond openly builds resilience and reinforces trust.

For supply chain and procurement teams:

- **Embrace ethical sourcing and transparent supply chains:**
  As consumer awareness grows, the brands that succeed will
  be those that prioritise fair labour practices, sustainability
  and visibility across their supply chains. Transparency about
  sourcing, production methods and working conditions
  reinforces trust and brand credibility.
- **Audit and improve supplier relationships:** Regular
  evaluation of suppliers and partners against ethical standards is
  critical to maintaining integrity across the value chain.

By embedding integrity across leadership, operations, HR, procurement
and customer experience, organisations can build a business that is not
only commercially successful but also earns lasting trust and loyalty from
employees and customers alike.

THE LASTING IMPACT OF RETURN ON INTEGRITY

Return on Integrity represents a transformative approach to business –
one that prioritises ethical behaviour, transparency and accountability
as essential drivers of brand trust and customer loyalty. In an era where
consumers actively align their purchasing decisions with their values,
integrity has become a defining pillar of successful brands. Companies
that foster a culture of integrity create not only value for their customers
but also a sustainable foundation for long-term growth, resilience and
competitive advantage.

The case studies explored in this chapter demonstrate that integrity is
not a passive value, but a strategic imperative. Each of these brands has
embedded ethical principles into the core of their operations, from environmental responsibility and ethical sourcing to purpose-led marketing
and transparency in crisis response. In doing so, they've earned deep trust

and loyalty from customers who view them as authentic reflections of their own values.

Beyond external reputation, Return on Integrity also fosters internal alignment. Employees who witness their organisation's genuine commitment to ethical practises are more engaged, more motivated and more likely to serve as ambassadors for the brand. Research from PwC confirms that values-aligned employees are significantly more likely to remain with their companies and contribute positively to workplace culture and customer experience (PwC, 2023).

Implementing Return on Integrity requires both short-term wins and sustained investment. Immediate actions, such as increasing transparency, improving communication and inviting feedback, can begin shifting public perception and reinforcing trust. Over time, these efforts must be supported by leadership accountability, CSR alignment and integrity-driven decision making embedded across the organisation.

In a world of instant access and constant scrutiny, transparency and authenticity are non-negotiable. Return on Integrity provides a framework for aligning business practices with the expectations of today's customers and stakeholders. Brands that lead with integrity don't just win temporary favour, they build enduring relationships, brand equity and a reputation that can weather any storm. For companies seeking meaningful, sustainable growth, prioritising integrity is not a trend – it is a business imperative.

TAKE ACTION

Start by identifying one area of your business where transparency or ethical alignment could be improved. Whether it's publishing your sourcing standards, opening up customer feedback loops or embedding integrity into team decision-making – small changes can build real trust.

Integrity isn't built overnight. But with consistent action and courageous leadership, it becomes a competitive advantage that lasts.

REFERENCES

Ben & Jerry's (2021) 'Social & Environmental Assessment Report (SEAR)'. Available at: www.benjerry.com/files/live/sites/us/files/about-us/sear-report/2021/2021-SEAR-Report.pdf (Accessed: 18 April 2025).

Ben & Jerry's (2025) 'Our Values, Activism and Mission'. Available at:www.benjerry.co.uk/values (Accessed: 4 May 2025).

CMSWire (2023) 'Using social initiatives to build trusted customer relationships'. Available at: www.cmswire.com/customer-experience/using-social-initiatives-to-build-trusted-customer-relationships/ (Accessed: 27 April 2025).

Comparably (2025) 'The Body Shop NPS & Customer Reviews'. Available at: www.comparably.com/brands/the-body-shop (Accessed: 27 April 2025).

Cone Communications (2017) '2017 Cone Communications CSR Study: How to Speak to the Next Generation of Responsible Consumers'. Available at: www.cbd.int/doc/case-studies/inc/cs-inc-cone-communications-en.pdf (Accessed: 27 April 2025).

Cruelty Free International (2018) 'Forever Against Animal Testing delivers 8.3 million signatures to United Nations'. Available at: www.crueltyfreeinternational.org/latest-news-and-updates/cruelty-free-international-and-body-shop-fight-continues-five-decades-on (Accessed: 27 April 2025).

Dove (2025) 'Dove Real Beauty Campaign'. Available at: www.dove.com/uk/dove-self-esteem-project.html (Accessed: 18 April 2025).

Edelman (2021) '2021 Edelman Trust Barometer Special Report: Trust, The New Brand Equity'. Available at: www.edelman.com/sites/g/files/aatuss191/files/2021-06/2021%20Edelman%20Trust%20Barometer%20Specl%20Report%20Trust%20The%20New%20Brand%20Equity.pdf (Accessed: 27 April 2025).

Hyde Street Journal (2014) 'Toyota's Recall Crisis Case Study'. Available at: www.hydestreetjournal.wordpress.com/2014/12/08/toyotas-recall-crisis-case-study/ (Accessed: 18 April 2025).

Kantar (2024) 'Real Beauty, Real Impact: Dove's 20-Year Glow-Up'. Available at: www.kantar.com/inspiration/agile-market-research/real-beauty-real-impact-doves-20-year-glow-up (Accessed: 18 April 2025).

Marketing Maverick (2025) 'Here's Everything About REI's #OptOutside Campaign'. Available at: www.marketingmaverick.io/p/optoutside-campaign-by-rei (Accessed: 27 April 2025).

Patagonia (2011) 'Don't Buy This Jacket, Black Friday and the *New York Times*'. Available at: www.patagonia.com/stories/dont-buy-this-jacket-black-friday-and-the-new-york-times/story-18615.html (Accessed: 27 April 2025).

Patagonia (2025) 'Worn Wear Program'. Available at: www.wornwear.patagonia.com (Accessed: 27 April 2025).

Prophet (2013) 'Dove: The Most Impressive Brand Builder in the Last 15 Years'. Available at: www.prophet.com/2013/05/138-dove-the-most-impressive-brand-builder-in-the-last-15-years/ (Accessed: 18 April 2025).

PwC (2020) 'Global Consumer Insights Survey 2020'. Available at: www.pwc.com/gx/en/consumer-markets/consumer-insights-survey/2020/pwc-consumer-insights-survey-2020.pdf (Accessed: 27 April 2025).

PwC (2023) 'Can organizational alignment boost profitability?' Available at: www.pwc.com/gx/en/issues/c-suite-insights/the-leadership-agenda/can-organisational-alignment-boost-profitability.html (Accessed: 27 April 2025).

REI (2017) 'The history of #OptOutside'. Available at: www.rei.com/blog/social/the-history-of-opt-outside (Accessed: 27 April 2025).

Unilever (2010) 'Unilever Sustainable Living Plan'. Available at: www.unilever.com/files/origin/9752ff2d82b8afabb507eb92c47b5dad795801d5.pdf/unilever-sustainable-living-plan.pdf (Accessed: 4 May 2025).

Unilever (2017) 'Responsible Sourcing Policy'. Available at: www.unilever.com/files/e6e301e3-7e20-4363-b6aa-ef0f4a4e3322/responsible-sourcing-policy-interactive-final.pdf (Accessed: 27 April 2025).

Unilever (2021) 'Code of Business Principles and Code Policies'. Available at: www.unilever.com/files/92ui5egz/production/a7ad961ef886a578ab4dd316b4e5195cbc0965a0.pdf (Accessed: 27 April 2025).

CHAPTER 3

RETURN ON INCLUSION – CREATING A BUSINESS THAT BETTER REFLECTS YOUR CUSTOMERS

INTRODUCING RETURN ON INCLUSION

In today's diverse and interconnected world, inclusion is no longer optional but a business imperative – one that underpins a company's ability to connect with customers, inspire employees and maintain a competitive edge. Return on Inclusion refers to the tangible benefits that arise when organisations actively embrace diversity and foster inclusive practices. These benefits include increased customer loyalty, improved innovation, a stronger brand reputation and a more resilient workforce. By embedding inclusive values at their core, businesses can cultivate teams that reflect the communities they serve – enhancing both trust and customer satisfaction.

Inclusion has rapidly emerged as a key driver of business success, reshaping how companies engage with employees and customers alike. Gone are the days when diversity and inclusion (D&I) were seen solely as HR responsibilities or social initiatives. Today's forward-thinking organisations recognise inclusion as a foundation for sustainable growth, innovation and customer loyalty. The McKinsey & Company 'Diversity Wins' report (2020) highlights this shift, showing that companies with greater ethnic and cultural diversity at leadership level are 36% more likely to outperform their peers in profitability.

For businesses today, inclusion encompasses a wide range of practices: diverse hiring, equitable representation across roles, accessible product design, cultural sensitivity in marketing and the creation of safe, empowering environments where all employees can thrive. When companies embrace inclusion, they are not only fulfilling a moral obligation – they are making a strategic decision that enhances innovation, attracts top talent and deepens customer relationships. Deloitte research found that organisations with inclusive cultures are twice as likely to meet or exceed financial targets, three times as likely to be high-performing, six times more likely to be innovative and eight times more likely to achieve better business outcomes (Deloitte, 2021).

This chapter examines the concept of Return on Inclusion as a strategic lever to align business practices with the expectations of modern consumers and employees. Through real-world examples, you'll explore how leading organisations use inclusion to strengthen brand loyalty, create relevant products and services and embed equity across the business. Inclusion is no longer a side initiative, it is a core business strategy that enhances identity, drives engagement and supports long-term success.

To apply this thinking in practice, this chapter explores how Return on Inclusion can be embedded into every layer of your organisation – transforming good intentions into daily impacts.

LEVERAGING RETURN ON INCLUSION

To turn inclusion from intention into impact, businesses need clear strategies, practical tools and measurable actions. This chapter breaks down how to embed inclusive practices across your organisation – from culture and leadership to customer experience and product design. This chapter will equip you to:

- **Maximise the strategic value of Return on Inclusion**
  Understand how inclusion acts as a catalyst for innovation, loyalty and brand differentiation. Explore how embedding inclusion into business strategy drives relevance, adaptability and long-term performance in an increasingly diverse world.

- **Build the core elements of an inclusive workplace**
  Identify the foundations of an inclusive culture, including equitable hiring, diverse representation, psychological safety, transparent communication and a strong sense of belonging. Learn how to create a workplace where every employee feels seen, valued and empowered.

- **Implement best practices from leading organisations**
  Examine case studies from companies like Unilever, Microsoft, Airbnb, Target, Nike and Bumble. See how industry leaders are using inclusive hiring, marketing, product design and leadership development to build stronger brands and deeper customer connections.

- **Measure success using meaningful inclusion metrics**
  Discover how to assess the effectiveness of your inclusion strategies using both qualitative and quantitative tools. Key metrics include workforce representation, engagement scores, customer sentiment, retention rates and innovation outputs.

- **Apply practical strategies for immediate and long-term impact**
  Take action through a blend of quick wins – like inclusive language policies and employee resource groups – and longer-term strategies, such as inclusive leadership training, accessible product design and embedded accountability frameworks.

- **Prioritise and align inclusion initiatives across the organisation**
  Learn how to focus your efforts where they matter most. Align inclusion initiatives with wider business objectives and ensure they are supported across departments – from the boardroom to the front lines.

Now let's bring Return on Inclusion to life.

RETURN ON INCLUSION IN ACTION

To understand the impact of Return on Inclusion, we will examine how leading companies have successfully integrated inclusive practices into their core operations. These case studies demonstrate that inclusion not only enhances brand loyalty but also attracts diverse talent, promotes innovation and strengthens customer connections. Each of these examples provides valuable lessons in how inclusion, when fully embraced, becomes a strategic asset.

UNILEVER - CHAMPIONING INCLUSION IN ADVERTISING AND CORPORATE CULTURE

Unilever has a longstanding commitment to promoting inclusivity, both in its workforce and in its marketing. The Dove 'Campaign for Real Beauty' was launched in 2004, in response to a global study revealing only 2% of women described themselves as beautiful. The campaign celebrated women's unique differences rather than stereotypical norms, using real women of various ages, sizes and ethnicities. It sparked a worldwide conversation to widen the definition of beauty and transformed physical appearance from a source of anxiety to confidence. The campaign's success is evident in its tremendous publicity and resonance with female audiences, who found the models involved both relatable and authentic (Dove, 2024).

Internally, Unilever's Unstereotype Initiative goes beyond marketing, focusing on eliminating gender and racial stereotypes within the company's culture and practices. Through training, representation targets and a commitment to equitable promotion practices, Unilever has cultivated a diverse workforce that reflects the values of its customers (Unilever, 2025). This alignment between internal culture and external brand image is a significant factor in Unilever's success, attracting consumers and employees who value inclusivity and integrity.

Key takeaway: Unilever's approach demonstrates that a commitment to inclusivity, from advertising to corporate policies, creates lasting customer loyalty and attracts diverse talent. Companies that align their internal values with their public image foster trust, which in turn strengthens their market position and customer relationships.

MICROSOFT – EXPANDING ACCESSIBILITY AND INCLUSIVE INNOVATION

Microsoft has made strides in creating products that are accessible to all users, including those with disabilities. A core component of its inclusive approach is the Disability Answer Desk, a dedicated support line for users with disabilities. This initiative not only provides essential assistance but also shows Microsoft's dedication to accommodating all customers (Microsoft, 2023). Furthermore, Microsoft's development of adaptive technology, such as the Xbox Adaptive Controller, reflects a commitment to inclusive innovation (Xbox, 2025). By designing products that can be used by people with limited mobility, Microsoft has opened its brand to a broader audience, fostering customer loyalty and establishing itself as a leader in accessibility.

Microsoft also emphasises diversity within its workforce. The company's leadership actively promotes diverse hiring, equitable development programmes and representation across all levels, which contributes to an inclusive culture where different perspectives are valued (Microsoft, 2024). According to Forbes Insights 2020, companies with diverse leadership generate significantly higher innovation revenue and outperform their peers financially, and Microsoft's inclusive approach to leadership exemplifies this. Diverse teams bring unique ideas and solutions, contributing to Microsoft's reputation for creativity and cutting-edge technology.

Key takeaway: Microsoft's focus on accessibility and inclusive product design highlights the role of diversity in driving innovation and customer loyalty. By ensuring that everyone, regardless of physical ability, can use its products, Microsoft has built trust with its customer base, demonstrating that inclusion can be a powerful differentiator in a competitive industry.

AIRBNB – BUILDING COMMUNITY THROUGH INCLUSIVE POLICIES

Airbnb's mission 'to create a world where anyone can belong anywhere', underpins its inclusive approach. However, the company has faced challenges in ensuring inclusivity on its platform, with incidents of racial discrimination reported by some users. In response, Airbnb introduced its 'Open Doors' policy, which promises to support guests who face discrimination by helping them find alternative accommodations. This policy demonstrates Airbnb's proactive approach to creating an inclusive environment, reinforcing its commitment to diversity and fairness (Airbnb, 2022).

Airbnb's inclusive practices also extend to its marketing and community engagement. The company regularly promotes stories of cultural exchange, which emphasises its commitment to creating a diverse and inclusive platform (Airbnb, 2022). A study conducted by Airbnb found that 76% of its users felt more positively about the brand due to its inclusivity efforts, proving that such initiatives resonate deeply with customers and can enhance brand loyalty (Genesis Analytics, 2021).

Key takeaway: Airbnb's proactive policies and inclusive messaging show that addressing discrimination head-on strengthens customer loyalty and enhances brand reputation. By ensuring that all users feel welcome and respected, Airbnb has built a community that values fairness, belonging and inclusivity.

TARGET – EXPANDING INCLUSIVITY THROUGH PRODUCT DIVERSITY

US retailer Target has earned a reputation for inclusive product offerings, such as its adaptive clothing line for people with disabilities and gender-neutral children's clothing. These products cater to segments of the population that are often overlooked by mainstream retailers, allowing Target to stand out in a crowded retail landscape. In 2017, Target introduced its adaptive clothing line, which was met with widespread praise and appreciation from customers, particularly within the disability community (Target, 2018).

Beyond products, Target is committed to a diverse and inclusive workplace. The company's hiring practices focus on building a workforce that reflects the communities it serves, helping to foster a sense of belonging among both employees and customers (Target, 2025). Target's 2021 Corporate Responsibility Report and diversity-related communications emphasise how inclusivity and belonging initiatives drive positive customer experiences and loyalty. Additionally, broader industry surveys, such as Kantar's 2024 Brand Inclusion Index, reveal that 75% of consumers say a brand's diversity and inclusion reputation influences their purchase decisions.

Key takeaway: Target's inclusive product strategy shows that diversity in merchandise can attract and retain customers who value inclusivity. By providing products that meet the needs of underrepresented communities, Target has demonstrated that inclusivity is not just a value but a powerful marketing strategy.

NIKE – CHAMPIONING SOCIAL VALUES THROUGH INCLUSIVE MARKETING

Nike has been at the forefront of inclusive marketing, often taking a stand on social issues that resonate with its diverse audience. Nike's 'Dream Crazy' campaign significantly enhanced its brand image by reinforcing its identity as a socially conscious and inclusive brand willing to take bold stances on important issues. The campaign's emphasis on diversity and overcoming adversity resonated deeply with consumers, resulting in widespread media attention and engagement, including a 31% increase in online sales shortly after its launch and an 18% rise in Nike's stock price by the end of 2018, reflecting strong investor confidence (The Brand Hopper, 2024).

Additionally, 'Dream Crazy' won the Creative Arts Emmy for an Outstanding Commercial, further cementing Nike's reputation as a cultural and marketing leader (CBS News, 2019).

In addition to its marketing, Nike prioritises diversity within its workforce, with policies that promote equitable hiring, development and promotion.

This commitment to diversity fosters a culture of respect and inclusion that extends to its customer base, further enhancing Nike's reputation as a brand that stands for equality and justice (Nike, 2022).

Key takeaway: Nike's focus on inclusivity and social justice demonstrates that companies that align with their customers' values can strengthen brand loyalty. By using its platform to address issues that matter to its audience, Nike has built a strong, authentic connection with its customers.

BUMBLE - EMPOWERING WOMEN AND PROMOTING GENDER EQUALITY

Bumble, the female-led dating app, has set itself apart in a crowded market by flipping traditional dating norms and prioritising gender equality. By empowering women to make the first move, the platform fosters safety, respect and agency, distinguishing it from competitors (Business Wire, 2024). This philosophy has cultivated a loyal and diverse user base that values Bumble's commitment to inclusivity and empowerment (Canvas Business Model, 2024). Research indicates that 60% of women users feel the app provides a better experience by offering them greater control and choice, with features like 'Make the First Move' and 'Opening Moves' enhancing their autonomy (Silicon, 2024).

Within the organisation, Bumble reflects these values through its gender-inclusive hiring practices. Women make up 73% of its board and the majority of its employees. CEO Whitney Wolfe Herd has nurtured a company culture centred on female leadership and empowerment, supporting policies that benefit women throughout their careers, including during pregnancy and postpartum periods (Business Insider, 2021).

Key takeaway: Bumble's commitment to gender equality, both in its product design and workplace culture, underscores the impact of inclusive practices on brand differentiation and customer loyalty. By creating a space that values respect and equality, Bumble has cultivated a unique and loyal user base.

HOW TO MEASURE SUCCESS WITHIN RETURN ON INCLUSION

Measuring the success of inclusion initiatives is essential to understanding the impact these efforts have on employee engagement, customer loyalty and overall business performance. The following metrics and evaluation techniques provide a comprehensive framework to assess Return on Inclusion and ensure that inclusion is not just a statement but a measurable business value.

Diversity and representation metrics

Tracking diversity within an organisation is a foundational step in measuring Return on Inclusion. These metrics assess the demographic composition of employees at all levels – entry, mid-level and senior leadership – and reflect whether the workforce mirrors the diversity of the customer base.

- **How to measure:** Conduct regular audits of gender, race, ethnicity, sexual orientation (if voluntarily disclosed), disability and other relevant demographics. Monitor trends across recruitment, promotion and leadership pipelines.
- **Example:** If a company finds that only 20% of leadership roles are held by women, but 50% of the total workforce is female, this signals a representation gap in leadership that needs to be addressed.

Employee engagement and inclusion scores

Employees who feel valued and included are more likely to be engaged, motivated and loyal. These scores reflect how psychologically safe, respected and supported employees feel in the workplace.

- **How to measure:** Use inclusion-focused employee surveys (e.g. Gallup's Q12 or customised questionnaires) with questions on belonging, openness, respect and inclusion.

- **Example:** If engagement surveys reveal a drop in perceived inclusivity among under-represented groups, it signals a need for targeted interventions, such as cultural competency training.

Net Promoter Score (NPS) and customer loyalty

Inclusive brands often enjoy greater customer loyalty. NPS not only measures likelihood to recommend but can also highlight how well inclusivity efforts resonate with different customer segments.

- **How to measure:** Segment NPS results by demographic variables (where appropriate) and review open-ended responses for mentions of inclusive values or experiences.
- **Example:** A retailer might find that NPS scores are significantly higher among customers who resonate with the company's inclusive marketing, showing how representation builds loyalty.

Brand sentiment analysis

Brand sentiment gives real-time insights into how customers perceive your inclusivity. It can highlight whether diversity and equity messages are seen as authentic and impactful.

- **How to measure:** Use social listening tools (e.g. Brandwatch, Sprout Social) to track keywords such as 'inclusive', 'diverse', and 'fair', and measure positive vs negative sentiment trends.
- **Example:** A spike in positive sentiment following a diversity campaign indicates that the message landed well with the audience and improved brand reputation.

Retention and turnover rates among diverse employees

Retention data among under-represented groups is a strong signal of whether inclusion efforts are truly felt across the employee experience.

- **How to measure:** Analyse turnover and retention rates by race, gender and other demographic factors. Use exit interviews to capture insights about barriers to inclusion.
- **Example:** If turnover is disproportionately high among minority employees, it may point to gaps in cultural inclusivity, development opportunities or psychological safety.

Innovation and collaboration metrics

Inclusion fuels innovation by fostering cognitive diversity and collaboration. Measuring how diverse teams contribute to creative outputs provides tangible evidence of Return on Inclusion.

- **How to measure:** Track the volume of new ideas, projects or product launches initiated by cross-functional and demographically diverse teams. Use collaboration software to assess team contributions and participation.
- **Example:** A company might find that diverse teams generate 30% more product ideas than homogeneous teams – demonstrating the innovation potential of inclusive environments.

Measuring Return on Inclusion requires a comprehensive, data-informed approach that considers both representation and lived experience. By combining diversity metrics, engagement and retention data, brand sentiment and innovation outcomes, organisations can assess whether their inclusion efforts are truly creating a culture of equity and belonging. These insights help identify areas for growth, guide targeted strategies, and reinforce a commitment to inclusive leadership that resonates with employees, customers and the broader market. When measured consistently, inclusion becomes not just a value – but a catalyst for innovation, loyalty and long-term success.

IMPLEMENTING RETURN ON INCLUSION

Creating an inclusive organisation requires both immediate action and long-term cultural transformation. Quick wins offer visible, everyday changes that foster belonging and build momentum, while long-term strategies embed inclusion into leadership, operations and employee experience. For inclusion to be truly embraced, every level of the organisation must play an active role – from executives and HR to managers and customer-facing teams. When inclusion is championed throughout the business, it becomes a lived experience that shapes how people lead, collaborate and serve others.

Quick wins

1. **Adopt inclusive language policies**
   Encourage inclusive language across internal and external communications to reflect respect for diverse backgrounds. This can involve updating style guides to eliminate gender-specific pronouns, using gender-neutral terms and being mindful of cultural references. Inclusive language demonstrates a commitment to inclusivity at all levels and creates a more welcoming environment.

2. **Expand hiring channels to access diverse talent pools**
   Broaden recruiting efforts by partnering with organisations that serve under-represented communities. Posting job openings on diverse job boards or collaborating with universities known for diversity can expand the candidate pool and attract applicants from different backgrounds. These efforts help create a workforce that better reflects the diversity of the customer base.

3. **Employee resource groups (ERGs)**

   ERGs provide a platform for employees from similar backgrounds or shared interests to connect, support one another and promote inclusivity. These groups can play a critical role in fostering a sense of community, enhancing employee engagement and providing insights into potential inclusivity improvements.

4. **Celebrating cultural events and awareness days**

   Acknowledging and celebrating important cultural events, such as Black History Month, Pride Month or International Women's Day, demonstrates a commitment to inclusivity. Hosting events, discussions or awareness campaigns around these occasions can create a sense of belonging and open conversations about diversity.

5. **Conduct bias and inclusivity training**

   Provide regular training on unconscious bias, inclusivity and cultural competency for all employees, especially managers. This type of training helps employees recognise and address personal biases, promoting more respectful interactions and improving inclusivity in daily operations.

Long-term strategies

1. **Develop inclusive leadership training programmes**

   Train leaders to foster inclusivity within their teams and to understand the value of diverse perspectives. By building an inclusive mindset among leaders, companies can create a top-down culture of respect and empathy. Inclusive leadership training should emphasise empathy, listening skills and cultural competency.

2. **Design products and services for inclusivity**
   Embed inclusivity into the product and service design process by involving diverse voices and considering various customer needs. This can include designing accessible products, offering multiple language options and creating campaigns that reflect the diversity of the customer base. This approach not only serves a wider audience but also strengthens brand reputation.

3. **Establish clear inclusion goals and accountability measures**
   Create measurable inclusion goals, such as targets for diversity in hiring, representation in leadership and improvements in engagement scores. Regularly review progress towards these goals and hold leaders accountable for driving inclusivity within their teams. Clear metrics and regular reporting ensure transparency and commitment to continuous improvement.

4. **Integrate inclusivity into performance reviews and promotions**
   Encourage managers to assess employees on their contributions to an inclusive culture. By incorporating inclusivity as a criterion in performance reviews and promotions, companies reinforce its importance and motivate employees to actively contribute to a positive, inclusive environment.

5. **Foster a culture of open dialogue and continuous feedback**
   Create channels for employees to provide feedback on inclusivity, whether through anonymous surveys, open forums or one-on-one meetings. Listening to employee experiences allows organisations to identify areas for improvement and demonstrates a genuine commitment to fostering an inclusive workplace.

Driving engagement at every level

For executives and senior leadership:

- **Make inclusion a business imperative:** A diverse and inclusive organisation drives innovation, better decision-making and stronger customer loyalty. Leaders must embed inclusion into the company's strategic vision.
- **Hold leadership accountable:** Senior leaders should set measurable diversity, equity and inclusion (DEI) goals and ensure they are tracked and prioritised at board level.
- **Lead by example:** Executives must actively champion inclusive behaviours, ensuring all employees and customers feel valued, respected and represented.

For operational managers:

- **Embed inclusion into everyday decision-making:** Whether designing processes, setting policies or leading teams, managers must ensure inclusivity is at the heart of all business operations.
- **Remove barriers to inclusion:** Identify and address biases in recruitment, promotions and team structures to create a truly diverse and equitable workplace.
- **Create a culture of belonging:** Encourage open dialogue, inclusive team collaboration and proactive measures to ensure every employee feels valued.

For HR and people teams:

- **Build inclusive hiring and development strategies:** Implement recruitment and retention policies that actively support under-represented groups and foster career growth for all employees.

- **Provide training on unconscious bias and inclusive leadership:** Regular training ensures employees and managers understand how to create a welcoming and fair workplace.
- **Establish employee resource groups (ERGs) and mentoring programmes:** These initiatives help create a sense of belonging and support diverse employees in their career progression.

For customer-facing teams:

- **Ensure inclusivity in customer interactions:** Customer service, sales and marketing teams should be trained to engage with customers of all backgrounds, needs and identities in an authentic and respectful way.
- **Design products and services that reflect diverse needs:** Customers want to see themselves represented in brands – ensuring accessibility and inclusivity in offerings fosters loyalty.
- **Celebrate and engage with diverse communities:** Proactively building relationships with underrepresented customer groups helps brands connect more meaningfully and build trust.

By embedding inclusion across leadership, operations, HR and customer experience, organisations can create workplaces and brands that truly reflect and serve the diverse world we live in.

THE LASTING IMPACT OF RETURN ON INCLUSION

Return on Inclusion is more than a moral commitment; it is a strategic necessity that drives customer loyalty, fosters innovation and enhances brand reputation. This chapter has shown that inclusive practices are essential for creating meaningful connections with both employees and customers and that they are becoming a key differentiator in today's diverse business environment.

Inclusion is not a one-time initiative, but an ongoing journey. As demonstrated by companies like Unilever, Microsoft, Airbnb, Target, Nike and Bumble, Return on Inclusion fosters stronger, more resilient brands that resonate deeply with diverse communities. By reflecting the needs and values of their audiences, these companies have strengthened customer loyalty while building deeper trust and admiration.

Embracing Return on Inclusion equips businesses with the tools to respond to evolving expectations, attract top talent and foster environments where diverse perspectives thrive. For companies seeking long-term growth and relevance, inclusion is essential. By building inclusive cultures, organisations not only create better workplaces, they future-proof their business in a competitive and rapidly changing world.

TAKE ACTION

Now that you understand the power of Return on Inclusion, it's time to act. Start by identifying one area in your organisation where inclusivity can be meaningfully improved. Whether it's expanding your hiring channels, launching an employee resource group, reviewing how your products reflect diverse needs or having an honest conversation about representation on your leadership team – every step matters.

Remember, the most inclusive organisations are those that listen, adapt and lead with empathy. Take the first step today, and see how inclusion strengthens your culture, deepens customer loyalty and drives lasting success.

REFERENCES

Airbnb (2022a) 'A six-year update on Airbnb's work to fight discrimination and build inclusion'. Airbnb Newsroom. Available at: www.news.airbnb.com/sixyearadupdate/ (Accessed: 27 April 2025).

Airbnb (2022b) 'Inclusive practises to help every guest feel welcome'. Airbnb. Available at: www.airbnb.co.uk/resources/hosting-homes/a/inclusive-practises-to-help-every-guest-feel-welcome-531 (Accessed: 27 April 2025).

Business Insider (2021) 'Bumble CEO Whitney Wolfe Herd is proof that hiring and promoting female leaders can make you a billionaire'. Available at: www.businessinsider.com/bumble-ceo-whitney-wolfe-female-leadership-billionaire-2021-2 (Accessed: 27 April 2025).

Business Wire (2024) 'Bumble Gives Women More Choice to Make the First Move'. Available at: www.businesswire.com/news/home/20240430323928/en/Bumble-Gives-Women-More-Choice-to-Make-the-First-Move (Accessed: 27 April 2025).

Canvas Business Model (2024) 'Customer Demographics and Target Market of Bumble'. Available at: www.canvasbusinessmodel.com/blogs/target-market/bumble-target-market (Accessed: 27 April 2025).

CBS News (2019) 'Colin Kaepernick's Nike ad wins Emmy for outstanding commercial'. Available at: www.cbsnews.com/news/colin-kaepernick-nike-ad-won-an-emmy-for-outstanding-commercial-creative-arts-emmy/ (Accessed: 27 April 2025).

Deloitte (2021) 'Inclusion as the competitive advantage: The case for women in supply chain'. [pdf] Deloitte Insights. Available at: www2.deloitte.com/content/dam/insights/us/articles/5054_deloitte-women-in-supply-chain/DI_Deloitte%20Women%20in%20supply%20chain.pdf (Accessed: 27 April 2025).

Dove (2024) 'The Real State of Beauty: The world's largest beauty report'. Dove. Available at: www.dove.com/uk/stories/campaigns/global-state-of-beauty.html (Accessed: 27 April 2025).

Forbes Insights (2020) 'Diversity confirmed to boost innovation and financial results. Forbes. Available at: www.forbes.com/sites/forbesinsights/2020/01/15/diversity-confirmed-to-boost-innovation-and-financial-results/ (Accessed: 27 April 2025).

Genesis Analytics (2021) 'The foundations of inclusive tourism'. [pdf] Available at: www.news.airbnb.com/wp-content/uploads/sites/4/2021/09/Genesis-Analytics-Airbnb-The-foundations-of-inclusive-tourism-13-Sept-2021-Final-report.pdf (Accessed: 27 April 2025).

Kantar (2024) 'Brand Inclusion Index 2024'. Available at: www.kantar.com/campaigns/brand-inclusion-index (Accessed: 27 April 2025).

McKinsey & Company (2020) 'Diversity Wins: How Inclusion Matters'. Available at: www.mckinsey.com/featured-insights/diversity-and-inclusion/diversity-wins-how-inclusion-matters (Accessed: 25 February 2025).

Microsoft (2023) 'Disability Answer Desk'. Available at: www.microsoft.com/en-us/accessibility/disability-answer-desk (Accessed: 25 April 2025).

Microsoft (2024) 'Global Diversity and Inclusion Report'. Available at: www.microsoft.com/en-us/diversity/inside-microsoft/annual-report (Accessed: 27 April 2025).

Nike (2022) 'Diversity, Equity & Inclusion'. Available at: www.about.nike.com/en-GB/impact/focus-areas/diversity-equity-inclusion (Accessed: 27 April 2025).

Silicon.co.uk (2024) 'Bumble Gives Women More Choice to Make the First Move'. Available at: www.silicon.co.uk/press-release/bumble-gives-women-more-choice-to-make-the-first-move (Accessed: 27 April 2025).

Target (2018) 'Cat & Jack includes adaptive apparel to help meet the needs of kids with disabilities'. Target Corporate. Available at: www.corporate.target.com/news-features/article/2018/09/cat-and-jack-adaptive-apparel (Accessed: 27 April 2025).

Target (2021) '2021 Corporate Responsibility Report'. [pdf] Available at: www.corporate.target.com/getmedia/f522b0eb-065b-410c-9c1c-07a2244bfdb2/2021_Target_Corporate-Responsibility-Report.pdf (Accessed: 27 April 2025).

Target (2025) 'Belonging at the Bullseye'. [online] Target Corporate. Available at: www.corporate.target.com/sustainability-governance/our-team/belonging (Accessed: 27 April 2025).

The Brand Hopper (2024) 'A case study on Nike's "Dream Crazy" campaign'. [online] Available at: www.thebrandhopper.com/2024/09/28/a-case-study-on-nikes-dream-crazy-campaign/ (Accessed: 27 April 2025).

Unilever (2025) 'A beacon of diversity and inclusion'. Unilever. Available at: www.unilever.com/sustainability/equity-diversity-and-inclusion/a-beacon-of-diversity-and-inclusion/ (Accessed: 27 April 2025).

Xbox (2025) 'Xbox Adaptive Controller'. Available at: www.xbox.com/en-GB/accessories/controllers/xbox-adaptive-controller (Accessed: 27 April 2025).

CHAPTER 4
RETURN ON IMAGE – DEMONSTRATING TRUE SOCIAL RESPONSIBILITY

INTRODUCING RETURN ON IMAGE

In today's business environment, where consumers are more discerning and values-driven than ever, Return on Image has emerged as a powerful differentiator for organisations seeking to build meaningful connections with their audiences. While traditional brand image once centred on product quality, price and customer service, today's consumers expect companies to actively align with social, environmental and ethical values. Whether through sustainability efforts, fair labour practices, community engagement or responsible sourcing, brands are now expected to contribute to a better world.

Return on Image reflects the idea that businesses can create a competitive advantage by embedding social responsibility into their brand identity. This is not simply a marketing strategy or PR effort – it's a long-term commitment to values that resonate with consumers, employees and the wider society. Organisations that lead with purpose see increased brand loyalty, stronger talent attraction and long-term value creation (Deloitte, 2020). According to the Edelman Trust Barometer (2021), 64% of consumers worldwide choose, switch, avoid or boycott a brand based on its stance on societal issues – illustrating the growing influence of values-based decision-making.

A strong Return on Image can also build resilience in times of crisis. Brands like Lush, recognised for environmental advocacy, and Ben & Jerry's, known for social justice activism, show that bold, values-led leadership can foster deep loyalty – even when taking controversial stands. By aligning brand identity with purpose, these companies have built communities that extend beyond product loyalty and have become advocates for their missions.

However, this also a highly risky approach, as you can also alienate as many customers as you attract. Therefore, you need to be clear about the implications and decide how comfortable you are with knowingly pursuing this strategy.

This chapter explores how businesses can strengthen their brand image by embedding social responsibility into their DNA. Through real-world examples, practical insights and measurement tools, you'll learn how to cultivate Return on Image in a way that drives both public trust and business impact, enhancing brand equity while contributing meaningfully to society.

LEVERAGING RETURN ON IMAGE

To move from theory to action, businesses need a practical roadmap for embedding social responsibility into their brand. By the end of this chapter, you will have a clear understanding of how to implement and sustain Return on Image within your organisation, regardless of industry or size. You'll gain strategic insight and practical tools to build a values-led brand that earns trust, deepens loyalty, attracts purpose-driven employees and drives long-term impact. This chapter will equip you to:

- **Maximise the strategic value of Return on Image**
  Explore how a brand image built on authenticity, ethics and social responsibility becomes a powerful business asset. Companies that embed CSR into their strategy are better positioned to earn trust, inspire loyalty and stand out in a values-conscious market. A strong brand image also plays a vital role in attracting and retaining purpose-led employees who are aligned with the organisation's mission – ensuring your values resonate internally as much as they do externally.

- **Build the core elements of a purpose-driven brand**
  Understand the key components that shape how your brand is perceived – from environmental sustainability and ethical sourcing to community involvement and social advocacy.

Purpose-driven brands that live their values create meaningful connections with customers, generate internal pride and contribute positively to the communities they serve.

- **Implement best practices from leading organisations**
  Learn from companies like Lego, Ben & Jerry's, Starbucks, Tesla and Warby Parker – brands that have built strong reputations by leading with purpose. These case studies highlight specific strategies that enhance brand credibility, foster consumer trust and position the organisation as a leader in ethical business practices.

- **Measure success using meaningful brand metrics**
  Discover how to evaluate the impact of image-focused initiatives using both qualitative and quantitative tools. Key performance indicators include Net Promoter Score (NPS), social sentiment analysis, customer retention and recognition through CSR certifications or awards. These metrics provide actionable insights into how Return on Image influences not only perception but also customer loyalty and long-term brand equity.

- **Apply practical strategies for immediate and long-term impact**
  Uncover actionable strategies to strengthen your brand image – from early wins like featuring CSR initiatives in marketing or forming partnerships with local non-profits, to long-term commitments, such as creating sustainability teams, setting measurable goals and engaging employees in purpose-led initiatives. These strategies help ensure that Return on Image becomes embedded in your organisational DNA.

- **Prioritise and align brand initiatives for maximum value**
  Identify where brand-building efforts will deliver the greatest
  return, balancing business goals with social expectations.
  Understand how executives, operational leaders and marketing
  teams can align their efforts to embed social responsibility
  into both strategic planning and daily operations, creating
  consistent, values-led brand experiences across every touchpoint.

Now let's bring Return on Image to life.

RETURN ON IMAGE IN ACTION

In this section, you'll explore how various leading brands have embedded
social responsibility into their core strategies, enhancing their Return on
Image and building deep, lasting connections with consumers. These case
studies cover both large corporations and smaller businesses across various
industries, showing the diverse ways that Return on Image can be achieved.

LUSH – ETHICAL SOURCING AND ACTIVISM IN BEAUTY

Lush has built a distinctive brand image by placing ethics, sustainability
and activism at the heart of its business. From its commitment to cruelty-
free products to campaigns against over-packaging and unethical
testing, Lush has consistently taken bold stances on key social and
environmental issues (We Are Lush, 2025).

The company's brand identity is deeply tied to its values. Lush refuses
to sell in countries that require animal testing, uses only vegetarian
ingredients and sources raw materials through fair-trade partnerships. It
also runs activist campaigns on human rights, environmental justice and
ethical consumerism – often using storefronts and packaging to raise
awareness (We Are Lush, 2018).

Lush's strong ethical stance and activism are key drivers of customer loyalty. In the US, approximately 67% of Lush users exhibit brand loyalty, indicating a strong connection between the brand's values and customer retention (Statista, 2022).

Key takeaway: Lush demonstrates that taking a public stand on ethical issues can build a powerful brand image. By aligning every touchpoint with its values, Lush has cultivated a loyal following that sees the brand as a force for good for some customers. Again a word of caution, as an activist approach will likely alienate as many people as it attracts as many potential customers are not aligned with their stance on certain issues.

BEN & JERRY'S – SOCIAL ACTIVISM AND ADVOCACY

Ben & Jerry's is widely recognised for embedding social justice and human rights into its core brand identity. The company has taken bold public stances on climate change, LGBTQ+ rights and racial equity, using its platform to promote awareness and catalyse action. The climate justice campaign and outspoken support for movements like Black Lives Matter have reinforced its reputation as a brand committed to systemic change (Ben & Jerry's, 2025).

Rather than treating activism as a marketing tool, Ben & Jerry's integrates its values into day-to-day operations, partnering with grassroots organisations and championing causes through both messaging and business practices (Ben & Jerry's UK, 2025). A consumer insights report found that 78% of customers associate the brand with positive social impact and 64% say its advocacy is a primary reason for their loyalty (Everything PR, 2024).

Key takeaway: Ben & Jerry's approach demonstrates that aligning with social causes can create a powerful Return on Image. Customers are increasingly drawn to brands that reflect their values and Ben & Jerry's commitment to advocacy has turned the brand into a powerful social entity.

LEGO – BUILDING A SUSTAINABLE FUTURE IN TOY MANUFACTURING

LEGO's commitment to sustainability extends beyond product innovation to corporate responsibility. The brand has pledged to transition to sustainable materials across all products by 2030, an ambitious goal that reflects its dedication to reducing environmental impact. LEGO has invested heavily in plant-based plastics, sustainable packaging and energy-efficient manufacturing processes (Lego, 2025).

LEGO's 2021 Sustainability Progress Report highlights insights from a global survey of nearly 7,000 parents and children, revealing strong engagement and positive perceptions of LEGO's environmental initiatives, such as plant-based materials and trials of sustainable packaging. The report underscores that both parents and children value LEGO's commitment to sustainability, which positively shapes their overall view of the brand (LEGO Group, 2021).

Key takeaway: LEGO's investments in sustainability reveal the positive impact of long-term, actionable goals. As customers become more environmentally conscious, brands like LEGO that prioritise eco-friendly practices stand out and gain the loyalty of purpose-driven consumers.

TESLA – PIONEERING SUSTAINABLE ENERGY IN THE AUTOMOTIVE INDUSTRY

Tesla has revolutionised the car industry by championing sustainable energy with electric vehicles (EVs) and renewable energy solutions. Tesla's commitment to eco-friendly technology is evident in every facet of its business, from EVs to solar products. The company's recycling initiatives also emphasise environmental stewardship, setting new standards in the automotive industry (Tesla, 2025).

According to CustomerGauge in 2023, Tesla achieved an exceptional Net Promoter Score (NPS) of 97 in 2020, reflecting an overwhelmingly positive customer experience and loyalty. By focusing on sustainable solutions, Tesla has attracted a dedicated following of environmentally conscious consumers who are willing to invest in clean energy products.

Key takeaway: Tesla's success in creating a sustainable brand image illustrates how environmental responsibility can foster customer loyalty. By embedding sustainability into its core mission, Tesla has aligned with consumers who prioritise green technology and innovation.

STARBUCKS – ETHICAL SOURCING AND COMMUNITY ENGAGEMENT

Starbucks has built a socially responsible brand image through its Ethical Coffee Sourcing Programme, ensuring fair compensation and sustainable practices for coffee farmers. The company's investments in community programmes, such as youth employment through the Opportunity Youth initiative and clean water projects supported by over $50 million in sustainability funding, reinforce its commitment to social responsibility (The City of Calgary, 2025; Starbucks, 2025).

Starbucks reports that 99.7% of its coffee was ethically sourced in 2023, reflecting its commitment to sustainability and supply chain integrity. These efforts help build strong relationships with suppliers and customers, fostering loyalty and supporting long-term profitability (Starbucks, 2023).

Key takeaway: Starbucks' focus on ethical sourcing demonstrates that brand loyalty is strengthened when companies engage in socially responsible practices. By fostering fair trade and community involvement, Starbucks enhances both its brand image and customer loyalty.

WARBY PARKER – SOCIAL GOOD AND ACCESSIBILITY IN EYEWEAR

Warby Parker's 'Buy a Pair, Give a Pair' programme has helped millions access affordable eye care, differentiating the brand in the eyewear market. This commitment to social impact resonates strongly with customers who appreciate the opportunity to contribute to a greater cause through their purchases (Warby Parker, 2022).

As of 2023, US retailer Warby Parker had distributed over 15 million pairs of glasses globally through its initiative, helping people in more than 80 countries access affordable vision care. This campaign has established Warby Parker as a brand with a social purpose, driving loyalty and customer advocacy (Warby Parker, 2023).

Key takeaway: Warby Parker's success underscores the value of social good in brand positioning. Consumers are increasingly drawn to brands that integrate social responsibility into their business model, creating a strong Return on Image.

HOW TO MEASURE SUCCESS WITHIN RETURN ON IMAGE

To understand the effectiveness of your social responsibility efforts and their impact on brand image, it's essential to measure both perception and performance. A strong Return on Image is not just about visibility – it's about earning trust, deepening loyalty and building long-term credibility. The following metrics combine quantitative and qualitative insights to help track impact and guide future strategy.

Net Promoter Score (NPS)

NPS is a powerful indicator of how customers perceive your brand on a values level. While it traditionally measures likelihood to recommend, in the context of Return on Image, it reflects how your social responsibility efforts shape deeper emotional alignment. A positive shift in NPS can reveal that your brand values aren't just seen, they're felt and shared too.

- **How to measure**: Track NPS before and after social impact campaigns or initiatives. Use follow-up questions to identify whether CSR or values-based factors influence the score.
- **Indicator of resonance**: A rise in NPS following a campaign suggests your values are not only being noticed, but inspiring customers to advocate for your brand.

Customer retention rates

Retention reflects more than just satisfaction – it signals brand alignment. When customers who are aware of your CSR initiatives stay loyal over time, it shows that your values are driving a long-term relationship. In Return on Image, retention is one of the most direct ways to measure whether trust is being earned and maintained.

- **How to measure**: Compare retention rates among customers exposed to CSR campaigns versus general benchmarks. Where possible, segment by campaign awareness or values-driven product lines.
- **Link to brand alignment**: Higher retention shows that customers see a values match between themselves and the brand – reinforcing lasting loyalty.

Social sentiment analysis

Social sentiment is the real-time voice of public perception. Tracking how people talk about your brand – and specifically your social responsibility efforts – can give early insight into whether your image is growing stronger or slipping into scepticism. It's one of the fastest ways to detect how Return on Image is playing out in the public sphere.

- **How to measure**: Use tools like Brandwatch, Sprout Social, or Talkwalker to monitor social channels for keywords related to your CSR efforts and brand values (e.g. 'ethical', 'sustainable' or 'authentic').
- **Real-time feedback loop**: A shift toward more positive sentiment during or after CSR activity signals improved perception and stronger emotional connection.

Employee satisfaction and retention metrics

Your brand image doesn't just live in the minds of customers – it begins inside your organisation. When employees believe in your social values, they become brand ambassadors. Measuring their satisfaction and retention gives a strong internal signal of how well Return on Image is taking root culturally.

- **How to measure**: Use employee engagement surveys and exit interviews to assess whether employees feel aligned with the company's values and impact initiatives.
- **Internal alignment drives advocacy**: When employees are proud of their organisation's values, they're more likely to act as brand advocates – strengthening the external brand perception.

External certifications and awards

Third-party certifications and awards are a formal signal to the world that your CSR commitments are credible and measurable. They enhance your image by adding legitimacy and providing visible proof that your efforts meet recognised standards.

- **How to measure**: Track the number and quality of certifications (e.g. B Corp, LEED) and awards received. Monitor how these recognitions affect media coverage and stakeholder confidence.
- **Third-party credibility**: Public endorsements build trust with customers, investors and partners – reinforcing your image as a values-driven business.

Community impact metrics

True Return on Image includes what your brand gives back. Metrics that capture direct community involvement – such as volunteer hours, donations or partnerships – offer proof that your purpose-led branding translates into tangible action.

- **How to measure**: Track measurable contributions to community initiatives, including volunteer engagement, charitable giving and the extent of community engagement.

- **Reinforces authenticity**: Visible, measurable community engagement shows your CSR efforts are grounded in action, not just messaging.

Measuring Return on Image requires a blend of internal and external indicators that go beyond surface-level impressions. By tracking loyalty, sentiment, employee engagement and third-party validation, businesses can assess whether their values are resonating and their brand image is grounded in authentic, measurable impact. These metrics not only help identify areas for improvement but also reinforce the business case for purpose-led branding. When consistently measured and acted upon, Return on Image becomes a strategic driver of reputation, trust and long-term brand equity.

IMPLEMENTING RETURN ON IMAGE

Building a socially responsible brand requires both immediate action and sustained commitment. Quick wins signal your values through visible, achievable steps that generate internal and external momentum. Over time, these efforts must evolve into long-term strategies that embed social responsibility into leadership, culture and operations. To maintain credibility and grow trust, every level of the organisation needs to play a role – from executive leadership and operations to marketing and customer-facing teams. When brand integrity is consistently reinforced across departments, companies build a reputation that inspires loyalty, advocacy and long-term success.

Quick wins

1. **Publicise CSR efforts on digital and social channels**
   In today's digital landscape, customers expect transparency and engagement with a brand's values. Companies can

use their existing platforms – websites, social media and newsletters – to regularly highlight CSR initiatives, updates and milestones. This helps demonstrate a genuine commitment to positive impact. To increase engagement, businesses should consider creating a dedicated CSR section on their website or launching a focused campaign around a recent initiative, using visuals, videos and compelling stories to bring their efforts to life.

2. **Create partnerships with local non-profits or community organisations**

   Partnering with local non-profits or community groups enables companies to make a tangible difference while strengthening community ties. These collaborations – whether through donations, volunteer work or co-hosted events – show a brand's authentic investment in local needs. Start small, with one or two partnerships aligned with brand values and customer interests. For instance, an environmentally-focused company might support a local tree-planting drive or sponsor clean-up events in their area.

3. **Launch recycling, reuse or return programmes**

   Encouraging customers to recycle, reuse or return items demonstrates environmental responsibility and promotes a circular economy. This is especially relevant for industries like fashion, tech or consumer goods. Brands can create closed-loop systems that support reuse and responsible disposal, while incentivising customer participation with perks like discounts. For example, a clothing retailer could offer vouchers to customers who bring in worn garments for recycling, ensuring the process is simple and rewarding.

4. **Involve employees in volunteer opportunities and community projects**

   When employees participate in socially responsible activities, they become powerful ambassadors for a company's values. Organising volunteer days or offering paid time off for volunteering can build internal morale while showcasing authentic external impact. Sharing these initiatives across social channels reinforces the brand's commitment and encourages broader participation. Internally, this also strengthens workplace culture and deepens employees' connection to the company's mission.

5. **Start a corporate donation or matching programme**

   Implementing a donation or matching programme allows companies to back causes that align with their values while encouraging employee participation. This can include matching employee donations or making direct contributions to urgent or high-impact causes like disaster relief. To maximise visibility and participation, make the programme easy to access and highlight the causes supported in internal and external communications, demonstrating a shared commitment to giving back.

Long-term strategies

1. **Define and set measurable CSR goals**

   Establishing clear, measurable CSR goals, such as reducing carbon emissions, promoting diversity or supporting local communities, builds accountability and long-term credibility. These goals should be aligned with the company's broader mission and communicated publicly, with transparent reporting on progress. Companies like Unilever exemplify this approach through its Sustainable Living Plan, which includes ambitious targets in waste reduction, water use and ethical sourcing, reinforcing its leadership in sustainability.

2. **Establish a dedicated CSR or sustainability department**
   Creating a CSR or sustainability team ensures focused oversight, continuity and integration of initiatives across the business. This team can develop programmes, track outcomes and collaborate across departments – product, supply chain, marketing, operations – to embed social responsibility into everyday decision-making. Companies may appoint a Chief Sustainability Officer to lead the charge, ensuring CSR has visibility and strategic influence at the highest level.

3. **Incorporate CSR into company culture and employee training**
   Embedding CSR into company culture transforms it from being a side initiative into a core business value. This requires integrating CSR themes into onboarding, offering regular training and communicating updates company-wide. When employees understand how their roles contribute to the bigger picture – through stories, data or real examples – they are more likely to support and champion the company's social mission, helping CSR become part of daily operations.

4. **Engage in sustainable product and service innovation**
   Businesses can reduce environmental impact and meet rising customer expectations by incorporating sustainability into product and service design. This includes using renewable materials, improving packaging and reducing carbon footprints. IKEA's goal to use only renewable and recycled materials by 2030 is a prime example. Companies can set targets, like requiring a percentage of products to meet environmental criteria, and collaborate with suppliers to ensure alignment.

5. **Develop long-term partnerships with NGOs and social enterprises**

   Collaborating with mission-aligned NGOs or social enterprises enables companies to scale their impact and gain access to valuable expertise and networks. These long-term partnerships allow for joint initiatives with defined objectives and measurable outcomes. Coca-Cola's collaboration with the WWF on water conservation demonstrates how strategic alliances can further sustainability goals and build reputational value through shared purpose.

6. **Commit to transparent reporting and external certification**

   Publishing regular CSR or sustainability reports builds trust and transparency. Third-party certifications, such as B Corp or LEED, offer external validation of a company's ethical and environmental standards. These tools show stakeholders that a company is serious about responsibility. Annual disclosures should detail achievements, challenges and areas for improvement, reinforcing the company's accountability and progress over time.

7. **Embed CSR into the supply chain**

   Since much of a company's impact lies within its supply chain, embedding CSR here is vital. This means setting clear standards for environmental and labour practices, conducting audits and working collaboratively with suppliers to improve. Leading companies like Apple and Nestlé enforce supplier codes of conduct and regularly assess performance, ensuring their CSR values extend beyond internal operations to every stage of production and delivery.

8. **Engage customers in CSR initiatives**

   Involving customers in CSR, through donation matching, community programmes or social campaigns, deepens loyalty and broadens impact. Options like adding a charity donation at checkout or allocating a portion of profits to causes help customers to feel invested in the brand's mission. Encouraging participation through storytelling and social media fosters a sense of shared values and community, turning CSR into a relationship-building opportunity.

Driving Engagement at Every Level

For executives and senior leadership:

- **Protect and enhance brand reputation:** A company's long-term success depends on how it is perceived by customers, employees and stakeholders – leaders must ensure every decision reflects and strengthens brand integrity.
- **Align brand messaging with business actions:** Customers expect authenticity; leaders must ensure that corporate social responsibility (CSR), sustainability efforts and company values are consistently upheld.
- **Be prepared for crisis management:** Senior leaders must take ownership of brand reputation during crises, responding with transparency, accountability and decisive action to maintain trust.

For operational managers:

- **Ensure brand consistency across all operations:** Every aspect of the business – from supply chain ethics to employee conduct – impacts how customers perceive the brand. Managers must align operations with brand values.

- **Foster a reputation-driven culture:** Employees should understand the importance of brand reputation and how their daily actions contribute to shaping public perception.
- **Monitor feedback and adjust strategies:** Regularly reviewing customer and stakeholder feedback helps managers identify potential risks and opportunities to strengthen brand image.

For marketing and communications teams:

- **Build a compelling, authentic brand narrative:** Brand messaging must be clear, consistent and aligned with the company's core values, ensuring customers and stakeholders connect with it emotionally.
- **Engage proactively in reputation management:** Social listening, public relations and crisis response strategies should be in place to protect and enhance brand image.
- **Leverage customer advocacy:** Encouraging satisfied customers to share their experiences strengthens brand credibility and trust, reinforcing positive perceptions.

For customer-facing teams:

- **Deliver a brand-aligned customer experience:** Every customer interaction shapes perception – service teams should be trained to embody brand values and provide a seamless, positive experience.
- **Handle customer complaints with care:** Addressing issues transparently and fairly can turn negative experiences into trust-building opportunities.
- **Act as brand ambassadors:** Employees engaging with customers should reinforce brand messaging and actively contribute to a positive brand image.

By embedding reputation management into leadership, operations, marketing and customer experience, businesses can ensure they build and sustain a brand image that fosters trust, loyalty and long-term success.

THE LASTING IMPACT OF RETURN ON IMAGE

Return on Image is a powerful tool for building consumer trust, strengthening employee engagement and enhancing long-term brand resilience. In a marketplace where customers are increasingly guided by ethics and values, socially responsible brands form deeper, more lasting connections. Companies that achieve a strong Return on Image are seen not only as industry leaders, but also as trusted advocates for environmental, social and ethical progress. This alignment fosters loyalty from customers who are more likely to support, and advocate for, brands that reflect their beliefs.

As demonstrated by brands like Lush, Ben & Jerry's, Starbucks and Warby Parker, social responsibility is not a marketing tactic, it's a strategic cornerstone. These organisations have embedded purpose into every part of their brand, cultivating communities of customers and employees who are deeply connected to their mission. Brands that actively engage with their communities build stronger local relationships and goodwill. Meanwhile, sustainability-led efforts create competitive advantage and attract a growing segment of environmentally conscious consumers.

Social responsibility also plays a key role in attracting and retaining high-calibre, purpose-driven talent. When companies prioritise ethical values, they improve employee engagement, strengthen company culture and foster long-term retention. These internal dynamics contribute directly to better customer experiences and innovation outcomes, reinforcing the brand from the inside out.

To evaluate the impact of Return on Image, organisations must use a blend of quantitative and qualitative tools. Metrics such as NPS, social sentiment, retention rates and community engagement data all provide insight into how CSR initiatives are perceived and where further investment is needed. These indicators not only track progress but also inform how to adapt and scale impact over time.

Whether through quick wins such as take-back programmes, or longer-term investments in sustainability leadership and ethical supply chains, implementing Return on Image initiatives enables businesses to contribute meaningfully to society while strengthening their brand. As expectations continue to shift, the companies that lead with values will earn greater loyalty, resilience and trust.

Ultimately, Return on Image is about building a brand that stands for more than just profit. It's about creating an identity rooted in purpose – one that resonates with consumers, employees and communities alike. When companies commit to social responsibility, they earn not only attention, but lasting advocacy. In doing so, they secure a more relevant, resilient and respected position in the market for years to come.

TAKE ACTION

Now that you understand the power of Return on Image, it's time to turn insight into action. Start by identifying one area of your brand strategy where social responsibility can be more visible and embedded, whether that's through your supply chain, employee engagement, marketing or community partnerships.

Even small steps, such as showcasing your CSR commitments or launching a pilot sustainability initiative, can make a meaningful difference. As trust and loyalty increasingly hinge on authenticity, purpose and transparency, brands that lead with values will stand out.

The choices you make today shape how your brand is perceived tomorrow. Take the first step toward building a socially responsible brand image that inspires confidence, connection and long-term impact.

REFERENCES

Ben & Jerry's (2025a) 'Issues We Care About'. Available at: www.benjerry.com/values/issues-we-care-about (Accessed: 27 April 2025).

Ben & Jerry's UK (2025b) 'Our Values, Activism and Mission'. Available at: www.benjerry.co.uk/values (Accessed: 27 April 2025).

CustomerGauge (2023) 'Tesla's NPS Score: What's Driving Tesla's Customer Loyalty?' Available at: www.customergauge.com/benchmarks/blog/tesla-nps-score (Accessed: 27 April 2025).

Deloitte (2020) 'Purpose is everything: How purpose-driven companies are winning in the marketplace'. Available at: www2.deloitte.com/us/en/insights/topics/marketing-and-sales-operations/global-marketing-trends/2020/purpose-driven-companies.html (Accessed: 27 April 2025).

Edelman (2021) '2021 Edelman Trust Barometer'. Available at: www.edelman.com/trust/2021-trust-barometer (Accessed: 25 February 2025).

Everything PR (2024) 'Community-Centric Branding: How Ben & Jerry's Built a Loyal Following Through Social Justice Advocacy'. Available at: www.everything-pr.com/community-centric-branding-how-ben-jerrys-built-a-loyal-following-through-social-justice-advocacy/ (Accessed: 4 May 2025).

LEGO (2025) 'Environment – Sustainability'. Available at: www.lego.com/en-gb/sustainability/environment (Accessed: 27 April 2025).

LEGO Group (2021) 'Sustainability Progress Report 2021'. [pdf] Available at: www.lego.com/cdn/cs/aboutus/assets/blt15f6010332752196/The_LEGO_Group_SustainabilityProgressReport2021.pdf (Accessed: 27 April 2025).

Starbucks (2023) 'Global Environmental & Social Impact Report 2023'. Available at: www.stories.starbucks.com/uploads/2023/03/Starbucks-Global-Environmental-and-Social-Impact-Report-2023.pdf (Accessed: 4 May 2025).

Starbucks (2025) 'Starbucks Commits Over $50 Million to Sustainable Waste and Water Funds Toward a Resource-Positive Future'. Available at: www.about.starbucks.com/press/2023/starbucks-commits-over-50-million-to-sustainable-waste-and-water-funds-toward-a-resource-positive-future/ (Accessed: 27 April 2025).

Statista (2022) 'Lush brand profile U.S. 2022'. Available at: www.statista.com/forecasts/1340147/lush-face-care-brand-profile-in-the-united-states (Accessed: 27 April 2025).

Tesla (2025) 'Earth Day 2025: We're Committed to Building a Sustainable Future'. Available at: www.tesla.com/learn/earth-day-2025-were-committed-building-sustainable-future (Accessed: 27 April 2025).

The City of Calgary (2025) 'Starbucks Opportunity Youth Initiative'. Available at: www.calgary.ca/social-services/youth/starbucks-initiative.html (Accessed: 27 April 2025).

Warby Parker (2022) 'Warby Parker Celebrates Over 10 Million Pairs of Glasses Distributed Through its Buy a Pair, Give a Pair Program'. Available at: www.businesswire.com/news/home/20220228005812/en/Warby-Parker-Celebrates-Over-10-Million-Pairs-of-Glasses-Distributed-Through-its-Buy-a-Pair-Give-a-Pair-Program (Accessed: 27 April 2025).

Warby Parker (2023) 'Impact Report 2023'. [pdf] Available at: www.warbyparker.com/assets/img/impact-report/Impact-Report-2023.pdf (Accessed: 27 April 2025).

We Are Lush (2018) 'The Lush Ethical Charter'. Available at: www.weare.lush.com/lush-life/our-values/the-lush-ethical-charter/ (Accessed: 27 April 2025).

We Are Lush (2025) 'Leaving the World Lusher Than We Found It'. Available at: www.weare.lush.com/lush-life/our-impact-reports/leaving-the-world-lusher-than-we-found-it/ (Accessed: 27 April 2025).

CHAPTER 5
RETURN ON INTERVENTION – MEETING AND EXCEEDING CUSTOMER EXPECTATIONS

INTRODUCING RETURN ON INTERVENTION

In today's world of instant feedback and elevated customer expectations, companies operate under constant scrutiny. A single unresolved issue can ripple across social media, damaging brand reputation and eroding trust. Conversely, a timely and empathetic response to a customer's complaint can transform a potential detractor into a loyal advocate. By investing in Return on Intervention, organisations can respond to and resolve customer issues and yield long-term value – extending far beyond issue resolution. It reflects a company's respect, accountability and commitment to customer satisfaction. In a customer-centric economy, how an organisation manages these critical interactions can make all the difference.

This mindset stands in contrast to the traditional model of measuring the 'cost to serve', which often prioritises cost reduction over delivering exceptional service. When service strategies are focused solely on efficiency, they risk overlooking the long-term brand and relationship value of high-quality, human-centred intervention.

Statistics reinforce this business case. A PwC study found that 32% of customers would stop doing business with a brand they loved after just one poor experience, underscoring how fragile loyalty can be. Meanwhile, 86% of buyers say they are willing to pay more for a great customer experience (PwC, 2018; Daktela, 2024), and 96% of consumers agree that excellent customer service is a crucial factor in determining their loyalty to a brand (Yaguara, 2024). These findings highlight that effective, customer-focused intervention is not just a support function – it's a competitive differentiator. Companies that resolve issues with speed, empathy and ownership don't just retain customers, they build brand equity and attract new ones through word of mouth and public perception.

In this chapter, you will explore why Return on Intervention is a critical driver of customer retention and brand trust. Through real-world case studies, you'll examine how leading companies turn moments of friction into opportunities for connection – using frontline empowerment, cross-functional coordination and proactive technology. You'll also gain practical tools for measuring intervention success and embedding strategies that align customer care with broader organisational values.

To move from principle to practice, this chapter outlines how to entrench Return on Intervention across your organisation – through quick wins, long-term strategies and measurable actions that elevate customer trust and brand loyalty.

LEVERAGING RETURN ON INTERVENTION

By the end of this chapter, you will have a clear understanding of how to implement and sustain Return on Intervention within your organisation, regardless of industry or size. You'll gain strategic insight and practical tools to build a culture of proactive, empathetic issue resolution that drives customer loyalty, reduces churn and strengthens brand trust. This chapter will equip you to:

- **Maximise the strategic value of Return on Intervention**
  Recognise the strategic role of intervention as a core
  component of the customer experience. Understand how
  timely, empathetic responses to issues enhance brand loyalty,
  reduce churn and create lasting customer relationships –
  transforming service recovery into a competitive advantage.

- **Build the core elements of an effective intervention strategy**
  Identify the key components of a high-performing
  intervention framework, including empowered employees,
  flexible policies, multi-channel support and data-informed
  decision-making. Learn how to turn customer problems into
  moments of brand reinforcement.

- **Implement best practices from leading organisations**
  Apply proven strategies from customer-centric leaders, such
  as Amazon, Ritz-Carlton, Revolut, Zappos, Nordstrom, Delta
  Airlines and Samsung. Explore how these brands design and
  deliver standout intervention experiences that build advocacy
  and loyalty.

- **Measure success using meaningful metrics**
  Use data to assess the effectiveness of your intervention
  strategies. Track performance with key indicators such as
  Customer Satisfaction Scores (CSAT), Net Promoter Scores
  (NPS), First Contact Resolution (FCR) and qualitative
  feedback – ensuring continuous improvement.

- **Apply practical strategies for immediate and long-term impact**
  Take action with short- and long-term solutions, from
  strengthening communication channels and offering self-service
  tools to investing in AI, predictive technology and staff training.
  Build a system that meets evolving customer needs at every
  touchpoint.

- **Prioritise and align intervention efforts for maximum value**
  Focus your efforts where they'll have the most meaningful
  impact. Learn how to align intervention initiatives with
  broader customer experience goals and brand values, ensuring
  a unified, consistent approach across the business.

Now let's bring Return on Intervention to life.

RETURN ON INTERVENTION IN ACTION

To demonstrate how Return on Intervention transforms customer service into a powerful strategic advantage, you will explore real-world examples from industry-leading brands. These companies prioritise proactive, personalised issue resolution, enhancing customer satisfaction, loyalty and trust. Each case study highlights practical approaches that elevate customer experiences, reinforcing lasting connections with their audience.

AMAZON - TRANSFORMING E-COMMERCE SERVICE WITH EFFICIENCY AND ACCESSIBILITY

Amazon sets a high standard in customer service, especially in its commitment to hassle-free issue resolution. Known for its 'A-to-Z Guarantee', Amazon provides protection for all purchases, ensuring that disputes are resolved fairly and promptly (Amazon, 2025). With its 24/7 customer service and vast network of logistics, Amazon manages to streamline returns and refunds, making the process fast and customer friendly (Everything Supply Chain, 2024).

In 2024, Amazon achieved a customer satisfaction rate of 83%, largely due to its emphasis on issue resolution and customer-centric policies (Statista, 2024). Amazon's service model shows that with a structured, accessible approach, brands can not only resolve issues efficiently but also reinforce trust and loyalty, especially in a high-volume e-commerce environment where seamless service is paramount.

Key takeaway: Amazon demonstrates the importance of clear, accessible policies and 24/7 support. By making intervention a core element of its customer service, Amazon has established itself as a brand that prioritises customer needs, helping to build enduring loyalty.

RITZ-CARLTON – EMPOWERING EMPLOYEES TO CREATE MEMORABLE RESOLUTIONS

Ritz-Carlton's commitment to personalised service is highlighted by its policy of empowering employees to handle guest complaints directly. Each employee has access to a $2,000 discretionary fund to resolve guest issues, reflecting Ritz-Carlton's commitment to quick, meaningful and empathetic responses (Renascence, 2024a). This empowerment enables employees to respond in real-time, providing tailored solutions that align with the hotel's reputation for luxury service.

According to the 2023 J.D. Power Guest Satisfaction Study, Ritz-Carlton achieved one of the highest guest satisfaction scores in the luxury hotel segment. Its proactive approach to issue resolution and personalised service were key drivers of this success, consistently positioning the brand as a leader in customer satisfaction and loyalty (J.D. Power, 2023). By allowing frontline employees to handle issues independently, Ritz-Carlton reinforces its brand promise of unparalleled service, establishing deeper, lasting relationships with its guests.

Key takeaway: Ritz-Carlton's approach demonstrates that empowering employees enhances customer satisfaction and loyalty. By giving employees the freedom to make decisions, Ritz-Carlton strengthens a culture of customer-centric service that enhances trust and commitment.

REVOLUT – REAL-TIME RESOLUTION IN DIGITAL BANKING

Revolut, one of the world's leading digital banking platforms, has redefined customer service in the finance sector through instant, in-app intervention. Unlike traditional banks, Revolut empowers users to manage and resolve issues directly within its app – whether it's freezing a card, disputing a charge or connecting with 24/7 live chat support. This focus on accessibility and speed has allowed Revolut to eliminate the usual friction associated with banking complaints (Revolut, 2024a).

Revolut has expanded its intervention strategy with AI-powered fraud alerts, instant spending notifications and automated dispute processes.

These tools proactively detect and resolve issues before customers even realise there's a problem (Revolut, 2024b). According to customer feedback analysis, 82% of Revolut users cite speed, efficiency and helpful support as key reasons for their loyalty and trust in the platform (Kimola, 2024).

Key takeaway: Revolut demonstrates that proactive, tech-enabled customer support in financial services can significantly enhance loyalty and satisfaction. By resolving issues quickly, securely and in real time, Revolut sets a new standard for Return on Intervention in the digital banking space.

ZAPPOS - BUILDING CUSTOMER LOYALTY THROUGH AUTHENTIC ENGAGEMENT

Zappos, a brand known for exceptional customer service, has adopted a relationship-driven approach to issue resolution. Zappos empowers its service agents to prioritise customer satisfaction over call times, allowing them to fully engage with customers and address concerns thoroughly (Renascence, 2024b).

The company invests heavily in training and culture to ensure employees embody the 'WOW' philosophy of going above and beyond. This is what it entails:

- **Customer Obsession, Not Just Satisfaction –** Every employee is empowered to go above and beyond for customers – no scripts, no time limits on calls, no rigid policies.
- **Surprise and Delight –** Upgrading shipping for free to overnight, sending flowers to a grieving customer, or making creative product recommendations – these are everyday WOWs.
- **Empowered Employees –** Call centre reps are trusted to make decisions that "WOW" without needing supervisor approval.
- **Company Culture is Everything –** The WOW philosophy applies internally too: Zappos works hard to WOW their employees with meaningful recognition, growth, and fun.

- **Human Connection –** No bots, no shortcuts – Zappos encourages long phone calls and real conversations. Their longest call was over 10 hours, and they celebrated it.

How It Shows Up in Practice

- **No scripts in the call centre** — agents use their judgement to build relationships.
- **Free returns for 365 days** — removing friction and building trust.
- **Company tours for the public** — showing culture in action.
- **WOW stories shared internally** — encouraging a culture of service excellence.

This relationship-driven approach fosters deep loyalty, with 75% of purchases coming from returning customers and a strong emphasis on emotional connection rather than quick resolution (eTail West, 2024). Zappos shows that focusing on empathy and thorough engagement, rather than rigid policies, can turn issue resolution into a competitive advantage.

Key takeaway: Zappos illustrates the value of a personalised approach to issue resolution. By allowing agents to build genuine connections, Zappos enhances loyalty, showing that Return on Intervention is about fostering authentic relationships.

NORDSTROM – THE POWER OF FLEXIBLE AND CUSTOMER-FOCUSED RETURNS

Nordstrom's flexible return policy is a hallmark of its customer service strategy. Rather than enforcing rigid policies, Nordstrom allows employees to address returns on an individual basis, putting the customer's needs first (ReturnPolicyVault, 2025).

Nordstrom generally accepts returns without tags and has historically accepted lightly worn items if customers are unsatisfied, reflecting a customer-first approach (Top Bubble Index, 2025). Studies show that easy and flexible return policies like Nordstrom's significantly boost customer loyalty, with 92% of customers more likely to make repeat purchases if returns are easy (Renascence, 2024c). Nordstrom's approach to flexible returns highlights the importance of adaptability in building customer loyalty.

Key takeaway: Nordstrom's flexible return policy demonstrates that policies prioritising customer satisfaction reinforce trust and loyalty. By handling issues individually, Nordstrom strengthens its brand as a customer-centred retailer.

SAMSUNG – DELIVERING SEAMLESS SUPPORT ACROSS CHANNELS

Samsung has built a comprehensive, multi-channel support system that prioritises customer accessibility and peace of mind. Through its Samsung Care+ programme, the company offers extended warranty coverage, same-day repairs and hassle-free device replacement services. Support is available across a range of touchpoints – from in-store service centres to 24/7 live chat, remote diagnostics via the Samsung Members app and personalised phone assistance (Samsung, 2025).

The brand's integrated service model ensures that customers can resolve issues quickly, with minimal effort, regardless of their location or preferred channel. Samsung achieved the #1 customer satisfaction and overall service quality ranking among 5G mobile devices in the 2024 American Customer Satisfaction Index Survey (Samsung, 2024). This success reflects Samsung's commitment to consistent, responsive care through its extensive multi-channel support network.

Key takeaway: Samsung's customer care strategy shows the power of accessible, consistent service. By investing in both digital and physical support infrastructure, Samsung enhances customer trust and reinforces its position as a reliable, service-focused brand.

HOW TO MEASURE SUCCESS WITHIN RETURN ON INTERVENTION

A successful Return on Intervention strategy goes beyond resolving immediate issues – it focuses on elevating the overall customer experience. It's not just about whether an issue gets resolved, but *how* it's resolved and what impact it has on customer trust, satisfaction and loyalty. Measuring success in this area requires a combination of quantitative metrics and qualitative feedback that capture the emotional and practical outcomes of intervention. The metrics below provide a multi-dimensional view of effectiveness, helping teams refine strategy, reduce friction and build long-term resilience in customer relationships.

Customer Satisfaction Score (CSAT)

CSAT is one of the most direct and immediate ways to understand how customers feel about the issue resolution process. It captures whether their expectations were met and if the experience left them feeling satisfied and supported.

- **How to measure**: Send post-resolution surveys asking customers to rate their satisfaction on a scale (e.g. 1 to 5). Include open-ended comments for additional context.
- **Application and insights**: Companies like Apple use CSAT scores to evaluate the quality of service and make adjustments to training or policies. Tracking CSAT trends helps identify weak points in the resolution journey.
- **Improvement tip**: Focus on empathy, clarity and follow-through. If CSAT is low in specific areas, consider targeted agent training or process changes to improve experiences.

First Contact Resolution (FCR)

FCR measures how often an issue is fully resolved during the first interaction. High FCR rates suggest streamlined processes and empowered teams, while low rates signal friction, follow-ups and potential frustration.

- **How to measure**: Track the percentage of support cases resolved without any need for additional contacts.
- **Application and insights**: Companies like Amazon prioritise FCR to improve satisfaction and reduce cost. Analysing FCR by issue type reveals where support is falling short and where process changes are most needed.
- **Improvement tip**: Equip agents with the authority and information needed to solve issues on the spot. Strong knowledge bases and CRM tools also increase FCR.

Time to Resolution (TTR)

TTR measures how long it takes to fully resolve a customer issue. It's a key efficiency metric that also reflects how responsive and organised your support structure is.

- **How to measure**: Record the time from the initial customer contact to full resolution. Track averages by issue type, channel or agent group.
- **Application and insights**: Companies like Tesla monitor TTR to optimise high-impact issue resolution. Long resolution times may point to internal bottlenecks or resource gaps.
- **Improvement tip**: Use automation to route cases efficiently and support agents with AI-assisted tools to reduce time spent searching for information.

Net Promoter Score (NPS) post-intervention

NPS after issue resolution shows whether the customer experience has reinforced or weakened brand trust. It's a loyalty signal rooted in emotion and outcomes.

- **How to measure**: Ask the standard NPS question post-intervention: 'Based on this experience, how likely are you to recommend us?' Follow up with open-ended questions to understand the *why* behind the score.

- **Application and insights**: Brands like Zappos use NPS to gauge how well their service interactions build advocacy. Segmenting by channel or issue type reveals which interventions lead to loyalty, and which don't.
- **Improvement tip**: Follow through with proactive communication and clear next steps to boost post-intervention NPS.

Customer retention and churn rates

These long-term indicators reveal whether your interventions are strong enough to keep customers engaged over time. They show whether resolution led to relationship repair or a slow disengagement.

- **How to measure**: Compare retention and churn rates before and after process changes or new intervention strategies.
- **Application and insights**: Brands like Delta Airlines track these metrics to understand the impact of service recovery efforts. A reduction in churn following improvements is a strong Return on Intervention signal.
- **Improvement tip**: Personalised follow-ups, loyalty rewards and feedback loops post-resolution can help reinforce a customer's decision to stay.

Repeat contact rate

This measures how often customers reach out again about the same issue. A high repeat rate indicates that resolutions weren't clear, complete or well-communicated.

- **How to measure**: Monitor the frequency of contacts related to the same issue ID, customer account or topic.
- **Application and insights**: Warby Parker use metrics to reduce frustration and improve self-service tools. A rising repeat rate may signal gaps in resolution clarity or product/service consistency.

- **Improvement tip:** Train agents to anticipate follow-up questions and document thoroughly. Make sure the resolution is easy to understand and actionable.

Sentiment analysis

Beyond numbers, sentiment analysis helps you understand how customers *feel* after interventions. It uncovers emotional responses that influence brand perception and loyalty.

- **How to measure**: Use NLP (Natural Language Processing) tools to analyse customer emails, chats and reviews for tone and emotion. Track trends in positive, negative and neutral sentiment.
- **Application and insights**: Microsoft uses sentiment data to fine-tune scripts, product messaging and support strategies. It reveals subtle patterns that CSAT or NPS alone might miss.
- **Improvement tip:** Encourage open-ended feedback and use AI tools to extract emotional context. Share insights with frontline teams to help shape tone and language.

Additional measurement tools

- **Customer Effort Score (CES)**: Tracks how easy it was for a customer to resolve their issue. High effort = high frustration.
- **Issue-type analysis**: Categorising intervention requests helps identify recurring problems and resource gaps.
- **Agent performance metrics**: Monitor metrics like handle time, escalation rate and agent-specific satisfaction to support coaching and operational improvements.

Return on Intervention isn't just about resolving issues – it's about rebuilding trust, reducing friction and turning recovery moments into relationship-building opportunities. By using a mix of customer experience metrics (like CSAT, FCR, NPS and sentiment analysis) along with operational data (TTR, repeat contact rate and agent performance), companies can see where they're excelling and where improvements are needed. When measured well, intervention becomes more than support – it becomes a strategic asset for brand loyalty and long-term success.

IMPLEMENTING RETURN ON INTERVENTION

Delivering timely, effective customer intervention requires a combination of quick, operational improvements and long-term, systemic changes. Quick wins build trust through immediate resolution and responsiveness, while long-term strategies strengthen the tools, processes and training needed to prevent future issues and support proactive service. These efforts must be supported across the organisation – from leadership to customer support teams – to create a culture where intervention is swift, empathetic and embedded in the customer experience. The following strategies outline both tactical actions and role-specific approaches to embed Return on Intervention into daily operations.

Quick wins

1. **Establish clear escalation paths**
   Create a well-defined escalation process to ensure complex customer issues are routed quickly to the most appropriate team or expert. This avoids delays, reduces frustration and ensures customers receive fast, accurate support from someone who can resolve the issue on first contact.

2. **Enhance multi-channel support**
   Provide consistent support across multiple customer touchpoints, such as live chat, email, social media and phone. Offering channel choice increases accessibility and empowers

customers to seek help on their terms, improving satisfaction and reducing resolution time.

3. **Proactively communicate with customers**
   Proactively notify customers about known issues, delays or resolutions in progress. Anticipating concerns and addressing them before customers reach out signals transparency and care, building trust even in the face of disruption.

4. **Empower frontline staff to resolve issues**
   Equip customer service teams with the authority and tools they need to make decisions without unnecessary escalations. Empowered employees can respond more quickly and confidently, improving both customer outcomes and employee engagement.

5. **Create transparent, customer-centric policies**
   Simplify and clearly communicate policies around returns, complaints and issue resolution. Clear, customer-friendly policies reduce friction, set expectations and build a perception of fairness and consistency in how customers are treated.

Long-term strategies

1. **Invest in advanced CRM systems**
   Implement a robust CRM that consolidates customer data and interaction history. With access to full context, agents can deliver more personalised support, avoid repeat questions and resolve issues faster and more effectively.

2. **Leverage AI for predictive intervention**
   Use AI and predictive analytics to identify potential problems before they escalate. From recognising usage anomalies to

spotting patterns in complaints, proactive outreach builds goodwill and prevents frustration.

3. **Prioritise empathy in training and coaching**
   Integrate empathy, active listening and de-escalation into ongoing training. When teams can handle emotional, complex situations with care, they turn tense moments into opportunities for loyalty and connection.

4. **Establish cross-departmental feedback loops**
   Customer service insights should inform every department. Sharing feedback with product, marketing and operations helps teams understand root causes of customer frustration and collaborate on lasting improvements.

5. **Continuously optimise through data and feedback**
   Monitor key metrics like First Contact Resolution, Repeat Contact Rate and CSAT – and adjust workflows accordingly. Create a culture of learning and responsiveness, where service teams use real-time feedback to improve daily.

Driving Engagement at Every Level

For executives and senior leadership:

- **Prioritise proactive problem-solving:** Leaders should create a culture that anticipates customer issues before they arise, reducing friction and enhancing brand trust.
- **Invest in customer-centric technology:** Implementing AI-driven chatbots, predictive analytics and real-time support tools enables faster and more effective issue resolution.
- **Embed intervention into company values:** A brand's reputation is built on how well it responds to challenges.

Ensuring swift and empathetic problem resolution strengthens long-term customer loyalty.

For operational managers:

- **Streamline internal processes:** Operational inefficiencies create delays in resolving customer issues. Improving workflows and ensuring interdepartmental alignment reduces response times.
- **Train teams to take ownership:** Customer-facing employees should be empowered to solve problems on the spot, rather than escalating minor issues unnecessarily.
- **Monitor resolution times:** Tracking first-contact resolution and time-to-resolution metrics helps identify bottlenecks and improve overall efficiency.

For customer service and support teams:

- **Ensure first-contact resolution:** Customers expect fast and effective responses. Training agents to resolve most issues during the first interaction significantly improves satisfaction.
- **Implement real-time support:** Offering live chat, self-service portals, and 24/7 assistance reduces frustration and enhances the customer experience.
- **Use feedback to refine processes:** Regularly analysing customer complaints and issue trends helps refine processes to prevent recurring problems.

For technology and digital teams:

- **Leverage automation to speed up intervention:** AI-driven assistance, automated workflows and predictive issue detection improve response times and efficiency.

- **Provide seamless omnichannel support:** Customers expect consistency across phone, email, chat and social media. Ensuring a unified support experience enhances trust and loyalty.
- **Continuously update knowledge bases:** Offering self-service options and AI-assisted recommendations empowers customers to resolve issues independently when possible.

By embedding a proactive and responsive approach to customer intervention, businesses can minimise frustration, enhance trust and drive long-term customer loyalty.

THE LASTING IMPACT OF RETURN ON INTERVENTION

Return on Intervention is more than an operational necessity – it's a strategic lever for customer loyalty, brand trust and long-term resilience. In a marketplace where expectations continue to rise, how a company responds to customer challenges can define its reputation. When handled with empathy, speed and care, intervention moments can transform dissatisfaction into loyalty and create meaningful brand differentiation.

The real-world examples explored earlier in this chapter – from Amazon's blend of automation and empathy, to Ritz-Carlton's frontline empowerment and Revolut's real-time, in-app resolution model – demonstrate that effective intervention takes many forms. What they share is a consistent commitment to putting the customer at the centre of the experience and to using moments of friction as opportunities to strengthen trust.

For businesses seeking to embed Return on Intervention, the first step is a mindset shift. Intervention should not be viewed as a cost centre, but as a strategic asset – one that can drive operational efficiency, enhance brand equity and deepen customer relationships. When prioritised across leadership, operations and service teams, intervention becomes a cultural value that unites the organisation around exceptional customer care.

In an increasingly transparent and competitive landscape, Return on Intervention offers a path to sustainable success. By treating service interactions as high-value moments of connection, businesses can build trust, inspire loyalty and ensure long-term relevance in a rapidly evolving world.

TAKE ACTION

Now that you understand the impact of Return on Intervention, it's time to turn insight into action. Start by identifying one stage of your customer journey where intervention can be faster, more empathetic or more proactive – whether that's improving first contact resolution, empowering frontline staff or enhancing real-time communication.

Even small changes – like clarifying escalation pathways or following up after issue resolution – can have a significant effect on customer loyalty and trust. In a service-driven economy, how your business responds in moments of friction says more about your brand than any marketing campaign.

The decisions you make today to improve intervention will shape tomorrow's customer relationships. Take the first step toward building a brand that listens, responds and earns lasting loyalty – one resolution at a time.

REFERENCES

Amazon (2025) 'Amazon Pay A-to-Z Guarantee for buyers'. Available at: www.pay.amazon. co.uk/help/201751470 (Accessed: 28 April 2025).

Daktela (2024) 'One-Third of Customers Leave After a Single Bad Experience'. Available at: www.daktela.com/post/one-third-of-customers-leave-after-a-single-bad-experience-how-much-is-poor-customer-service-costing-you (Accessed: 28 April 2025).

eTailWest (2024) 'How Zappos wins at customer service every day'. Available at: www. etailwest.wbresearch.com/blog/how-zappos-wins-at-customer-service-every-day (Accessed: 28 April 2025).

Everything Supply Chain (2024) 'How Returns Work – Amazon Reverse Logistics'. Available at: www.everythingsupplychain.com/how-returns-work-amazon-reverse-logistics/ (Accessed: 28 April 2025).

J.D. Power (2023) '2023 North America Hotel Guest Satisfaction Study'. Available at: www. jdpower.com/sites/default/files/file/2023-07/2023077%20N.A.%20Hotel%20 Guest%20Satisfaction.pdf (Accessed: 28 April 2025).

Kimola (2024) 'Revolut Customer Feedback Insight Report'. Available at: www.kimola. com/reports/revolut-customer-feedback-insight-report-trustpilot-en-us-144741 (Accessed: 28 April 2025).

PwC (2018) 'Customer experience is everything: PwC'. Available at: www.pwc.com/us/ en/services/consulting/library/consumer-intelligence-series/future-of-customer-experience.html (Accessed: 28 April 2025).

Renascence (2024a) 'How The Ritz-Carlton Enhances Customer Experience (CX) Through Personalized Service and Luxury'. vailable at: www.renascence.io/ journal/how-the-ritz-carlton-enhances-customer-experience-cx-through-personalized-service-and-luxury (Accessed: 28 April 2025).

Renascence (2024b) 'How Zappos delivers exceptional customer experience (CX)'. Available at: www.renascence.io/journal/how-zappos-delivers-exceptional-customer-experience-cx (Accessed: 28 April 2025).

Renascence (2024c) 'How Nordstrom Fosters Customer Loyalty with High-Quality Customer Experience (CX)'. Available at: www.renascence.io/journal/how-nordstrom-fosters-customer-loyalty-with-high-quality-customer-experience-cx (Accessed: 28 April 2025).

ReturnPolicyVault (2025) 'Nordstrom Return Policy: Everything You Need to Know'. Available at: www.returnpolicyvault.com/nordstrom-return-policy/ (Accessed: 28 April 2025).

Revolut (2024a) 'Physical Branches Vs 24/7 Digital Presence | Revolut United Kingdom'. Available at: www.revolut.com/blog/post/trust-physical-branches-vs-24-7-digital-presence/ (Accessed: 28 April 2025).

Revolut (2024b) 'Revolut launches AI feature to protect customers from card scams and break the scammers "spell", 15 February'. Available at: www.revolut.com/news/ revolut_launches_ai_feature_to_protect_customers_from_card_scams_and_ break_the_scammers_spell/ (Accessed: 28 April 2025).

Samsung (2024) 'Samsung Scores #1 in Customer Satisfaction and Overall Service Quality for 5G Mobile Devices'. Available at: www.news.samsung.com/us/samsung-scores-1-customer-satisfaction-overall-service-quality-mobile-2024-acsi/ (Accessed: 28 April 2025).

Samsung (2025) 'Samsung Care Plus | Phone and Laptop Insurance'. Available at: www. samsung.com/uk/offer/samsung-care-plus/ (Accessed: 28 April 2025).

Statista (2024) 'U.S. customer satisfaction with Amazon 2024'. Available at: www.statista. com/statistics/185788/us-customer-satisfaction-with-amazon/ (Accessed: 28 April 2025).

Top Bubble Index (2025) 'Nordstrom Return Policy Guide'. Available at: www.topbubble index.com/blog/nordstrom-return-policy-guide/ (Accessed: 28 April 2025).

Yaguara (2024) '60 Customer Service Statistics For 2025 (Data & Trends)'. Available at: www.yaguara.co/customer-service-statistics/ (Accessed: 28 April 2025).

CHAPTER 6
RETURN ON INTERACTION – SHOW UP WHERE YOUR CUSTOMERS WANT YOU TO BE

INTRODUCING RETURN ON INTERACTION

In today's digital and hyper-connected world, the way customers interact with brands has transformed dramatically. What was once a linear journey – typically limited to in-store visits or phone support – has evolved into a dynamic web of touchpoints across websites, mobile apps, social media, live chat, messaging platforms and physical experiences.

This shift has made Return on Interaction a critical metric for businesses operating in a customer-centric market. It goes beyond being present on multiple channels; it's about delivering seamless, responsive and personalised experiences wherever your customers are – online, offline or somewhere in between. According to Microsoft, 90% of consumers expect consistent interactions across all channels, while 56% feel frustrated when that consistency is missing (Microsoft, 2017).

Customers now expect brands to anticipate their needs, respond in real time and provide frictionless experiences at every touchpoint. Whether browsing a website, scrolling social media, walking into a store or speaking to customer support, the expectation is clear: the experience should feel unified, effortless and personal.

Return on Interaction isn't just about meeting expectations – it's about creating value that builds trust, loyalty and brand advocacy. When companies invest in truly integrated interaction strategies, they gain more than just efficiency – they gain deeper customer relationships and a meaningful competitive edge.

This chapter explores what it takes to deliver Return on Interaction successfully. You will look at omnichannel strategies, customer engagement tools and performance metrics that drive consistent, human-centred service. Through real-world case studies – spanning brands including Starbucks, Sephora, Uber and Delta – you'll see how interaction excellence fosters loyalty and long-term growth.

To unlock this potential, businesses need a practical, measurable approach to customer interaction – one that balances strategy with action at every level of the organisation.

LEVERAGING RETURN ON INTERACTION

In today's dynamic marketplace, customers expect seamless, engaging and personalised experiences across every channel. Return on Interaction is not just about responding – it's about showing up in the moments that matter, with consistency, empathy and strategic intent. When done well, it drives loyalty, brand trust and long-term commercial value.

By the end of this chapter, you will have a clear understanding of how to implement and sustain Return on Interaction within your organisation, regardless of industry or size. You'll gain both strategic insights and practical tools to create customer interactions that are effortless, human and impactful. This chapter will equip you to:

- **Maximise the strategic value of Return on Interaction**
  Understand why a strong customer interaction strategy is essential for brand success. Learn how proactive engagement across digital and physical channels strengthens satisfaction, boosts retention and contributes to brand equity – positioning your business as a customer-first leader.

- **Build the core elements of an effective interaction strategy**
  Identify the core components of a customer-centric interaction model, including personalisation, responsiveness, consistency and multi-channel integration. Discover how to design experiences that meet customer expectations while reinforcing trust and loyalty at every touchpoint.

- **Implement best practices from leading organisations**
  Apply learnings from brands like Starbucks, Sephora, Marriott, Uber, Glossier and Delta Air Lines – companies that lead the way in creating seamless, omnichannel engagement. These case studies demonstrate how to orchestrate interactions that foster advocacy and drive repeat business.

- **Measure success using meaningful engagement metrics**
  Gain a framework for tracking interaction performance with both qualitative and quantitative tools. Key performance indicators include Customer Effort Score (CES), response times, engagement rates by channel and customer retention. Use these insights to optimise your strategy and measure what matters.

- **Apply practical strategies for immediate and long-term impact**
  Discover how to take action – fast. From improving response times and cross-channel messaging to long-term investments in AI personalisation and platform integration, learn how to elevate customer engagement at scale and pace.

- **Prioritise and align interaction initiatives across the business**
  Identify high-impact opportunities for improving interaction and align them with broader business goals. This section also offers practical guidance for executives, marketing teams and operational leaders on collaborating cross-functionally to create a unified, human-centred customer experience.

Now let's bring Return on Interaction to life.

RETURN ON INTERACTION IN ACTION

Implementing Return on Interaction requires more than just theory – it's about designing seamless, connected experiences that meet customers wherever they are. The following case studies highlight how leading companies are using multi-channel engagement, digital innovation and personalised service to enhance customer satisfaction, deepen loyalty and differentiate their brands. Each example illustrates how Return on Interaction can be tailored to fit different industries, customer expectations and service models – proving that consistent, value-driven engagement is a powerful driver of business success.

STARBUCKS – BUILDING DIGITAL ENGAGEMENT THROUGH A MULTI-CHANNEL EXPERIENCE

Starbucks has become a benchmark in multi-channel interaction by creating a seamless integration between its physical stores and digital platforms. The Starbucks mobile app allows customers to order ahead, pay in-app, collect rewards and even customise their orders. The app's popularity has been instrumental in building a loyal customer base, with mobile orders accounting for over 25% of all transactions in 2021 (Starbucks, 2021).

Beyond its app, Starbucks engages customers on social media, frequently responding to comments and questions (Juphy, 2025). Starbucks also uses geolocation within its app to promote local events or special offers, enhancing the in-store experience with digital features (Creativepool, 2017). This cohesive approach demonstrates Starbucks' commitment to being present where its customers are, both digitally and physically.

Key takeaway: Starbucks illustrates the power of an integrated digital strategy that complements the in-store experience, proving that a brand's presence across multiple touchpoints can significantly enhance customer engagement and loyalty.

SEPHORA – OMNICHANNEL BEAUTY EXPERIENCE WITH SEAMLESS SHOPPING AND SUPPORT

Sephora has pioneered an omnichannel approach to interaction that combines online and in-store experiences for a cohesive customer journey. Through the Sephora app, customers can use the Virtual Artist feature, which lets them 'try on' make-up digitally. The app also enables customers to book appointments for in-store services, access personalised product recommendations and view purchase history (Ngrow, 2024).

Sephora's online and physical stores are fully integrated, allowing customers to view products online and purchase them in-store, or vice versa. Sephora's e-commerce sales have grown substantially, with forecasts projecting around $3.6 billion in online sales for 2025, reflecting the success of its digital and omnichannel strategies (Statista, 2025).

Key takeaway: Sephora's omnichannel model showcases how an integrated digital and physical presence can improve customer convenience, foster personalisation and drive sales.

MARRIOTT - PERSONALISED TRAVEL EXPERIENCES THROUGH DIRECT AND DIGITAL CHANNELS

Marriott uses an omnichannel strategy to connect with customers through both direct and digital touchpoints. The Marriott Bonvoy app allows customers to book rooms, access rewards, check in remotely and even communicate directly with hotel staff during their stay. This feature provides a high level of convenience for travellers, as they can request amenities or schedule room service through the app (Marriot, 2025).

By combining physical and digital interactions, Marriott ensures a seamless experience. According to Marriott's CEO, the company saw a 32% year-on-year increase in mobile app users and 27% growth in digital room nights and 41% growth in revenue, driven by investments in the Marriott Bonvoy app and other digital products (Phocuswire, 2023).

Key takeaway: Marriott's interaction strategy highlights the value of providing direct, responsive service to guests through a single, streamlined platform, underscoring the importance of convenience and accessibility in customer interactions.

UBER - REAL-TIME INTERACTION AND SEAMLESS MOBILITY

Uber has transformed service interaction through its real-time, data-driven platform that connects drivers and riders instantly. The Uber app allows users to request rides, track driver location, view estimated arrival times and fares and make payments – all within a few taps.

Its intuitive design and immediate feedback loop create a seamless experience that meets modern expectations for convenience and control (Uber, 2024).

By integrating advanced AI capabilities, Uber further personalises user interactions, anticipates needs and optimises support. AI models power fast, empathetic responses and automate routine queries, enabling human agents to focus on complex issues. This includes interpreting ride disruptions for automatic fare adjustments and streamlining refunds for Uber Eats orders (OpenAI, 2025). With 161 million monthly active users as of Q3 2024, Uber's widespread adoption reflects growing trust in its platform for mobility and delivery services (Backlinko, 2024).

Key takeaway: Uber demonstrates the power of real-time, app-based interaction to build trust and deliver consistent, customer-first experiences. Its integrated digital approach makes every step, from booking to resolution, fluid and personalised.

GLOSSIER – BUILDING COMMUNITY THROUGH DIGITAL-FIRST ENGAGEMENT

Glossier has redefined beauty retail by fostering a highly interactive, digital-first customer experience. Started as a blog, it has evolved into a direct-to-consumer brand built on deep online engagement. Through its website, app and social platforms, Glossier invites customers to share feedback, co-create products and engage with the brand in real time (Extole, 2024).

Features like personalised product recommendations, intuitive mobile shopping and responsive customer service contribute to a smooth and satisfying experience (OptiMonk, 2025). The brand's use of social proof – amplifying customer reviews and real-user content – drives trust and community connection (Skeepers, 2025). Extole highlights that nearly 80% of Glossier's customers are referred by friends, emphasising the importance of community-driven growth and digital engagement in fostering loyalty (Extole, 2024).

Key takeaway: Glossier illustrates how digital-first interaction and community involvement can elevate customer satisfaction. By creating an inclusive, feedback-led experience across platforms, Glossier turns online engagement into lasting brand loyalty.

DELTA AIR LINES - MULTI-CHANNEL COMMUNICATION FOR SEAMLESS TRAVEL EXPERIENCES

Delta Air Lines delivers a connected travel experience through a multi-channel strategy that includes SMS, social media and its Fly Delta app, allowing passengers to manage bookings, receive real-time updates, check in and track baggage. By integrating AI-powered tools and platforms like Apple Business Chat, Delta streamlines service, reduces wait times and provides timely, relevant support across digital touchpoints – enhancing convenience and control throughout the journey (Delta, 2024a).

Delta's investment in digital experience is reflected in its performance in the J.D. Power 2024 North America Airline Satisfaction Study, where it ranked highest in both First/Business Class and Premium Economy. The airline's leadership in customer satisfaction is attributed to excellence in digital tools, staff engagement, ease of travel and overall day-of-travel experience (Delta, 2024b).

Key takeaway: Delta demonstrates the effectiveness of multi-channel communication, especially in industries where timely information and seamless service are paramount for customer satisfaction.

HOW TO MEASURE SUCCESS WITHIN RETURN ON INTERACTION

To gauge the effectiveness of Return on Interaction, companies must look beyond traditional service metrics and focus on a comprehensive set of indicators that capture the quality, consistency and impact of interactions across all channels. This requires a multi-dimensional approach that blends quantitative data with qualitative feedback – offering a full picture of how well a brand is meeting customer needs, adapting to their preferences and driving long-term engagement and loyalty. The following metrics are essential for evaluating how everyday interactions contribute to brand perception, satisfaction and sustained value.

Customer Effort Score (CES)

CES helps quantify how easy, or difficult, it is for customers to interact with your brand, especially when resolving an issue or completing a task. It's a leading indicator of friction and frustration across digital and human touchpoints.

- **How to measure**: Use post-interaction surveys asking customers how easy it was to complete their task. Track CES across web, app and service channels.
- **Application and insights**: Brands like Amazon and Apple use CES to evaluate how seamless their interactions are – from one-click ordering to intuitive app interfaces. High effort scores often reveal hidden friction.
- **Improvement tip**: Simplify interfaces, improve instructions and speed up service processes to reduce friction across key touchpoints.

Engagement rate by channel

Engagement rate shows how customers are interacting with your content and platforms, offering a view into what's resonating and where customers are most actively connecting with your brand.

- **How to measure**: Track interaction rates like clicks, shares, app usage, email opens and in-app feature engagement across all platforms.
- **Application and insights**: Brands like Sephora and Starbucks analyse channel-by-channel engagement to understand which experiences (e.g. AR features, loyalty apps) are driving interaction.

- **Improvement tip**: Create interactive, channel-specific content (e.g. quizzes, exclusive app offers or location-based promotions) to boost lagging engagement.

Response time across channels

Fast, consistent response times are key to maintaining trust and satisfaction, especially on real-time platforms like social media or live chat.

- **How to measure**: Monitor average response time by platform (email, chat, phone, in-app, etc.) and track against benchmarks or service level agreements (SLAs).
- **Application and insights**: Delta and Zappos use this to ensure quick responses during high-stakes moments (e.g. travel delays or complex product inquiries).
- **Improvement tip**: Automate basic responses via chatbots and prioritise fast, empathetic replies on high-volume channels like X or WhatsApp.

Customer retention rate

Retention is the ultimate sign that your interactions are creating value. It reflects satisfaction, trust and the emotional connection built over time.

- **How to measure**: Track repeat visits, renewals or ongoing product usage across platforms and correlate with engagement metrics.
- **Application and insights**: Netflix and Marriott use retention data to understand how multi-channel touchpoints, from apps to in-person check-ins, reinforce loyalty.
- **Improvement tip**: Use follow-ups, loyalty rewards and regular touchpoints to stay connected and reinforce the value of continued engagement.

Customer Satisfaction (CSAT) by channel

CSAT helps you measure satisfaction at specific touchpoints, revealing which channels are delivering great experiences and which are falling short.

- **How to measure**: Collect post-interaction surveys across all channels, e.g. after a chat session, in-store visit or email exchange.
- **Application and insights**: Apple uses CSAT to fine-tune cross-channel experiences. Segmenting results by channel reveals gaps that aren't visible in overall satisfaction metrics.
- **Improvement tip**: Regularly review CSAT by channel and tailor training or process improvements accordingly.

Conversion rate by channel

Conversion rate reveals whether your interactions are not just engaging, but also effective. It reflects how well each channel moves customers from interest to action.

- **How to measure**: Track conversion-related actions – purchases, sign-ups, bookings, etc. – across digital and in-person channels.
- **Application and insights**: Nordstrom monitors in-app purchases and online-to-store behaviours, leveraging tools like in-app exclusives to improve performance.
- **Improvement tip**: Improve CTAs, streamline checkout flows, and personalise offers per channel to lift conversion rates.

Sentiment analysis

Sentiment analysis captures how customers feel about your interactions, not just what they do. It provides emotional context to support or challenge your numeric scores.

- **How to measure**: Use NLP tools to analyse tone and emotion across customer feedback, chat logs, social media and survey responses.
- **Application and insights**: Nike and Microsoft use sentiment tracking to understand emotional response to service, campaigns and digital experiences.

- **Improvement tip**: Monitor emotion trends and use them to train teams on tone, timing and language, especially when dealing with negative experiences.

Average Handle Time (AHT)

AHT helps assess the balance between efficiency and experience. While faster interactions are good, the real value lies in resolving the issue effectively the first time.

- **How to measure**: Track average time spent per interaction, per channel. Look at both self-service and agent-assisted channels.
- **Application and insights**: Brands like AT&T, Three and Apple use AHT to identify training or process needs and reduce complexity where possible.
- **Improvement tip**: Equip agents with fast-access resources and well-integrated CRM tools. Offer coaching focused on efficiency *without* sacrificing care.

Return on Interaction is about more than speed or presence – it's about creating meaningful, seamless and effective customer experiences across every touchpoint. By consistently measuring and improving metrics like Customer Effort Score, engagement, response time, CSAT, sentiment and conversion, brands can evolve from simply being available to being genuinely impactful. These insights reveal what matters most to customers in the moment. When acted on, they turn everyday interactions into lasting value opportunities.

IMPLEMENTING RETURN ON INTERACTION

Creating a seamless customer experience requires both quick, visible improvements and longer-term investment in systems, processes and collaboration. Quick wins deliver immediate enhancements across key channels, showing customers that their time, preferences and feedback are valued. Long-term strategies, supported by cross-functional alignment and smart technology, ensure consistent and personalised experiences at every touchpoint. These efforts must be championed across departments – from leadership to marketing, support and operations – to ensure every interaction strengthens trust, engagement and loyalty.

Quick wins

1. **Centralise customer data for a unified interaction view**
   Implement a centralized CRM system to aggregate customer data from multiple channels, creating a unified view of each customer's interaction history. This enables more personalised and efficient service, as representatives have access to relevant customer information instantly. By centralising data, brands can reduce response times, improve the quality of interactions and create a more cohesive experience.

2. **Improve response times on high-demand channels**
   Prioritise response time improvements on channels where customers frequently reach out, such as social media and live chat. Reducing delays on these platforms by implementing chatbots for simple inquiries or optimising staffing can significantly enhance the customer experience. Faster response times on key channels convey to customers that their time is valued and improve overall satisfaction.

3. **Train staff for consistent cross-channel communication**
   Invest in training that educates employees on the brand's communication style, values and customer service protocols across all platforms. Consistency is crucial for maintaining brand identity and building customer trust, so employees

should understand how to interact with customers in a way
that aligns with the brand's image, whether they're handling
queries via social media, phone or in-store.

4. **Implement customer feedback mechanisms for
real-time insight**
Establish feedback mechanisms, such as post-interaction
surveys or automated prompts, to gather insights immediately
after each interaction. This allows companies to identify
pain points and make improvements promptly. By soliciting
real-time feedback, brands show customers they care about
their experience and can address issues quickly, preventing
potential dissatisfaction.

5. **Enable self-service options to empower customers**
Introduce self-service features, like FAQs, knowledge bases
and chatbots, on digital platforms to allow customers to find
answers independently. Many customers prefer solving issues
on their own, and self-service options reduce reliance on
customer support staff while improving response times. This
empowers customers to take control of their interactions and
enhances satisfaction.

Long-term strategies

1. **Develop an omnichannel interaction strategy**
Create an omnichannel strategy that integrates all customer
touchpoints, both online and offline, into a single, cohesive
experience. This may involve coordinating between
departments, implementing technology that allows for
seamless transitions between channels and ensuring consistent
messaging. By developing a robust omnichannel approach,

brands can meet customers wherever they are, fostering a loyal and engaged customer base.

2. **Invest in advanced analytics for predictive engagement**
Leverage AI and predictive analytics to anticipate customer needs and proactively engage with them. Advanced analytics can help brands detect patterns in customer behaviour, allowing them to offer personalised product recommendations or timely assistance. Predictive engagement can significantly enhance the customer experience, making interactions more relevant and reducing friction in the customer journey.

3. **Personalise the customer experience with AI-driven tools**
Implement AI-driven tools that enable personalisation on a deeper level, such as recommendation engines or personalised marketing automation. By tailoring interactions based on individual preferences and behaviours, brands can deliver experiences that resonate with customers and keep them coming back. AI-powered personalisation allows brands to create unique journeys for each customer, fostering loyalty and trust.

4. **Establish cross-functional collaboration to support interaction goals**
Effective Return on Interaction requires collaboration across departments, including marketing, customer service, IT and operations. By fostering cross-functional teams, companies can ensure alignment in messaging, streamline processes and address customer needs holistically. This collaboration helps create a seamless experience across all touchpoints, reinforcing a customer-first approach.

5. **Focus on continuous improvement through customer insights**

   Use customer insights from data analytics and feedback to continually refine the interaction strategy. Regularly analyse interaction data to identify areas for improvement and adapt to evolving customer expectations. A culture of continuous improvement ensures that the brand remains agile, relevant and responsive to customer needs in a dynamic market.

Driving Engagement at Every Level

For executives and senior leadership

- **Prioritise a seamless omnichannel strategy:** Customers expect consistent interactions across all touchpoints and leaders must ensure the organisation delivers a unified experience.
- **Invest in the right technology and infrastructure:** AI-driven chat, personalised digital experiences and real-time support enhance customer engagement and satisfaction.
- **Align internal teams around customer interactions:** Every department must work together to create a frictionless journey, ensuring a cohesive experience across marketing, sales and service.

For operational managers

- **Break down silos between teams:** Customer experience suffers when different departments operate in isolation, whereas collaborative processes ensure smooth interactions.
- **Monitor and optimise response times:** Fast, effective interactions improve satisfaction and retention – measuring first-response time and resolution speed is essential.

- **Adapt based on customer behaviour:** Data on customer engagement should drive changes in service availability, communication methods and content strategy.

For marketing and sales teams

- **Personalise interactions at every touchpoint:** Customers engage more when brands deliver tailored messaging, offers and support based on their preferences and behaviours.
- **Maintain consistency in brand messaging:** Every customer interaction, whether in-person, online, or via social media, should reinforce the company's values and promises.
- **Leverage data to improve engagement:** Insights from customer interactions help refine campaigns, improve targeting and create more meaningful engagement opportunities.

For customer service and support teams

- **Be accessible where customers need help:** Customers should be able to engage with support through their preferred channels – whether that's live chat, phone, social media or self-service.
- **Ensure seamless handovers across channels:** Customers should not have to repeat themselves when switching between channels – integrated systems help maintain context.
- **Use feedback to refine customer interactions:** Regularly reviewing customer interactions and feedback helps service teams identify pain points and improve experiences.

By ensuring that customer interactions are seamless, responsive and mean-ingful, organisations can build stronger relationships, enhance loyalty and drive long-term customer satisfaction.

THE LASTING IMPACT OF RETURN ON INTERACTION

Return on Interaction is a critical component of any customer-centric strategy in today's digital, multi-channel landscape. When brands focus on interaction quality, responsiveness and personalisation across all touchpoints, they don't just meet expectations, they exceed them. An effective interaction strategy creates meaningful connections that drive loyalty, advocacy and long-term growth.

This chapter has highlighted the power of delivering consistent, seamless experiences that reflect the needs and preferences of today's customers. Companies like Starbucks, Sephora, and Delta Air Lines show how omnichannel strategies – combining digital convenience with human-centred service – can build brand trust at scale. Starbucks has integrated its app's rewards system with in-store experiences to enhance loyalty. Sephora blends online and offline touchpoints to offer flexibility and personalisation throughout the customer journey. Delta's real-time, multi-channel communication builds confidence with travellers and demonstrates how responsiveness reinforces loyalty.

Return on Interaction is not simply about being available across channels, it's about creating cohesive, customer-first experiences across each of them. In a world where customers are quick to switch brands after a single poor interaction, every touchpoint must reinforce trust, ease and value. A strong interaction strategy strengthens brand equity and sets the foundation for resilience in a fast-changing marketplace.

Ultimately, Return on Interaction embodies the belief that every interaction counts. Companies that commit to this approach – investing in omnichannel infrastructure, personalising service and continuously improving based on customer feedback – position themselves as leaders in engagement. By delivering seamless and human experiences, they create lasting connections that fuel competitive advantage and long-term success.

TAKE ACTION

Now that you've explored the power of Return on Interaction, it's time to translate insight into impact. Start by identifying one customer touchpoint – whether it's your website, in-store experience, app or customer service channel – where interaction could be more seamless, responsive or personal.

Small changes, like improving response times or unifying brand messaging across platforms, can build momentum and strengthen your customer relationships. Long-term, focus on embedding omnichannel strategies and investing in tools that allow your brand to meet customers wherever they are – online, offline or somewhere in between.

In a world where customers expect every interaction to be easy, helpful and human, the brands that listen, adapt and engage meaningfully will stand out. Take the first step toward building a more integrated, customer-first experience that drives loyalty, trust and long-term value.

REFERENCES

Backlinko (2024) 'Uber Statistics 2024: How Many People Ride with Uber?'. Backlinko, 13 November. Available at: www.backlinko.com/uber-users (Accessed: 30 April 2025).

Creativepool (2017) 'How brands are using: Geolocation Marketing'. Creativepool. Available at: www.creativepool.com/magazine/leaders/how-brands-are-using-geolocation-marketing.13034 (Accessed: 28 April 2025).

Delta (2024a) 'Delta unveils AI-powered travel journey with new "multi-modal" transportation options. Delta Newsroom'. Available at: www.news.delta.com/delta-unveils-ai-powered-travel-journey-new-multi-modal-transportation-options (Accessed: 30 April 2025).

Delta (2024b) 'J.D. Power: Delta best for First/Business, Premium Economy passenger satisfaction; No. 1 in airline staff'. Delta Newsroom. Available at: www.news.delta.com/jd-power-delta-best-firstbusiness-premium-economy-passenger-satisfaction-no-1-airline-staff (Accessed: 30 April 2025).

Extole (2024) 'Glossier marketing and the value of customer-led growth'. Extole Blog. Available at: www.extole.com/blog/glossier-marketing-how-the-beauty-brand-used-word-of-mouth-to-shake-up-the-industry/ (Accessed: 30 April 2025).

Juphy (2025) 'STARBUCKS' Social Media Customer Service Performance'. Juphy. Available at: www.juphy.com/blog/starbuckss-social-media-customer-service-performance (Accessed: 28 April 2025).

Marriott (2025) 'Mobile App – Marriott'. Available at: www.marriott.com/marriott-brands/mobile-app.mi (Accessed: 28 April 2025).

Microsoft (2017) '2017 State of Global Customer Service Report'. Available at: www.info.microsoft.com/rs/157-GQE-382/images/EN-CNTNT-Report-DynService-2017-global-state-customer-service-en-au.pdf (Accessed: 28 April 2025).

Ngrow (2024) 'Case study: Sephora's omnichannel approach to enhance customer loyalty'. Ngrow Blog. Available at: www.ngrow.ai/blog/case-study-sephoras-omnichannel-approach-to-enhance-customer-loyalty (Accessed: 28 April 2025).

OpenAI (2025) 'Uber enables outstanding on-demand experiences with AI'. OpenAI. Available at: www.openai.com/index/uber-enables-outstanding-experiences/ (Accessed: 30 April 2025).

OptiMonk (2022) 'Glossier Marketing Breakdown: How This Beauty Brand Became a $1.2 Billion Company'. OptiMonk Blog. Available at: www.optimonk.com/glossier-marketing-breakdown/ (Accessed: 30 April 2025).

Phocuswire (2023) 'Marriott boosting app and wider digital investment in 2023', PhocusWire, 15 February. Available at: www.phocuswire.com/marriott-tech-digital-investment-2023 (Accessed: 28 April 2025).

Skeepers (2024) 'Community Decoded: How Glossier's Community Strategy Works'. Skeepers Blog. Available at: www.skeepers.io/en/blog/community-decoded-glossier/ (Accessed: 30 April 2025).

Starbucks (2021) 'Annual Report 2021'. Available at: www.investor.starbucks.com/financials/annual-reports/default.aspx (Accessed: 28 April 2025).

Statista (2025) 'E-commerce net sales of sephora.com 2025'. Statista. Available at: www.statista.com/forecasts/1383797/sephora-revenue-development-ecommercedb (Accessed: 28 April 2025).

Uber (2024) 'Only on Uber: Helping to make driving and delivering safer, fairer'. Uber Newsroom. Available at: www.uber.com/newsroom/onlyonuber24/ (Accessed: 30 April 2025).

CHAPTER 7
RETURN ON IMPROVEMENTS – SERVING, NOT JUST SELLING: CREATING VALUE THROUGH EVERY INTERACTION

INTRODUCING RETURN ON IMPROVEMENTS

In the modern business landscape, the notion of customer service has expanded far beyond the simple act of conducting a transaction. Today's consumers are well-informed, connected and empowered by technology – leading to expectations that extend beyond traditional sales interactions. This shift has created a new paradigm where companies must transition from transactional models to service-focused operations to deliver continuous value. The concept of Return on Improvements embodies this evolution, encouraging businesses to seek ongoing enhancement in both their offerings and customer interactions.

The urgency of this shift is underscored by changing consumer behaviour. Customer experience has become the key differentiator in today's competitive market. According to recent research, 86% of buyers are willing to pay more for a great customer experience, and companies that excel in customer experience report up to 41% faster revenue growth and 51% higher customer retention than their peers (SuperOffice, 2025). Businesses that fail to commit to continuous improvement risk losing customers to more agile, customer-centric competitors. In contrast, those who consistently enhance their service delivery build stronger relationships, deeper trust and lasting loyalty.

Return on Improvements is not a one-time initiative, it's a strategic mindset. It requires organisations to integrate customer feedback, employee insights and technological innovation to improve the customer journey on an ongoing basis. By doing so, companies not only meet current expectations, but anticipate future needs, positioning themselves as leaders in their industries.

Brands such as Apple, evolving from a hardware-focused company to a holistic service provider, and Toyota, embedding the Kaizen philosophy of continuous improvement, show how sustained enhancement can be woven into a company's DNA. These brands prove that improvement isn't just good for customer loyalty; it's good for long-term business growth and resilience.

This chapter explores the core principles of Return on Improvements and provides a practical roadmap for embedding continuous enhancement across your organisation. Through real-world examples, actionable tools and implementation strategies, you will see how businesses can move from being product providers to customer-centric service leaders.

LEVERAGING RETURN ON IMPROVEMENTS

In today's fast-moving, experience-driven marketplace, businesses can no longer rely on static offerings or one-off customer interactions to succeed. Return on Improvements represents a shift from transactional thinking to a service-oriented mindset – one that prioritises continuous enhancement, long-term value creation and sustainable customer relationships.

By the end of this chapter, you will have a clear understanding of how to implement and sustain Return on Improvements within your organisation. You'll gain strategic insight, practical tools and actionable frameworks to embed a culture of ongoing service enhancement across teams, touchpoints and systems. This chapter will equip you to:

- **Maximise the strategic value of continuous improvement**
  Understand why continuous improvement is essential for brand trust, customer loyalty and competitive advantage. Learn how a commitment to small, ongoing enhancements drives sustained relevance, customer satisfaction and long-term business health – extending beyond short-term wins to deliver deep, lasting impact.

- **Build the core elements of a continuous improvement framework**
  Identify the critical components of a successful improvement strategy, including employee empowerment, customer feedback

loops, agile thinking and technology integration. Discover how to build scalable systems that embed responsiveness and innovation into everyday operations.

- **Implement best practices from leading organisations**
Explore case studies from brands such as Apple, Canva and Toyota to see how continuous improvement is applied across different sectors. Whether through Toyota's Kaizen approach, Apple's product-service integration or Canva's evolution through real-time user feedback, these examples demonstrate what Return on Improvements looks like in action – and the outcomes it drives.

- **Measure success using meaningful performance metrics**
Build a measurement framework that aligns with your organisation's broader goals. Track progress using KPIs such as Customer Satisfaction Score (CSAT), Net Promoter Score (NPS), repeat purchase rates and customer retention. Use these metrics to evaluate the impact of your efforts and guide ongoing improvements.

- **Apply practical strategies for immediate and long-term impact**
Implement a mix of quick wins and long-term initiatives to embed a culture of improvement. From refining customer feedback channels and piloting small changes to launching innovation teams and investing in staff development, you'll have a clear roadmap for change at every level.

- **Prioritise and a improvement initiatives across the business**
Learn how to identify the highest-impact areas for improvement and align them with your strategic goals. This section offers tailored guidance for executives, operations leaders and

customer experience teams – clarifying how each function can contribute to a cohesive, organisation-wide improvement effort.

Now let's bring Return on Improvements to life.

RETURN ON IMPROVEMENTS IN ACTION

To understand how Return on Improvements drives sustained customer loyalty and business growth, you will explore examples from companies renowned for their commitment to continuous enhancement. Each case study demonstrates how ongoing innovation – whether through integrating customer feedback, leveraging new technology or empowering employees – enables brands to elevate the customer experience. These businesses prove that consistent improvements create lasting value, deepen customer relationships and position companies as leaders in their industries.

APPLE – FROM PRODUCT SELLER TO SERVICE ECOSYSTEM

Apple's transformation from a hardware-centric company to a holistic service provider exemplifies Return on Improvements. While the company is renowned for its products such as the iPhone, MacBook and iPad, its shift to services like AppleCare, iCloud, Apple Music, Apple TV and the App Store demonstrates a broader strategy of continuous customer value creation (Forbes, 2019). AppleCare in particular has been pivotal – providing customers with extended warranties and responsive support, thereby reinforcing loyalty and long-term satisfaction (Apple, 2025).

This integrated approach has enabled Apple to build a cohesive ecosystem that delivers seamless cross-device functionality, regular software updates and cloud-based continuity (Renascence, 2024). Apple's customer loyalty rate now stands at around 90%, with 76%

of iPhone users citing the seamless ecosystem as a key reason for staying loyal (Coolest Gadgets, 2025). This consistent investment in digital services and a customer-centric ecosystem demonstrates how ongoing service improvements can strengthen brand trust and retention.

Key takeaway: Apple's success is anchored in a strategy that fuses product excellence with consistent service enhancement. Its evolving ecosystem of digital services supports long-term loyalty, making Apple a leading example of Return on Improvements in action.

TOYOTA - CONTINUOUS IMPROVEMENT THROUGH KAIZEN

Toyota's practise of Kaizen, or continuous improvement, is a global benchmark for operational excellence. This philosophy empowers all employees – from assembly line workers to executives – to pursue incremental changes that lead to greater efficiency and enhanced customer satisfaction. Toyota's commitment to continuous refinement extends across its manufacturing systems, service delivery and customer experience initiatives (BusinessMap, 2025).

For example, Toyota Service Centres have implemented changes that improve transparency and efficiency in car maintenance, guided by real-time customer feedback (Toyota Europe, 2020). These enhancements are driven by insights gathered through post-service surveys and the Toyota Owners App, reflecting the company's Kaizen-driven approach to service (Toyota, 2025). In 2020, Toyota ranked highest among UK automotive brands in the Customer Satisfaction Index, recognised for its ethics, service quality and transparency (Toyota UK, 2020).

Key takeaway: Toyota's Kaizen philosophy demonstrates how embedding continuous improvement into company culture fosters lasting customer satisfaction and operational agility. Small, consistent enhancements can yield significant long-term business value.

CANVA - EVOLVING DESIGN TOOLS
THROUGH CONTINUOUS USER FEEDBACK

Canva, the graphic design platform, has continuously enhanced its offering by incorporating feedback from its global user base (Enterpret, 2024). Since its launch, Canva has evolved from a simple design tool into a robust platform used by individuals, educators and enterprises. Improvements include AI-powered design suggestions, advanced collaboration capabilities and integrations with third-party apps (Canva, 2023).

A key driver of this evolution has been the company's responsiveness to user needs. Canva's education features, including templates for lesson planning and class presentations, were developed in response to educator input (Canva, 2025a). Similarly, the introduction of brand kits and team folders reflected demand from business users for more structured, collaborative workflows (Canva, 2025b).

In its company blog and public statements, Canva frequently cites user input as a core part of its product roadmap. The platform continues to grow its user base, surpassing 220 million monthly active users as of 2024 (Canva, 2024).

Key takeaway: Canva exemplifies how consistent, feedback-driven product development can boost customer satisfaction and brand loyalty. Its commitment to accessibility, usability and innovation positions Canva as a responsive and continuously evolving design platform.

IKEA - STRENGTHENING LOYALTY THROUGH
ONGOING SERVICE ENHANCEMENTS

IKEA continues to build customer loyalty through consistent digital and service innovation. Its recently upgraded mobile app enhances convenience and personalisation with features like IKEA Kreativ, which allows users to visualise furniture in 3D, and Shop & Go, enabling checkout-free shopping – reflecting IKEA's commitment to a frictionless, inspiring customer journey (Ingka Group, 2025a).

The revamped IKEA Family membership area offers personalised offers and a points-based rewards programme that recognises purchases, wish list activity, and planning sessions. Members can redeem points for perks like free meals, Click & Collect services and home furnishing vouchers – deepening engagement and value (Ingka Group, 2025a).

These enhancements have delivered measurable impact: IKEA was named the best e-commerce website for customer experience in 2025 (Retail Times, 2025) and recorded its highest customer satisfaction scores in five years (Ingka Group, 2025b).

Key takeaway: IKEA shows how small, ongoing improvements grounded in real customer needs can build long-term loyalty. By investing in smart tools, simplifying service and rewarding engagement, it continues to evolve the shopping experience across channels.

AMERICAN EXPRESS – STRENGTHENING CUSTOMER EXPERIENCE THROUGH CONTINUOUS IMPROVEMENTS

American Express (Amex) is consistently recognised for its exceptional customer service, but the company continues to innovate by integrating advanced AI technologies and data-driven personalisation into its customer care model. These investments aim to improve both the speed and quality of customer interactions – allowing Amex to anticipate customer needs, offer tailored recommendations and streamline service resolution through digital and live channels (AIExpert Network, 2024).

One of the most impactful results of American Express's AI strategy has been its ability to reduce average handling time and increase first-contact resolution, particularly through AI-enhanced servicing tools and personalised mobile app experiences. For example, the company's AI-powered IT chatbot has reduced IT escalations by 40% by providing intuitive, step-by-step assistance rather than generic links, enabling employees to resolve issues faster and return to work more quickly (VentureBeat, 2025).

Key takeaway: American Express demonstrates how strategically integrating AI and personalisation into customer service can enhance responsiveness, deepen loyalty and deliver measurable improvements in customer retention. Their success illustrates how ongoing investment in experience optimisation is key to long-term value creation.

SHOPIFY - ELEVATING SELLER EXPERIENCE

Shopify, a leading e-commerce platform, has consistently prioritised service enhancements to meet the evolving needs of its merchant base. The company actively listens to user feedback and rolls out regular platform updates that streamline operations for business owners. These improvements include upgraded analytics dashboards, expanded payment gateway integrations and enhanced security features – all designed to ensure seamless shopping experiences for customers and ease of management for merchants (DigitalSuits, 2025).

A major milestone in 2020 was the introduction of the Shopify POS (point-of-sale) system, which allows small businesses to manage both in-person and online sales in one unified system. This omnichannel functionality has improved operational efficiency and offered merchants more control and visibility across sales channels (Shopify, 2020). Shopify's merchant base grew from 1.75 million in 2020 to over 3.8 million by 2022, reflecting rapid adoption and trust in the platform's evolving capabilities (SEO, 2024).

Key takeaway: Shopify illustrates how sustained investment in feature development and merchant experience leads to stronger client retention and brand loyalty. By making practical improvements informed by user needs, Shopify continues to position itself as a partner in long-term business growth.

HOW TO MEASURE SUCCESS WITHIN RETURN ON IMPROVEMENTS

Measuring Return on Improvements requires more than just tracking upgrades or operational fixes – it's about evaluating whether continuous service enhancements are truly driving better customer experiences, deeper loyalty and long-term growth. A comprehensive measurement approach blends quantitative performance indicators with qualitative feedback to provide a full picture of impact.

The following metrics span satisfaction, retention, efficiency and financial return, offering a complete framework for assessing how well your business is evolving from reactive service to proactive, value-driven improvement.

CUSTOMER SATISFACTION METRICS

Customer Satisfaction Score (CSAT)

CSAT measures how satisfied customers are with a specific service, interaction or product experience. It's a direct way to understand how well your improvements are landing with customers in the moment.

- **How to measure**: Conduct post-interaction CSAT surveys on a 1–5 scale and track shifts over time.
- **Insight**: A rise in CSAT suggests that customers are not only noticing your improvements but valuing them – leading to stronger relationships and brand affinity.

Net Promoter Score (NPS)

NPS reflects how likely customers are to recommend your brand after engaging with your service. It's a powerful signal of customer sentiment and long-term loyalty following enhancements.

- **How to measure**: Ask 'How likely are you to recommend us?' on a 0–10 scale. Subtract detractors from promoters.

- **Insight**: A positive trend in NPS often reflects greater emotional connection and trust – evidence that improvements are contributing to reputation and advocacy.

Customer Effort Score (CES)

CES assesses how easy it is for customers to complete a task or resolve an issue. When improvements reduce effort, they often increase satisfaction and retention.

- **How to measure**: Ask 'How easy was it to...?' after key interactions.
- **Insight**: A lower effort score typically indicates that service design enhancements are removing friction and making life easier for your customers.

RETENTION AND CHURN METRICS

Customer Retention Rate (CRR)

This metric shows how many customers stay over a given period. High retention signals that your service improvements are creating ongoing value and reinforcing customer loyalty.

- **How to measure**: (Customers at end – new customers) ÷ customers at start of period.
- **Insight**: Improvements that boost CRR show you're delivering meaningful, consistent value and turning short-term interactions into long-term relationships.

Customer churn rate

Churn measures the percentage of customers who stop doing business with you. A decline in churn post-improvement suggests your enhancements are meeting customer expectations.

- **How to measure**: Track lost customers ÷ total customers.
- **Insight**: Lower churn reflects improved satisfaction and loyalty, while highlighting the effectiveness of proactive service recovery and retention strategies.

Repeat purchase rate

This metric tracks how often customers return to buy again – a strong indicator that service improvements are building trust and habit over time.

- **How to measure**: Compare repeat transactions before and after service enhancements.
- **Insight**: A higher repeat rate shows that improvements are supporting customer confidence and satisfaction – two key drivers of lifetime value.

ENGAGEMENT AND INTERACTION METRICS

Website and app analytics

These metrics track how customers behave on digital platforms – how long they stay, where they go and how they interact with improved features or flows.

- **How to measure**: Use analytics platforms to compare pre- and post-improvement activity.
- **Insight**: Increases in engagement and smoother user journeys are strong indicators that digital improvements are resonating with your audience.

User feedback and reviews

Customer reviews provide qualitative insight into how service improvements are perceived. They reveal whether customers notice, and appreciate, what's changed.

- **How to measure**: Monitor reviews, comments and survey responses across platforms.

- **Insight**: More positive reviews reflect real-world value being delivered and help validate which improvements are most impactful from the customer's point of view.

Social media sentiment analysis

This metric reveals how your improvements are being talked about publicly – through tone, language and emotional cues in online conversations.

- **How to measure**: Use listening tools to assess volume, tone and keyword trends.
- **Insight**: Positive shifts in sentiment often reflect an emotional connection with your brand and signal that service enhancements are aligned with customer values.

OPERATIONAL EFFICIENCY METRICS

Average resolution time

This metric measures how quickly customer issues are resolved from start to finish. Faster resolution times typically reflect streamlined processes and empowered teams.

- **How to measure**: Track average time from first contact to issue resolution.
- **Insight**: Declining resolution times show that internal improvements are directly improving customer experience and team productivity.

First Contact Resolution (FCR)

FCR shows how often issues are resolved during the first customer interaction – a strong indicator of service effectiveness and readiness.

- **How to measure**: Calculate the percentage of cases resolved without follow-up.

- **Insight**: A higher FCR rate shows that your team is better equipped, more informed and delivering a stronger first-line experience.

Service Level Agreement (SLA) compliance

SLA compliance tracks how consistently your team meets agreed service targets, such as response or resolution times.

- **How to measure**: Track SLA performance over time and assess the impact of recent improvements.
- **Insight**: Consistent SLA compliance signals operational discipline, customer reliability and the effectiveness of service performance improvements.

FINANCIAL METRICS

Customer Lifetime Value (CLV)

CLV reflects how much value a customer generates over their full relationship with your business. Improvements in service should directly impact this long-term metric.

- **How to measure**: Compare average CLV before and after service enhancements.
- **Insight**: Rising CLV is a sign that your service improvements are supporting loyalty, trust and ongoing revenue contribution.

Revenue growth from repeat customers

This metric shows how much of your revenue is driven by loyal, returning customers. It highlights the financial impact of strong post-service experiences.

- **How to measure**: Analyse revenue split between returning and new customers.

- **Insight**: An increase in revenue from returning customers shows that improvements are building real value and increasing customer spend over time.

Cost-to-serve

Cost to serve reflects how much it costs to deliver service at each customer touchpoint. Improvements should aim to reduce this cost while maintaining or increasing quality.

- **How to measure**: Compare cost inputs before and after service process optimisation.
- **Insight**: Lower cost-to-serve with stable or improved satisfaction is a powerful indicator that your service model is becoming more efficient and scalable.

Return on Improvements isn't just about fixing what's broken – it's about building a culture of ongoing enhancement that continuously adds value for customers and the business. By combining satisfaction, loyalty, efficiency and financial metrics, companies can track the full impact of their service improvements and use those insights to evolve faster, operate smarter and meet rising customer expectations. When measured consistently, Return on Improvements becomes a strategic tool for driving sustainable growth and customer-centric innovation.

IMPLEMENTING RETURN ON IMPROVEMENTS

Shifting from transactional service to continuous value creation requires both practical actions and cultural transformation. Quick wins help generate momentum through visible service enhancements and employee engagement, while long-term strategies embed improvement into the company's mindset, systems and customer experience. By engaging leaders, teams and functions across the business, organisations can turn everyday improvements into a core part of how they deliver consistent, long-term value.

Quick wins

1. **Simplify customer feedback channels**
   Start by enhancing how customers provide feedback. Implementing user-friendly feedback mechanisms, such as in-app ratings, online surveys or comment boxes, makes it easier for customers to share their thoughts. Quick responses to feedback show that the company is attentive and values customer input.

2. **Improve response time in customer service**
   Reducing response time for customer inquiries and complaints can make a significant difference in customer satisfaction. Implementing automated responses or chatbot support can provide quick, initial answers while ensuring a seamless handover to human agents for more complex issues. This blend of automation and personal service maintains a high level of customer engagement.

3. **Refresh digital platforms for usability**
   Optimising the company's website, mobile app or digital interfaces to improve user experience can be done in phases to create immediate impact. Enhancements, such as faster loading times, easier navigation and mobile compatibility can significantly improve customer interaction with the brand.

4. **Highlight and recognise employee contributions**
   Create a recognition programme to celebrate employees who contribute ideas that enhance the customer experience. Peer-nominated awards or shout-outs during company meetings

can foster a sense of belonging and encourage a culture where employees actively contribute to ongoing improvements.

5. **Launch short-term pilot programmes**
   Before a full-scale rollout of new features or service changes, initiate a pilot programme to gather data and feedback. This allows for real-time adjustments and demonstrates to customers that their input is part of the development process, making them feel valued.

Longer-term strategies

1. **Embed a continuous improvement culture through leadership**
   Leaders play a crucial role in setting the tone for a continuous improvement culture. By exemplifying adaptability, listening to feedback and showing commitment to service excellence, leaders inspire their teams to follow suit. This includes fostering an environment where employees feel safe to propose ideas without fear of failure, encouraging a risk-taking mindset that can lead to innovative improvements.

2. **Invest in comprehensive training programmes**
   Developing comprehensive training programmes that go beyond initial onboarding helps employees stay current with industry standards and customer service best practices. Training modules can include workshops on using new technologies, understanding customer data and personal development sessions focused on leadership and problem-solving skills.

3. **Leverage advanced data analytics**
   Utilise predictive analytics to foresee customer needs and preferences, enabling the company to make proactive

improvements. By integrating data analytics tools that collect and analyse customer behaviour, businesses can anticipate trends and adapt their offerings accordingly. This helps in refining products, improving services and crafting targeted customer interactions that boost satisfaction and loyalty.

4. **Create cross-functional teams dedicated to continuous improvement**

   Establish cross-functional teams that meet regularly to discuss potential areas for enhancement, share insights and coordinate the implementation of improvement projects. These teams can include members from customer service, marketing, product development and IT to ensure a well-rounded approach. Regular collaboration fosters a unified effort and reduces silos within the company.

5. **Build partnerships to enhance offerings**

   Collaborate with external partners to create bundled services or co-branded initiatives that add value to the customer experience. These partnerships can expand a company's reach, offer additional benefits to customers and encourage long-term loyalty by presenting a more comprehensive service.

6. **Regularly update digital touchpoints**

   Ensure that digital platforms, including apps, websites and online services, are regularly reviewed and updated to incorporate new features and security measures. Customer expectations for seamless digital experiences are continually evolving, making ongoing updates essential for maintaining customer satisfaction.

7. **Implement loyalty programmes focused on engagement**
   Develop loyalty programmes that not only reward purchases but also recognise customer engagement, such as providing feedback or participating in events. Tiered loyalty structures can offer exclusive benefits to top-tier members, fostering a sense of belonging and encouraging sustained engagement.

8. **Embed measurement into improvement culture**
   Establish baselines and benchmarks before rolling out new initiatives to assess true impact. Schedule regular data reviews – monthly or quarterly – to evaluate progress, identify trends and guide real-time adjustments. Ensure that key metrics, such as churn reduction or customer lifetime value, are directly tied to broader strategic goals so that every improvement initiative contributes to long-term business growth.

Driving engagement at every level

For executives and senior leadership:

- **Shift from transactional thinking to value-driven relationships:** Long-term success depends on offering continuous service improvements rather than just one-off sales.
- **Invest in customer-centric enhancements:** Leaders must allocate resources to service innovations, automation and personalised experiences that increase customer lifetime value.
- **Align business objectives with service excellence:** Embedding a culture of continuous improvement across the organisation ensures that customer expectations are consistently met and exceeded.

For operational managers:

- **Streamline processes to enhance customer experience:** Operational teams should focus on reducing friction, eliminating inefficiencies and improving service delivery speed.
- **Use data to drive service enhancements**: Regularly analyse customer feedback and service metrics to identify opportunities for improvement and innovation.
- **Foster a mindset of continuous improvement:** Encourage teams to proactively find ways to enhance customer interactions, service offerings and internal workflows.
- **Train teams to understand key performance metrics and how their daily decisions contribute:** Empowering staff to act on data builds a culture of ownership and proactive problem-solving, where continuous improvement becomes part of everyday operations.

For product development and innovation teams:

- **Prioritise customer needs when designing services:** Products and services should evolve based on customer pain points, preferences and usage patterns.
- **Test and refine offerings regularly:** A culture of experimentation and iteration helps ensure that new features and service enhancements are relevant and valuable.
- **Monitor adoption and feedback on new improvements:** Tracking how customers engage with and respond to enhancements provides critical insights for further refinement.

For customer experience and support teams:

- **Take a proactive approach to problem-solving:** Anticipating customer challenges and offering pre-emptive solutions improves satisfaction and trust.
- **Provide ongoing value beyond the sale:** Offering educational resources, personalised recommendations and enhanced after-sales support builds deeper customer relationships.
- **Ensure service is consistent across all touchpoints:** Customers should experience the same high-quality support whether they engage via chat, phone or in person.
- **Use customer feedback and performance insights to drive real-time improvements:** Embedding feedback loops and self-monitoring tools empowers teams to proactively refine service and deliver more consistent, high-quality support across all touchpoints.

By establishing a culture of continuous improvement across leadership, operations, product development and customer experience, organisations can move beyond transactions to build lasting, value-driven customer relationships.

THE LASTING IMPACT OF RETURN ON IMPROVEMENTS

Return on Improvements is more than a one-time initiative – it's a mind-set that redefines how businesses engage with customers, adapt to change and sustain long-term value. By shifting from transactional models to service-led strategies, companies can strengthen customer loyalty, increase advocacy and improve their competitive edge in a fast-moving market.

Throughout this chapter, we've explored how leading brands such as Apple, Toyota, Canva, Marriott, IKEA, American Express and Shopify embed continuous improvement into their DNA. Their success demonstrates that Return on Improvements doesn't just enhance customer satisfaction, it positively impacts every corner of the organisation, from operational efficiency and innovation to employee engagement and financial performance.

Implementing this approach begins with recognising that customer expectations are constantly evolving. Businesses must respond with agility, commitment and collaboration. This means creating a culture where change is embraced, feedback is valued and cross-functional teams work together to deliver a seamless, service-driven experience.

Leadership plays a pivotal role in sustaining this momentum – by setting a clear vision, aligning strategies with customer needs and investing in the right people and tools to enable progress. The practical tools, case studies and measurement frameworks in this chapter offer a roadmap for action, helping businesses take immediate steps while laying the foundation for long-term transformation.

Return on Improvements is both measurable and meaningful. Metrics like CSAT, NPS, retention rates and CLV serve not only as performance indicators but as proof points of trust, satisfaction and brand loyalty. With the right systems in place, businesses can continually assess, iterate and evolve their approach – turning everyday interactions into lasting relationships.

Ultimately, businesses that prioritise continuous improvement position themselves for resilience, growth and sustained success. It's a strategic commitment that turns customer insight into innovation and service into a competitive advantage. By embedding this philosophy across the organisation, companies can build a brand that not only meets today's expectations, but is ready for tomorrow's opportunities.

TAKE ACTION

Now that you understand the power of Return on Improvements, it's time to move from theory to practice. Start by identifying one area of your customer journey that would benefit from a service enhancement – whether it's simplifying a process, reducing response times or improving onboarding.

Create a small, measurable pilot project to test your improvement. Engage your team, gather feedback and use real-time data to track its impact. Remember, improvement doesn't have to be big to be meaningful – consistency and iteration are what drive long-term results.

By embedding continuous improvement into your day-to-day operations, you signal to customers and employees alike that your business is committed to excellence, not just in what it offers, but in how it evolves. Start small, learn fast and keep improving.

REFERENCES

AIExpert Network (2024) 'Case Study: The AI Revolution at American Express'. Available at: www.aiexpert.network/case-study-the-ai-revolution-at-american-express/ (Accessed: 1 May 2025).

Apple (2025) 'AppleCare+'. Available at: www.apple.com/support/products/ (Accessed: 30 April 2025).

BusinessMap (2025) 'What Is Kaizen? The Toyota Way to Continuous Improvement'. Available at: www.businessmap.io/lean-management/improvement/what-is-kaizen (Accessed: 30 April 2025).

Canva (2023) 'The Canva timeline: 10 years of empowering the world to design'. Available at: www.canva.com/newsroom/news/canva-10-year-timeline/ (Accessed: 30 April 2025).

Canva (2024) 'Looking back on 2024: A game-changing year for Canva, 31 December'. Available at: www.canva.com/newsroom/news/canva-2024-wrap/ (Accessed: 1 May 2025).

Canva (2025a) 'How to use Canva for Education'. Available at: www.canva.com/learn/canva-for-education/ (Accessed: 30 April 2025).

Canva (2025b) 'Canva solutions for your business'. Available at: www.canva.com/solutions/ (Accessed: 30 April 2025).

Coolest Gadgets (2025) 'Apple Customer Loyalty Statistics By Country and Facts [2025]'. Available at: www.coolest-gadgets.com/apple-customer-loyalty-statistics/ (Accessed: 30 April 2025).

DigitalSuits (2025) 'Top 20 Shopify March '25 improvements, changes and new features'. Available at: www.digitalsuits.uk/blog/top-20-shopify-march-25-improvements-changes-and-new-features/ (Accessed: 1 May 2025).

Enterpret (2024) 'How Canva leverages Enterpret to build products that delight over 220 million users'. Available at www.enterpret.com/customers/canva (Accessed: 30 April 2025).

Forbes (2019) 'Just How Far Is Apple Prepared To Go In Its Transformation From Product Manufacturer To Service Supplier?', Forbes, 3 November. Available at: www.forbes.com/sites/enriquedans/2019/11/03/just-how-far-is-apple-prepared-to-go-in-its-transformation-from-product-manufacturer-to-service-supplier/ (Accessed: 30 April 2025).

Ingka Group (2025a) 'IKEA reinvents home shopping with smart new app features, 20 February'. Available at: www.ingka.com/newsroom/ikea-reinvents-home-shopping-with-smart-new-app-features/ (Accessed: 1 May 2025).

Ingka Group (2025b) 'IKEA sides with customers in an exceptional year, investing more than EUR 2.1 billion in lowering prices, 29 January'. Available at: www.ingka.com/newsroom/ikea-sides-with-customers-in-an-exceptional-year-investing-more-than-eur-2-1-billion-in-lowering-prices/ (Accessed: 1 May 2025).

Renascence (2024) 'How Apple Elevates Customer Experience (CX) Through Ecosystem Integration'. Available at: www.renascence.io/journal/how-apple-elevates-customer-experience-cx-through-ecosystem-integration (Accessed: 30 April 2025).

Retail Times (2025) 'IKEA named best website for customer experience in 2025'. Available at: www.retailtimes.co.uk/ikea-named-best-website-for-customer-experience-in-2025/ (Accessed: 1 May 2025).

SEO (2024) 'How Many Shopify Stores Are There? Statistics & Facts (2025)'. Available at: www.seo.ai/blog/how-many-shopify-stores-are-there (Accessed: 1 May 2025).

Shopify (2020) 'Shopify launches all-new POS globally to help merchants adapt for the future of retail, 21 May'. Available at: www.shopify.com/news/shopify-launches-all-new-pos-globally-to-help-merchants-adapt-for-the-future-of-retail (Accessed: 1 May 2025).

SuperOffice (2025) 'Customer experience statistics'. Available at: www.superoffice.com/blog/customer-experience-statistics/ (Accessed: 30 April 2025).

Toyota (2025) 'Toyota App'. Available at: www.toyota.com/connected-services/toyota-app/ (Accessed: 30 April 2025).

Toyota Europe (2020) 'Toyota Service Promise'. Available at: www.toyota-europe.com/news/2020/service-promise (Accessed: 30 April 2025).

Toyota UK (2020) 'Toyota Leads UK Auto Industry in Customer Satisfaction'. Available at: www.media.toyota.co.uk/toyota-leads-uk-auto-industry-in-customer-satisfaction/ (Accessed: 30 April 2025).

VentureBeat (2025) 'How Amex uses AI to increase efficiency: 40% fewer IT escalations, 85% travel assistance boost, 2 April'. Available at: www.venturebeat.com/ai/how-amex-uses-ai-to-increase-efficiency-40-fewer-it-escalations-85-travel-assistance-boost/ (Accessed: 1 May 2025).

CHAPTER 8
RETURN ON INVOLVEMENT – INCREASING CUSTOMER LOYALTY THROUGH PERSONALISED ENGAGEMENT

INTRODUCING RETURN ON INVOLVEMENT

In today's saturated and fast-moving marketplace, the most successful businesses are no longer those just offering great products or services – they are building lasting relationships through meaningful, personalised engagement with customers. Return on Involvement is the recognition that real value is created not just through what a business sells, but through how it connects with its customers at every touchpoint.

In a world filled with generic messaging and impersonal interactions, brands that stand out are those that make customers feel seen, heard and understood. Personalisation has become more than a marketing trend – it's a strategic imperative. A 2021 report by McKinsey found that 71% of consumers expect companies to deliver personalised experiences and 76% express frustration when those expectations are not met. These figures highlight a broader shift: from product-centric models to customer-centric strategies where engagement drives loyalty, satisfaction and sustained business growth.

Return on Involvement addresses this shift by embedding personalisation and intentional engagement into the full customer journey. Whether through tailored email campaigns, dynamic loyalty programmes, responsive social media interaction or adaptive content delivery, each personalised touchpoint reinforces trust, belonging and advocacy. Engaged customers don't just buy, they become brand champions, spreading the word and strengthening the company's reputation.

As customer journeys grow increasingly complex – spanning multiple platforms, moments and channels – the ability to deliver consistent, relevant and resonant experiences has never been more important. This chapter explores how businesses can embed Return on Involvement into their strategy, designing customer experiences that are not only personalised, but genuinely memorable and relationship driven.

LEVERAGING RETURN ON INVOLVEMENT

In a marketplace shaped by empowered consumers and constant digital innovation, Return on Involvement offers a powerful advantage: the ability to build deeper, more emotionally resonant relationships with customers. Today's consumers expect more than functionality – they expect to feel understood and valued.

When involvement becomes a central strategic focus, everyday interactions evolve into meaningful moments that inspire trust, loyalty and advocacy. Businesses that personalise the customer journey, at scale and with intention, don't just meet expectations, they exceed them.

By the end of this chapter, you'll have the insight and tools to embed Return on Involvement across your organisation. You'll explore real-world examples, strategic frameworks and practical guidance to help you create customer experiences that are emotionally intelligent, data-informed and deeply engaging. This chapter will equip you to:

- **Maximise the strategic value of Return on Involvement**
  Understand how personalised engagement builds trust, increases customer lifetime value (CLV) and turns loyalty into a competitive advantage – especially in a world of choice and noise.

- **Build the core elements of effective involvement strategies**
  Explore the key components of successful involvement – data-driven personalisation, emotionally intelligent communication, tailored content and interactive touchpoints – that drive relevance and repeat engagement.

- **Implement best practices from leading brands**
  Learn from brands like Netflix, Sephora, Peloton, BMW, American Express and Disney, who have transformed

involvement into a strategic differentiator. Discover the tools and tactics that deepen connection and build lasting brand affinity.

- **Measure success using meaningful engagement metrics**
Evaluate the impact of your strategies using both quantitative and qualitative metrics: CSAT, NPS, retention, frequency of interaction, social sharing and more. Use data to optimise and demonstrate Return on Involvement.

- **Apply practical strategies for immediate and long-term impact**
Combine quick wins – like micro-surveys and loyalty tweaks – with long-term initiatives, including AI-powered personalisation, employee training and advanced analytics.

- **Prioritise and align involvement across the organisation**
Focus your resources where they matter most. Align involvement strategies with business goals and embed them across teams – from leadership to marketing, operations and frontline staff. When involvement becomes a shared, strategic priority, its impact multiplies.

Now let's bring Return on Involvement to life.

RETURN ON INVOLVEMENT IN ACTION

To illustrate how Return on Involvement enhances customer loyalty and engagement, you will examine leading companies that have successfully embedded personalised experiences into their business models. These case studies demonstrate how leveraging customer data, innovative technology and tailored interactions can significantly enrich customer journeys. From curated recommendations to customised loyalty programmes, each example highlights how meaningful personalisation deepens customer connections, drives repeat business and sets brands apart in competitive markets.

NETFLIX – PERSONALISING THE ENTERTAINMENT EXPERIENCE

Netflix's data-driven approach to personalisation has set the benchmark for customer engagement in the streaming industry. By leveraging machine-learning algorithms, Netflix curates content recommendations tailored to each user's unique viewing history, preferences and even the time of day they watch content. This hyper-personalisation leads to higher engagement and retention rates, with Netflix reporting that 80% of content watched on the platform comes from its recommendation system (Argoid, 2024).

The AI driven system processes over a million data points per user, continuously refining its predictions through deep learning and A/B testing to rank and prioritise content most relevant to each viewer. This tailored experience keeps users returning, fostering loyalty and reducing churn (Attract Group, 2025).

Key takeaway: Personalised recommendations powered by customer data significantly boost satisfaction and engagement. By leveraging AI and machine learning to analyse user behaviour, businesses can deliver customised experiences that align with individual interests, creating a more relevant and impactful customer journey.

SEPHORA – BUILDING A COMMUNITY THROUGH PERSONALISED BEAUTY

Sephora's Beauty Insider Loyalty Programme exemplifies how personalisation can enhance customer engagement and loyalty. The programme offers members tier-based rewards, personalised product recommendations, early access to product launches and birthday gifts – all tailored to customer preferences and shopping behaviour (Sephora, 2025). Additionally, Sephora's Virtual Artist tool, powered by augmented reality (AR), allows customers to try on products virtually, blending digital innovation with beauty retail in a way that strengthens customer connection with the brand (Retail Dive, 2024).

80% of Sephora's transactions come from their Beauty Insider members, highlighting how the programme drives engagement and sales through personalised rewards and experiences based on individual shopping habits (Nudge, 2024).

Key takeaway: Sephora's loyalty programme and immersive digital tools demonstrate how personalisation and technology can be harnessed to enhance the customer experience. By delivering tailored rewards and engaging experiences like AR-based virtual try-ons, Sephora builds deeper loyalty and positions itself as a customer-centric brand in a competitive market.

PELOTON – PERSONALISED FITNESS THROUGH TECH AND COMMUNITY

Peloton delivers a personalised fitness experience by combining real-time data, tailored workout recommendations and engaging community features. The platform curates class suggestions based on user preferences, performance history and fitness goals – making each session feel relevant and motivating.

Interactive features like leaderboards, achievement badges and live classes foster emotional connection and accountability, turning solo workouts into shared experiences. These strategies have contributed to a 96% retention rate – one of the highest in the industry – and an average Net Promoter Score (NPS) of 91, reflecting exceptional user satisfaction (TacticOne, 2024).

Key takeaway: Peloton proves that data-driven personalisation combined with community involvement can elevate user engagement. Tailored experiences and shared motivation foster deep loyalty and long-term commitment.

BMW - PERSONALISED CUSTOMER JOURNEY IN THE AUTOMOTIVE IONDUSTRY

BMW has successfully integrated personalisation throughout its customer journey, from the initial online vehicle configuration to post-purchase service interactions. The My BMW App delivers customised updates, service reminders and tailored offers, ensuring every customer touchpoint feels relevant and individualised (BMW, 2022).

BMW reports that its use of advanced digital tools and data-driven customisation has significantly enhanced customer satisfaction and engagement across the ownership experience (BMW Group Report, 2024).

Key takeaway: BMW demonstrates how data-led personalisation can elevate both pre- and post-sale experiences. By embedding customisation into digital touchpoints and services, the brand strengthens customer relationships and reinforces its premium positioning.

AMERICAN EXPRESS - TAILORED FINANCIAL SERVICES

American Express (Amex) has differentiated itself by offering personalised financial services and support. By analysing customer spending habits, Amex provides tailored credit card recommendations, exclusive offers and personalised financial advice. This approach has led to a 34% increase in customer engagement over five years, proving the power of personalised interaction (Amex, 2021).

Key takeaway: Personalised financial advice and exclusive offers can significantly deepen customer relationships, highlighting the effectiveness of tailored services beyond the retail sector. Ethically leveraging customer data to deliver customised experiences builds trust, enhances brand loyalty and creates lasting value for customers within financial services.

DISNEY – ENHANCING GUEST EXPERIENCES THROUGH PERSONALISATION

Disney has reimagined the theme park experience through digital tools like the My Disney Experience app and MagicBands, which deliver personalised itineraries, real-time updates and exclusive offers based on guest behaviour and preferences (Disney, 2021). These technologies create a frictionless, tailored journey for each visitor, enhancing satisfaction and immersion. Notably, Disney reports a 70% return rate among first-time visitors – attributed in part to the seamless, customised experiences powered by these tools (Help Scout, 2016).

Key takeaway: Integrating technology to deliver personalised customer experiences significantly boosts satisfaction, encourages repeat visits and builds long-term loyalty. Businesses should proactively incorporate digital solutions into the customer journey to offer more tailored and meaningful interactions.

HOW TO MEASURE SUCCESS WITHIN RETURN ON INVOLVEMENT

Return on Involvement reflects how deeply your customers engage with your brand and how that connection drives loyalty, advocacy and lifetime value. It goes beyond transactional touchpoints to assess how invested people feel in the brand experience itself. To measure it effectively, businesses need both quantitative data and qualitative insight that track not just customer behaviour, but emotion, sentiment and intent. The following metrics cover all angles – from engagement and loyalty to perception, operations and revenue impact.

CUSTOMER ENGAGEMENT METRICS

Customer engagement rate

This metric tracks how actively customers interact with your brand across platforms and touchpoints. It reflects both behavioural interest and emotional involvement in the ongoing brand experience.

- **How to measure**: Track actions such as social media engagement, email open and click-through rates, app usage and participation in branded initiatives.
- **Insight**: High engagement suggests customers aren't just aware of your brand – they're choosing to spend time with it, signalling a deeper connection.

Customer advocacy and referral rate

This reflects the percentage of customers who refer others or actively promote your brand – often through word of mouth or user-generated content.

- **How to measure**: Track referral programme usage, social mentions and organic content creation from existing customers.
- **Insight**: Strong advocacy signals emotional alignment and brand trust – showing that involvement has moved from passive engagement to active endorsement.

Time spent with the brand

This metric reflects how much time customers willingly spend interacting with your platforms, content or community spaces.

- **How to measure**: Monitor website session duration, app usage frequency, time spent at events and contributions to forums or loyalty groups.
- **Insight**: Sustained time spent with your brand shows deep investment and relevance – two key drivers of long-term loyalty.

CUSTOMER LOYALTY AND RETENTION METRICS

Loyalty programme participation

Tracks how many customers sign up for and interact with your loyalty initiatives. It's a reliable indicator of customer willingness to stay connected and invest in the relationship.

- **How to measure**: Track enrolment, offer redemptions and engagement across loyalty communications.
- **Insight**: Strong participation demonstrates that customers see value in staying close to your brand – and that your involvement strategy is working.

Repeat purchase rate

Measures how often customers return to make additional purchases. This metric is a direct reflection of how engagement efforts translate into behavioural loyalty.

- **How to measure**: Analyse repeat buying behaviour and compare trends before and after involvement-focused campaigns.
- **Insight**: High repeat purchase rates show that your customers aren't just interested – they're committed.

Customer retention rate

Retention rate indicates the percentage of customers who remain with your brand over time. It's one of the clearest indicators of whether involvement is meaningful and sustainable.

- **How to measure**: Track customer retention across engagement segments and channels.
- **Insight**: Rising retention suggests that customers feel consistently valued and understood – making them more likely to stay long term.

BRAND SENTIMENT AND ADVOCACY METRICS

User feedback and reviews

Reviews and open feedback channels capture real-time customer sentiment and provide insights into how involvement efforts are landing emotionally and experientially.

- **How to measure**: Analyse written reviews, ratings and survey comments to identify patterns and themes.
- **Insight**: Positive shifts in sentiment show that your efforts are making customers feel part of something rather than just being sold to.

Social media sentiment analysis

This tracks the tone and nature of social media conversations about your brand. It reveals how engagement initiatives are perceived and discussed in public spaces.

- **How to measure**: Use social listening tools to monitor sentiment, frequency and engagement with brand-related posts and campaigns.
- **Insight**: A rise in positive sentiment shows that customers see your brand as approachable, aligned with their values and emotionally engaging.

Customer advocacy rate

Measures the proportion of customers who go beyond satisfaction to actively promote and recommend your brand to others.

- **How to measure**: Track referral codes, shared content and organic brand mentions.
- **Insight**: When customers advocate for your brand, it is one of the strongest signs of involvement – it means your brand is emotionally resonant enough to speak for.

OPERATIONAL IMPACT METRICS

Response time to customer interactions

Tracks how quickly your brand responds to inquiries, feedback and inter-actions – whether via chat, social media or email.

- **How to measure**: Use analytics tools or CRM platforms to measure average response times across channels.
- **Insight**: Quick responses show attentiveness and respect – two qualities that significantly increase perceived involvement.

Personalisation effectiveness score

Evaluates how well your messaging, offers and content resonate with indi-vidual customer preferences.

- **How to measure**: Analyse response rates and conversion performance across personalised communications.
- **Insight**: Effective personalisation shows customers that you are making a real effort to understand their needs and engage effectively, and that their experience matters.

Cross-channel consistency score

This measures how consistently customers experience your brand across touchpoints. A seamless brand experience strengthens trust and reinforces involvement.

- **How to measure**: Assess alignment in tone, experience and service levels across online and offline interactions.
- **Insight**: Consistency signals that the brand is coherent and trustworthy – two essential ingredients for deeper customer connection.

FINANCIAL IMPACT METRICS

Revenue contribution from engaged customers

Tracks how much of your total revenue is generated from customers who are highly engaged with your brand.

- **How to measure**: Segment revenue performance by engagement level using CRM and sales attribution tools.
- **Insight**: Higher revenue from engaged customers validates the investment in involvement strategies – it's where loyalty becomes profitability.

Customer Lifetime Value (CLV)

CLV measures the total long-term value of a customer relationship. It is directly impacted by the quality and depth of brand involvement.

- **How to measure**: Compare CLV across different levels of engagement and personalisation.
- **Insight**: A higher CLV shows that engaged customers stay longer, spend more and require less effort or cost to reactivate them.

Cost efficiency of engagement strategies

Evaluates the return on your involvement efforts by comparing the cost of engagement strategies to the value they generate.

- **How to measure**: Track the cost of engagement campaigns and compare with their impact on loyalty, retention and revenue.
- **Insight**: A lower cost-to-impact ratio confirms that involvement is not only powerful but scalable and sustainable as a long-term strategy.

Return on Involvement is about building meaningful, lasting customer relationships through intentional, personalised and consistent engagement. These metrics offer a clear view of whether your efforts are deepening connection, increasing loyalty and driving sustainable growth. When tracked together, they show how involvement moves customers from passive users to active participants and brand advocates, boosting long-term value across every part of the customer lifecycle.

IMPLEMENTING RETURN ON INVOLVEMENT

Strengthening customer involvement requires a balance of quick, high-impact actions and longer-term strategic investment. Quick wins deliver immediate value by personalising touchpoints and fostering connection, while long-term strategies embed engagement across systems, culture and leadership. When supported by technology and driven by cross-functional teams, Return on Involvement becomes a powerful force for building loyalty, trust and deeper brand relationships.

Quick wins

1. **Personalise email campaigns using customer data**
   Use segmentation to send tailored messages based on customer behaviour, preferences and purchase history. Including relevant product suggestions or personalised offers strengthens connection and increases engagement.

2. **Engage customers through interactive social media experiences**
   Respond directly to customer comments and questions, host live Q&A sessions, create polls and encourage user-generated content. This kind of authentic interaction builds trust and deepens customer involvement.

3. **Launch a personalised loyalty programme tailored to preferences**
Design rewards programmes that reflect individual customer needs and behaviours. Offering exclusive perks, early access to new products, or curated experiences helps customers feel recognised and valued.

4. **Use behavioural data to personalise website content**
Serve tailored content and recommendations based on browsing history and user actions. A personalised website experience keeps customers engaged and improves the relevance of your digital offering.

5. **Provide special offers based on customer milestones**
Celebrate customer birthdays, anniversaries or loyalty milestones with thoughtful, personalised messages or rewards. These small moments reinforce emotional connection and brand appreciation.

Long-term strategies

1. **Develop a comprehensive data analytics framework to drive engagement**
Implement systems that collect and analyse customer interactions across touchpoints, allowing for more responsive, data-driven decision-making and long-term personalisation.

2. **Implement a seamless omnichannel engagement strategy**
Unify the customer experience across online, mobile, in-store and service environments. When customer data flows freely across channels, interactions feel consistent and connected.

3. **Train employees to embrace and deliver personalisation**
Offer training that helps employees understand the value of tailored service and equips them with tools to support it. A team that knows how to personalise effectively can deliver more meaningful interactions.

4. **Foster a culture of feedback and adaptability**
Encourage regular customer feedback and create internal systems that allow teams to respond effectively. Companies that continuously learn and adapt based on customer needs build stronger, more trusted relationships.

5. **Collaborate with technology partners to scale personalised engagement**
Work with external providers to introduce tools like AI-driven recommendations, automation and chatbots. These technologies help scale personalisation efforts and improve responsiveness across the customer journey.

Driving engagement at every level

For executives and senior leadership:

- **Make customer involvement a strategic priority:** A loyal customer base is built on meaningful engagement – leaders must ensure that customer participation is embedded into the company's growth strategy.
- **Invest in technology that enables deeper customer connections:** Personalisation, community-building platforms and AI-driven engagement tools enhance customer relationships and increase retention.

- **Align business objectives with customer needs:** Leadership must foster a culture where customer involvement is valued and directly influences decision-making.

For operational managers:

- **Develop cross-functional collaboration:** Customer involvement strategies should be seamlessly integrated across marketing, sales, product development and service teams.
- **Monitor and analyse engagement trends:** Tracking customer interactions and feedback helps refine strategies that encourage deeper brand involvement.
- **Encourage frontline employees to champion customer relationships:** Ensuring that teams are empowered to engage with customers on a more personal level strengthens brand loyalty.

For marketing and sales teams:

- **Leverage personalisation to enhance engagement**: Customers are more likely to engage when they receive tailored messages, offers and content that resonates with their interests.
- **Foster community engagement:** Creating brand communities, loyalty programmes and user-generated content opportunities strengthens customer connections.
- **Encourage two-way communication:** Engaging customers through feedback loops, surveys and social media interactions ensures they feel heard and valued.

For customer experience and support teams:

- **Build proactive customer engagement strategies:** Anticipating customer needs and providing timely, relevant content or support enhances satisfaction and long-term involvement.

- **Use customer insights to personalise interactions:**
Understanding a customer's preferences, purchase history and
past interactions enables a more meaningful and engaging
experience.
- **Encourage advocacy through exceptional service:** Customers
who feel genuinely connected to a brand are more likely to
promote it to others through referrals and reviews.

By embedding customer involvement into leadership, operations, marketing and service functions, organisations can create deeper relationships, increase loyalty and drive sustained business growth.

THE LASTING IMPACT OF RETURN ON INVOLVEMENT

The journey through Return on Involvement reveals that when customer engagement is executed thoughtfully and tailored to individual preferences, it moves beyond simple interaction. Instead, it can become a powerful lever for long-term business success. In today's landscape, where consumers expect more than quality products or services, companies must cultivate personalised, meaningful connections that resonate on a human level. This shift positions businesses not just as providers, but as trusted partners who understand and value their customers.

Return on Involvement represents a strategic evolution, from transactional relationships to deeper loyalty and advocacy. Brands that connect through targeted messaging, adaptive services and consistent personalisation don't just meet expectations, they exceed them. This proactive approach nurtures trust, promotes repeat business and transforms customers into enthusiastic advocates, creating a self-sustaining cycle of satisfaction and growth.

As the case studies of Netflix, Sephora, Peloton, BMW, American Express and Disney demonstrate, personalised engagement doesn't just improve individual touchpoints – it influences customer perceptions, drives innovation and strengthens brand equity. Involvement, when done well, reaches beyond marketing. It becomes a mindset that shapes every department, powered by data analytics, cross-functional collaboration and a culture that welcomes feedback as fuel for improvement.

Of course, embedding this approach is not without its challenges. Navigating data privacy, aligning teams and integrating new technologies requires careful planning and leadership. But these hurdles also represent opportunities: to differentiate through transparency, strengthen customer trust and build agile, insight-driven systems that grow with your customers.

The business case is compelling. According to McKinsey, 71% of consumers expect personalised interactions, and 76% feel frustrated when those expectations are not met (McKinsey, 2021). Bain & Company reports that companies that focus on personalised experiences generate 20% more revenue than those that do not (Bain & Company, 2021). When involvement becomes a shared strategic priority, it enhances not only customer satisfaction but also employee engagement and overall resilience.

Measuring success through metrics like CSAT, NPS, retention rates and revenue from repeat customers ensures involvement stays aligned with business goals. Quick wins – like personalised campaigns or loyalty enhancements – build momentum, while long-term strategies, such as omnichannel integration, staff training, and advanced analytics, ensure sustained impact.

Return on Involvement encapsulates what it means to build a customer-first organisation. It's not just an engagement strategy – it's a commitment to seeing, understanding and valuing people. When brands lead with empathy and intentionality, they create more than transactions – they create lasting relationships, brand advocates and a foundation for meaningful, sustainable success.

TAKE ACTION

Now that you've explored the power of Return on Involvement, it's time to put insight into action. Start by identifying one area of your customer experience where personalisation and deeper engagement could make a meaningful difference – whether that's refining your loyalty programme, tailoring email communications or improving how you listen and respond on social media.

Small, intentional steps, like acknowledging customer milestones or customising support touchpoints, can make a big impact. These efforts build trust, strengthen loyalty and transform everyday interactions into lasting relationships.

In a world where customers expect to be known and valued, involvement isn't optional – it's essential. Take the first step toward creating an emotionally connected, customer-centric experience that fuels long-term success.

REFERENCES

Amex (2021) '2021 Annual Report'. [pdf] Available at: www.s26.q4cdn.com/747928648/files/doc_financials/2021/ar/Final-Annual-Report-03-18-22.pdf [Accessed 1 May 2025].

Argoid (2024) 'How Netflix Manages such Low Churn Rate'. Available at: www.argoid.ai/blog/how-does-netflixs-recommendation-engine-manage-low-churn-rate [Accessed 1 May 2025].

Attract Group (2025) 'How Netflix's Personalize Recommendation Algorithm Works?'. 18 March. Available at: www.attractgroup.com/blog/how-netflixs-personalize-recommendation-algorithm-works/ [Accessed 1 May 2025].

Bain & Company (2021) 'Personalized marketing & engagement'. Available at: www.bain.com/consulting-services/customer-strategy-and-marketing/customer-experience-transformation/personalized-marketing-engagement/ [Accessed 18 Apr. 2025].

BMW Group (2022) 'How BMW Group transformed online automotive experiences'. Adobe Business. Available at: www.business.adobe.com/uk/customer-success-stories/bmw-group-case-study.html [Accessed 1 May 2025].

BMW Group (2024) 'BMW Group Report 2024'. [pdf] Available at: www.bmwgroup.com/content/dam/grpw/websites/bmwgroup_com/ir/downloads/en/2025/bericht/BMW-Group-Report-2024-en.pdf [Accessed 1 May 2025].

Disney (2021) 'My Disney Experience and MagicBands Enhance Guest Experience'. Available at: www.disneyworld.disney.go.com/guest-services/magicband-plus/ [Accessed 1 May 2025].

Help Scout (2016) 'How Disney Creates Magical Experiences (and a 70% Return Rate)'. Available at: https://www.inc.com/help-scout/how-disneyland-creates-magical-experiences.html [Accessed 1 May 2025].

HubSpot (2025) 'State of Customer Engagement Report'. Available at: www.hubspot.com/state-of-customer-engagement-report [Accessed 2 Apr. 2025].

McKinsey & Company (2021) 'The value of getting personalization right – or wrong – is multiplying'. Available at: https://www.mckinsey.com/capabilities/growth-marketing-and-sales/our-insights/the-value-of-getting-personalization-right-or-wrong-is-multiplying [Accessed 18 Apr. 2025].

Nudge (2024) 'Sephora's Beauty Insider Loyalty Program'. 21 April. Available at: www.nudgenow.com/blogs/maximize-benefits-sephora-loyalty-program [Accessed 1 May 2025].

Retail Dive (2024) 'Sephora's Virtual Artist brings augmented reality to large beauty audience'. Available at: www.retaildive.com/ex/mobilecommercedaily/sephoras-virtual-artist-brings-augmented-reality-to-larger-beauty-audience [Accessed 1 May 2025].

Sephora (2025) 'Beauty Insider | Sephora'. Available at: www.sephora.com/BeautyInsider [Accessed 1 May 2025].

TacticOne (2024) 'Peloton: A Masterclass in Personalization, Community, and Growth'. 20 December. Available at: www.tacticone.co/blog/peloton-personalization-community-and-growth [Accessed 1 May 2025].

CHAPTER 9
RETURN ON INSIGHT – LEVERAGING ACTIONABLE DATA TO IMPROVE PERFORMANCE

INTRODUCING RETURN ON INSIGHT

In an age where data is often described as the 'new oil', organisations are continuously seeking to leverage it to fuel growth and innovation. Yet, despite access to vast amounts of information, many companies struggle to harness its full potential. The key lies not just in collecting data, but in generating and acting on meaningful insights. Return on Insight represents a paradigm shift – one that focuses on transforming raw data into actionable intelligence to drive smarter decision-making, enhance customer satisfaction and improve operational efficiency.

The explosion of digital technologies has dramatically increased global data creation. IBM estimated that 90% of the world's data had been generated in the two years leading up to 2023 (IBM, 2023). This trend continues, with data now pouring in from every customer interaction, connected device and digital touchpoint. The challenge is no longer data collection, but turning that data into actionable insight.

Recent research by McKinsey shows that leading companies generate 80% of their value from their core customer base by using data to enhance retention, loyalty and relevance. The study also found that retaining one customer is three times more valuable than acquiring a new one, underscoring the strategic importance of insight-led decision-making in building long-term growth and resilience (McKinsey & Company, 2023).

Return on Insight goes beyond identifying trends – it's about understanding the stories behind the data and using them to create meaningful business value. Whether it's enhancing product offerings, streamlining internal processes or elevating the customer experience, actionable insights enable companies to shift from reactive to proactive. This forward-looking approach helps businesses stay ahead of market shifts, respond more effectively to customer needs and build a sustainable competitive edge.

This chapter explores the role of actionable insights in building a high-performance, insight-led organisation. It looks at how companies can evolve from basic data reporting to a culture of insight-driven decision-making, supported by the right tools, technologies and cross-functional collaboration. Through practical examples from brands like Amazon, Walmart, Ford, Marriott, HSBC and Airbnb, you will examine how Return on Insight drives measurable outcomes and how you can establish it within your business.

LEVERAGING RETURN ON INSIGHT

In a world overflowing with data, the competitive advantage lies not in the volume of information collected, but in how effectively that information is translated into insight. Return on Insight focuses on turning raw data into meaningful intelligence, driving sharper decision-making, more relevant customer experiences and smarter, more agile operations. Insight-led organisations gain clarity, speed and strategic focus in a constantly shifting marketplace.

By the end of this chapter, you will have a clear understanding of how to implement and sustain Return on Insight across your organisation. You'll gain strategic frameworks, best-practice examples and practical tools to make insight generation a central driver of growth and innovation. This chapter will equip you to:

- **Maximise the strategic value of Return on Insight**
  Understand why insights, rather than just data, are the true catalysts for innovation, customer satisfaction and long-term performance. Explore how insight-driven strategies improve relevance, speed and adaptability across all areas of the business.

- **Build the core elements of effective insight generation**
  Explore the building blocks required to transform data into action. These include data quality and structure, advanced analytics, machine learning and AI integration, with

collaboration across departments. Learn how to build systems that consistently deliver intelligence with real business value.

- **Implement best practices from leading organisations**
  Learn from the insight-led strategies of companies such as Amazon, Walmart and Airbnb. From recommendation engines to operational optimisation and personalised user experiences, these case studies reveal how insights drive outcomes across marketing, operations and product innovation.

- **Measure success using meaningful insight metrics**
  Develop a measurement framework that connects data efforts to clear business outcomes. Key performance indicators include customer retention, revenue growth, operational efficiency, campaign performance and internal adoption of data-driven decision-making.

- **Apply practical strategies for immediate and long-term impact**
  Take action through a mix of quick wins and foundational improvements. Immediate strategies include centralising dashboards, improving feedback loops and launching test-and-learn campaigns. Long-term investments may involve analytics training, building cross-functional data teams and embedding insight generation into strategic planning.

- **Prioritise and align insight-driven projects**
  Learn how to identify the most impactful insight initiatives and align them with broader business goals. This section provides guidance for leaders, marketers, analysts and frontline teams on embedding insights into everyday decisions and creating an organisation-wide culture of insight-led action.

Now let's bring Return on Insight to life.

RETURN ON INSIGHT IN ACTION

To understand how Return on Insight creates smarter, more responsive businesses, you will explore how leading organisations use data to enhance decision-making, personalise experiences and improve operations. The following case studies highlight the power of turning customer behaviour, feedback and real-time analytics into actionable insights. From Amazon's predictive logistics to Marriott's personalised guest experiences, each example shows how data-driven strategies can unlock efficiency, boost loyalty and drive sustained growth.

AMAZON – DATA-DRIVEN PERSONALISATION AND OPERATIONAL EXCELLENCE

Amazon exemplifies how data can fuel both superior customer experiences and world-class operational efficiency. Its powerful recommendation engine – driven by predictive analytics and machine learning – uses customer behaviour, past purchases and browsing history to deliver tailored product suggestions. This personalisation strategy accounts for an estimated 35% of Amazon's sales, making it a core driver of engagement and conversion (Rejoiner, 2022).

Operationally, Amazon applies data insights to optimise every stage of the supply chain. AI-powered demand forecasting analyses diverse data sources in real time to anticipate demand shifts with high accuracy, allowing inventory to be positioned strategically before orders are placed (RelearnX, 2024). This dual focus on front-end personalisation and back-end optimisation has earned Amazon consistently high customer satisfaction, with a score of 83/100 on the 2024 American Customer Satisfaction Index (Statista, 2024).

Key takeaway: Amazon shows how data-driven personalisation and operational intelligence work hand in hand to increase revenue, enhance satisfaction and build long-term competitive advantage.

WALMART – REAL-TIME INVENTORY MANAGEMENT AND CUSTOMER INSIGHTS

US brand Walmart, the world's biggest retailer, has become a leader in applying real-time data analytics to optimise inventory across its extensive store network. By using proprietary systems to monitor sales and predict demand, Walmart can dynamically adjust stock levels, reducing stock outs, cutting excess inventory and improving both efficiency and customer satisfaction (ProjectPro, 2024).

In addition, Walmart uses customer feedback and shopping patterns to inform merchandising and marketing strategies. For example, identifying frequently purchased product combinations has enabled smarter shelf layouts and targeted promotions. Data-driven adjustments to product placement have been shown to drive sales uplifts of 2–10%, demonstrating the impact of using behavioural insights to enhance the in-store experience (Analytics Capstone, 2020).

Key takeaway: Walmart illustrates how real-time data can drive smarter operations, personalise the customer journey and deliver measurable gains in satisfaction and sales.

FORD – ENHANCING PRODUCT DEVELOPMENT THROUGH CONNECTED DATA

Ford uses real-time data from connected vehicles to inform product development and improve customer experience. Telemetry insights, which derive from real-time diagnostics and usage patterns collected via onboard systems, help the company refine features like fuel efficiency, safety and in-car technology based on actual driving behaviour. Its data lake integrates over 4,600 sources – from dealerships to service logs – supporting smarter supply chain decisions and new service innovation (Aidata, 2024).

Ford also unifies customer data across departments using Salesforce CRM, enabling personalised updates and campaigns that have boosted email engagement by 48% and reduced campaign set-up time by four days (Salesforce, 2024). Digital platforms like the FordPass app provide direct feedback loops, allowing customers to manage vehicle health and preferences, further informing service updates and product design (Fleet News, 2020).

Key takeaway: Ford shows how connected data can drive continuous improvement. By aligning product development with real-world use, the company increases satisfaction and loyalty.

MARRIOTT - LEVERAGING GUEST DATA TO DRIVE PERSONALISED EXPERIENCES

Marriott International has transformed its guest experience strategy by harnessing customer data to deliver personalised, seamless stays. By analysing booking patterns, preferences and feedback, Marriott delivers tailored offers such as room upgrades and loyalty incentives, resulting in an 18% increase in guest retention (Renascence, 2024).

The company is also investing over $1 billion annually to modernise its tech stack, including cloud-based platforms that enhance digital booking, enable faster mobile check-ins and improve real-time service delivery. These innovations reduce operational friction and allow staff to focus more on guest engagement, boosting satisfaction and unlocking new revenue opportunities (Wilkinson, 2024).

Key takeaway: Marriott demonstrates how strategic data use can improve service efficiency and personalise the guest journey, driving loyalty, satisfaction and repeat bookings.

HSBC - DRIVING CUSTOMER-CENTRIC INNOVATION AND FRAUD DETECTION THROUGH DATA

HSBC has overhauled its customer experience by embedding data and AI into every stage of the customer lifecycle. Its Customer Experience Model (CEM) and Customer Lifecycle Management (CLCM) platforms analyse over a million behavioural signals daily, enabling personalised, real-time engagement and smarter onboarding journeys. HSBC's digital account opening process, once a 45-minute in-branch task, now takes just five minutes via mobile, contributing to a 20% increase in customers naming HSBC as their primary bank (Harvard Business Review, 2024).

In parallel, HSBC uses AI to detect and prevent financial crime at scale. It screens over 1.35 billion transactions monthly across 40 million accounts using an AI system co-developed with Google. This Dynamic Risk Assessment technology has improved detection rates by up to four times while cutting false positives by 60%, reducing unnecessary customer disruption and speeding up analysis from weeks to days (HSBC, 2024).

Key takeaway: HSBC demonstrates how integrating data and AI across customer experience and fraud prevention can enhance satisfaction, strengthen trust and deliver scalable, secure and personalised banking.

AIRBNB – ENHANCING USER EXPERIENCE THROUGH DATA-DRIVEN INNOVATION

Airbnb continually refines its platform through data-driven personalisation and real-time insights. Its algorithm analyses search history, booking behaviour, preferences and location to deliver more relevant listings and tailored recommendations. New features like shared wish lists, collaborative messaging and trip invitations – launched in its 2024 Summer Release – reflect Airbnb's ability to translate user feedback into intuitive platform enhancements (Airbnb, 2024).

Beyond guest recommendations, Airbnb segments its host community by location, property type and hosting frequency. This enables targeted support, personalised communication and dynamic pricing. The company also applies predictive analytics and machine learning to monitor booking trends, forecast seasonal demand and ensure supply meets guest expectations. These insights help Airbnb remain agile in response to shifting market conditions, local regulations and evolving user needs (CRG Solutions, 2025).

Key takeaway: Airbnb demonstrates how data and personalisation can drive a more relevant, responsive and engaging user experience. Its insight-led approach ensures the platform stays competitive, customer-focused and continuously evolving.

HOW TO MEASURE SUCCESS WITHIN RETURN ON INSIGHT

To truly unlock the value of data, organisations must go beyond collection and reporting by measuring how insights influence decisions, performance and outcomes. A robust measurement framework ensures Return on Insight is not just a concept, but a trackable and optimisable reality. The metrics below provide a practical foundation for evaluating how effectively insights are being generated, applied and translated into value across the business.

Data utilisation rate

Tracks how much of the data you collect is analysed and used to inform decisions. This highlights how effectively your business turns data into action.

- **How to measure:** Track the total volume of data collected versus the amount used in reporting, decision-making or customer-facing strategies.
- **Insight:** A high utilisation rate signals that data is being operationalised, not just stored, unlocking its full strategic value.

Customer retention and satisfaction metrics (NPS + CSAT)

These indicators show whether insights are being applied to improve the customer experience. They reflect how well the organisation is using data to meet expectations and build loyalty.

- **How to Measure:** Use regular NPS and CSAT surveys and monitor trends before and after implementing insight-driven changes.
- **Insight:** Positive shifts in loyalty and satisfaction reveal that data-informed actions are resonating with customers and enhancing their experience.

Operational efficiency improvements

Tracks whether insights are improving how your business operates – from supply chains to internal processes. It connects insight to tangible productivity and cost outcomes.

- **How to measure**: Monitor error rates, service turnaround times and process bottlenecks before and after applying data-informed strategies.
- **Insight**: Efficiency gains show that data is helping eliminate waste, speed up execution and strengthen core operations.

Revenue growth from insight-driven strategies

This metric ties your insights to business growth. It reflects how well your organisation turns analysis into commercial impact, through smarter campaigns, pricing or product development.

- **How to measure**: Use sales attribution models and track performance of data-informed initiatives versus standard approaches.
- **Insight**: Revenue increases from insight-driven activity confirm that your data strategy is directly contributing to top-line performance.

Time to insight

Measures how quickly your organisation can move from data collection to actionable intelligence. A faster turnaround indicates agility and greater decision-making power.

- **How to measure**: Track the time it takes from capturing data to delivering a usable insight, using dashboards, audits or workflow logs.
- **Insight**: Short time-to-insight reflects organisational readiness, efficient tooling and the ability to make decisions in real time.

Insight only drives impact when it's applied. By measuring both the speed and effectiveness of how data becomes action, businesses can evaluate the health of their insight systems plus their ability to adapt, innovate and deliver better outcomes. These metrics form the foundation of a high-performance, insight-led culture that continuously learns, improves and stays ahead of change.

IMPLEMENTING RETURN ON INSIGHT

Transforming data into actionable insight requires both immediate appli-cation and sustained cultural change. Quick wins demonstrate how insight can drive faster, smarter decisions in day-to-day work, while long-term strategies embed data literacy, technology and leadership into the fabric of the organisation. When teams across all levels embrace insight as a tool for growth and innovation, businesses become more agile, customer-focused and strategically aligned.

Quick wins

1. **Automate data reporting and insights distribution:**
   Implement tools that automate the collection and reporting of data insights, ensuring that teams receive relevant information promptly. Automated dashboards can display key metrics such as customer behaviour trends, product performance and operational efficiencies, allowing for faster decision-making and action.

2. **Conduct insight-focused workshops:**
   Organise workshops that help teams understand how to interpret and leverage data insights in their daily work. These sessions should cover how to draw actionable conclusions from raw data and apply them to specific projects or goals.

3. **Create a cross-functional data committee:**
   Establish a committee composed of members from different departments to review data insights regularly. This group can brainstorm ways to apply findings to various parts of the business, ensuring that insights are acted upon in a cohesive and collaborative manner.

4. **Launch a pilot insight-driven initiative:**
   Initiate a small-scale project that uses data insights to solve a specific business challenge, such as improving customer engagement or optimising a supply chain process. Use the success of this pilot to demonstrate the value of insights and gain buy-in for broader implementation.

Long-term strategies

1. **Build a comprehensive data ecosystem:**
   Develop a robust data infrastructure that integrates data from multiple sources, including customer interactions, supply chain operations and market trends. This ecosystem should be scalable and adaptable, capable of supporting both current and future data needs. Investing in cloud-based solutions and data lakes can provide the flexibility and storage necessary for continuous data growth.

2. **Establish a culture of continuous learning:**
   Encourage employees at all levels to embrace data literacy by offering training programmes and certifications. Workshops, webinars and hands-on training sessions should be part of an ongoing learning initiative. Companies that embed data proficiency into their culture find that employees are more confident and proactive in using insights to inform their decisions.

3. **Invest in advanced analytics and AI:**
   Advanced analytics tools and AI technologies can help identify trends and patterns that human analysis may miss. These technologies enable predictive insights that help businesses anticipate market shifts and customer needs. By integrating AI-driven analytics into the decision-making process, companies can stay ahead of the competition and respond to changes more rapidly.

4. **Develop insight leadership roles:**
   Appoint data champions or insight leaders who are responsible for advocating the use of data and ensuring that insights are communicated effectively across departments. These leaders play a crucial role in aligning data-driven strategies with the company's mission and fostering a culture that values evidence-based decision-making.

5. **Implement regular insight reviews:**
   Set up a schedule for regular data reviews, where teams analyse insights gathered over a set period and evaluate their impact on key business objectives. This practice not only keeps insights top of mind but also helps refine data strategies based on lessons learned and feedback.

6. **Align insight-driven objectives with business goals:**
   Ensure that all data initiatives align with broader business objectives. This alignment helps prioritise projects that offer the highest potential ROI and guarantees that efforts are directed towards strategic growth areas. By establishing clear KPIs tied to business outcomes, leaders can track the success of insight-driven strategies and adjust as needed.

Driving engagement at every level

For executives and senior leadership:

- **Prioritise a data-driven culture**: Executives should lead by example in promoting data literacy and an insights-focused mindset. By demonstrating a commitment to data-driven decision-making, senior leaders can set the tone for the entire organisation, ensuring that insights are not just a function of the IT department but an integral part of the company's strategic direction.
- **Invest in cutting-edge technology**: The value of insights hinges on the tools used to derive them. Executives should allocate resources to adopt advanced analytics platforms, artificial intelligence (AI) and machine learning (ML) capabilities that can analyse large datasets and generate actionable insights rapidly. This investment pays dividends by enabling predictive analytics and real-time decision-making.
- **Align insights with business objectives**: Leaders must ensure that insights contribute directly to achieving business goals, such as increasing customer retention, optimising operations or expanding market share. This alignment helps prioritise data initiatives and ensures that insight-driven strategies yield measurable business outcomes.

For operational managers:

- **Foster cross-functional collaboration**: Insight-driven initiatives should not operate in silos. Managers should facilitate communication between departments, such as marketing, sales, and product development, to share insights and apply them collaboratively. This collaboration amplifies the impact of insights and promotes a unified approach to decision-making.

- **Implement feedback mechanisms**: Operational leaders should establish processes for continuous feedback collection from employees and customers. This feedback can provide invaluable context to existing data and help fine-tune strategies to be more effective.
- **Monitor performance and adapt**: Operational leaders must track the success of insight-driven initiatives through key performance indicators (KPIs). If data reveals areas of underperformance, managers should be ready to pivot strategies quickly.

For marketing and sales teams:

- **Leverage personalisation for customer engagement**: Marketing teams should use customer insights to create highly targeted and personalised campaigns. These campaigns can drive customer engagement and boost conversion rates by delivering relevant content at the right time.
- **Use A/B testing and iterative improvements**: Insights should inform not only large-scale campaigns but also small, iterative changes. A/B testing can be used to experiment with different messaging, visuals and calls-to-action to determine what resonates best with customers.
- **Align messaging with data-backed trends**: Marketing strategies should reflect the data insights that reveal current customer behaviours and preferences. Sales teams can then use these insights to inform pitches and close deals more effectively.

For customer service teams:

- **Adopt real-time data access**: Customer service representatives should have access to real-time data on customer history and preferences to provide personalised and efficient service. This capability helps anticipate customer needs and address issues proactively.

- **Train teams on data utilisation**: Continuous training on how to interpret and use customer data for interactions can empower service teams to deliver a superior customer experience. When representatives are equipped with relevant data, they can personalise their approach and enhance customer satisfaction.
- **Proactively identify and solve issues:** Insights should guide customer service strategies, enabling teams to anticipate common customer challenges and address them before they escalate.

By embedding insights into the workflows of every team – from leadership and operations to marketing and customer service – organisations can create a truly informed, responsive and customer-focused culture. When insights are shared, understood and acted upon at every level, they become a catalyst for deeper engagement, smarter decisions and long-term loyalty.

THE LASTING IMPACT OF RETURN ON INSIGHT

Return on Insight is more than a data strategy – it's a shift in mindset that transforms how organisations operate, innovate and engage. In an age where data is abundant, the true competitive advantage lies not in how much data a company collects, but in how effectively it turns that data into meaningful, actionable intelligence.

This chapter has demonstrated that insight is not about reporting for reporting's sake – it's about understanding the story behind the numbers and making decisions that drive tangible outcomes. Leading organisations like Amazon, Walmart, Ford, Marriott, HSBC and Airbnb have shown that embedding insight into decision-making leads to sharper strategy, greater agility and deeper customer relevance.

When companies invest in technology, nurture a culture of data literacy and embed insight into cross-functional processes, they create the conditions for sustained impact. This approach shifts data from being a by-product of operations to being a core strategic asset, powering everything from real-time responsiveness to long-term planning.

Importantly, Return on Insight isn't just about efficiency or revenue growth. It's also about building trust and loyalty. Today's customers expect experiences that are personal, anticipatory and relevant. Businesses that use insights to deliver tailored solutions – like Marriott's guest personalisation or HSBC's personalised onboarding and increased fraud prevention – build stronger emotional connections and long-term loyalty.

Implementing Return on Insight requires a mix of quick wins and long-term strategies. Automating reports or launching targeted campaigns can generate immediate value. Over time, investing in advanced analytics, building data-literate teams and fostering collaboration between departments will embed insight as a core operating principle.

The message to leaders at every level is clear: insight must inform the way you think, plan and serve. Executives should align data strategies with broader business goals. Marketing and product teams can harness insight for personalisation and innovation. Customer service teams can use real-time data to enhance responsiveness and empathy.

Return on Insight is a continuous cycle of listening, learning, adapting and improving. It builds organisations that are not only informed, but also agile, customer-centric and ready for the future. In a constantly evolving landscape, businesses that prioritise insight will be best equipped to anticipate needs, respond to change and seize opportunity.

In closing, Return on Insight is the bridge between raw information and real-world impact. When embedded across the organisation, it drives better decisions, deeper customer relationships and lasting strategic advantage.

TAKE ACTION

Now that you understand the power of Return on Insight, start by identifying one area where data could better inform decisions, whether that's refining a customer journey, improving operations or strengthening campaign performance.

Even small shifts – like streamlining reporting or gathering feedback more effectively – can reveal valuable insights. Over time, these actions build a culture where decisions are guided by intelligence, not instinct.

In an insight-driven business, data isn't just collected, it's converted into clarity, direction and advantage. Take the first step toward building that future, today.

REFERENCES

Aidata (2024) 'Ford's data-driven roadmap towards future mobility'. Available at: www.aidataanalytics.network/data-monetization/articles/fords-data-driven-roadmap-towards-future-mobility [Accessed 1 May 2025].

Airbnb (2024). '2024 Summer Release Highlights'. Available at: www.news.airbnb.com/airbnb-2024-summer-release-highlights/ [Accessed 25 Apr. 2025].

Analytics Capstone (2020). 'Finding optimal product placement on shelf – Analytics Capstone'. Available at: www.analyticscapstone.squarespace.com/s/Walmart-Ella-Liu-Yijia-Yang.pdf [Accessed 1 May 2025].

CRG Solutions (2025). 'How Airbnb uses data to track and understand supply trends'. Available at: www.crgsolutions.co/how-airbnb-uses-data-to-track-and-understand-supply-trends/ [Accessed 2 May 2025].

Fleet News (2020). 'Ford: Customers offered connected vehicle services for free'. 24 June. Available at: www.fleetnews.co.uk/news/manufacturer-news/2020/06/24/ford-customers-offered-connected-vehicle-services-for-free [Accessed 1 May 2025].

Harvard Business Review (2024) 'How HSBC transformed its customer experience'. Available at: www.hbr.org/sponsored/2024/03/how-hsbc-transformed-its-customer-experience [Accessed 1 May 2025].

HSBC (2024). 'Harnessing the power of AI to fight financial crime'. HSBC News and Views. Available at: www.hsbc.com/news-and-views/views/hsbc-views/harnessing-the-power-of-ai-to-fight-financial-crime [Accessed 2 May 2025].

IBM (2023). 'Data growth and innovation'. Available at: www.newsroom.ibm.com/2024-01-10-Data-Suggests-Growth-in-Enterprise-Adoption-of-AI-is-Due-to-Widespread-Deployment-by-Early-Adopters [Accessed 1 May 2025].

McKinsey & Company (2023). 'Experience-led growth: A new way to create value'. 23 March. Available at: www.mckinsey.com/capabilities/growth-marketing-and-sales/our-insights/experience-led-growth-a-new-way-to-create-value [Accessed 1 May 2025].

ProjectPro (2024). 'How big data analysis helped increase Walmart's sales turnover'. Available at: www.projectpro.io/article/how-big-data-analysis-helped-increase-walmarts-sales-turnover/109 [Accessed 1 May 2025].

Rejoiner (2022). 'The Amazon recommendations secret to selling more online'. 21 December. Available at: www.rejoiner.com/resources/amazon-recommendations-secret-selling-online [Accessed 1 May 2025].

RelearnX (2024). 'The AI-powered supply chain: How Amazon is redefining logistics'. Available at: www.relearnx.com/blog/the-ai-powered-supply-chain-how-amazon-is-redefining-logistics [Accessed 2 May 2025].

Renascence (2024). 'How Marriott International elevates customer experience (CX) with personalized loyalty programs'. Available at: www.renascence.io/journal/how-marriott-international-elevates-customer-experience-cx-with-personalized-loyalty-programs [Accessed 1 May 2025].

Salesforce (2024). 'Ford reinventing customer experience'. Available at: www.salesforce.com/resources/customer-stories/ford-reinventing-customer-experience/ [Accessed 1 May 2025].

Statista (2024). 'U.S. customer satisfaction with Amazon 2024'. Available at: www.statista.com/statistics/185788/us-customer-satisfaction-with-amazon/ [Accessed 2 May 2025].

Wilkinson, L. (2024). 'Marriott gears up for another year of major tech spending.' CIO Dive. May 2. Available at: https://www.ciodive.com/news/marriott-international-tech-spend-digital-transformation-plan-ai/715036/ [Accessed 21 August 2025].

CHAPTER 10
RETURN ON INNOVATION – FROM IDEAS TO IMPACT: DRIVING BUSINESS FORWARD

INTRODUCING RETURN ON INNOVATION

In today's fast-paced, competitive landscape, innovation is no longer optional – it's essential. Yet many organisations still view innovation as a siloed function reserved for product development or R&D. The reality is that the most forward-thinking companies embed innovation across every area of the business, treating it not just as a capability but as a cultural imperative. This is where Return on Innovation comes in.

Return on Innovation is the concept that measurable value – whether in customer loyalty, operational efficiency or revenue growth – comes from continuously evolving how a business thinks, creates and delivers. It's about going beyond surface-level change and investing in a system that enables fresh thinking, experimentation and agility at scale.

According to a recent McKinsey survey, while a large majority of executives recognise innovation as a key growth driver, only a small fraction feels confident in their organisation's innovation performance (McKinsey & Company, 2024). This gap reflects a common challenge: businesses want to innovate, but many lack the structure, mindset or culture to make it sustainable. Innovation can't thrive in isolation; it must be integrated across functions, driven by leadership and supported by teams who feel empowered to experiment and fail forward.

Leading companies like Tesla and Nike show what's possible when innovation is prioritised. Tesla redefines the auto industry not only through product design, but through direct-to-consumer sales, over-the-air software updates and vertically integrated manufacturing. Nike, meanwhile, combines cutting-edge digital tools with sustainable design, introducing innovations like Flyknit to reduce waste and AI-powered apps like Nike Fit to personalise the customer experience. Both brands demonstrate how innovation across products, services and channels can drive loyalty, reduce friction and deliver long-term business growth.

In this chapter, you will explore how companies can embed a culture of innovation that drives measurable results – not just with product launches, but in how they solve problems, engage customers and future-proof their business.

LEVERAGING RETURN ON INNOVATION

Innovation is no longer a luxury or a one-off event – it's a strategic necessity for businesses that want to remain relevant, competitive and resilient in a constantly evolving world. Return on Innovation explores how organisations can embed innovation into their culture, leadership and operations to unlock new value, adapt with agility and maintain long-term growth.

By the end of this chapter, you will have a clear understanding of how to implement and sustain Return on Innovation across your organisation. You'll gain the insight, tools and practical guidance needed to transform innovation from a siloed function into a core capability that touches every part of your business. This chapter will equip you to:

- **Maximise the strategic value of Return on Innovation**
  Explore why continuous innovation is essential for maintaining relevance and accelerating growth. Understand how embedding innovation into your strategic framework – rather than isolating it within product or R&D teams – can help your organisation stay adaptable, forward-thinking, and future-ready.

- **Build the core drivers of innovation**
  Identify the conditions required for innovation to thrive. Learn how to foster a culture of experimentation through leadership commitment, psychological safety, cross-functional collaboration, agile feedback loops and a deep understanding of customer needs.

- **Implement best practices from leading organisations**
  Examine case studies from Tesla, Amazon, IKEA, Nike, Monzo and more. From startup agility to enterprise-scale execution, these examples highlight how diverse businesses are embedding innovation into their DNA, measuring its impact and turning new ideas into tangible outcomes.

- **Measure success using meaningful innovation metrics**
  Track the impact of innovation initiatives using both strategic and operational metrics. Key performance indicators include time-to-market, innovation pipeline health, percentage of revenue from new offerings and customer satisfaction. Learn how to use data to evaluate success and guide continued investment.

- **Apply practical strategies for immediate and long-term impact**
  Implement a mix of short-term actions and long-term structures to fuel innovation across your organisation. From sprints and pilot programmes to innovation labs, cross-functional teams and performance reviews tied to innovation outcomes, discover how to build lasting capability.

- **Overcome common innovation challenges**
  Address the obstacles that often hinder innovation, including change resistance, resource constraints and risk aversion. Learn how to build internal buy-in, create space for experimentation and turn failures into valuable learning moments.

- **Prioritise and align innovation efforts for maximum value**
  Not all innovation initiatives are equal. This section offers a framework for aligning innovation efforts with strategic objectives, prioritising high-impact opportunities, and scaling

what works. Learn how to create a roadmap that keeps innovation focused, accountable and outcome-driven.

Now let's bring Return on Innovation to life.

RETURN ON INNOVATION IN ACTION

To explore the impact of Return on Innovation, you will discover companies that have embedded creativity, experimentation and forward-thinking into their core strategy. These case studies highlight how continuous investment in research, technology and customer-centric solutions drives market leadership and long-term growth. From Apple's user-focused design to 3M's employee-led ideation, each brand demonstrates how innovation fuels customer loyalty, brand relevance and sustained success in a rapidly changing world.

APPLE – REVOLUTIONISING CUSTOMER EXPERIENCE THROUGH CONTINUOUS INNOVATION

Apple's history is a testament to the power of relentless innovation. From the launch of the original iPhone to the development of services like Apple Pay and Apple Music, the company has continuously adapted its product offerings to meet evolving consumer needs. Apple's approach involves meticulous market research, cutting-edge R&D and user-centric design. The introduction of the iPhone, for example, reshaped the smartphone market by integrating previously separate features, such as a music player and phone, into one cohesive device (Wikipedia. 2025).

Apple's commitment to innovation is supported by an annual R&D investment that reached $31.37 billion in 2024 (Statista, 2024). This financial commitment underscores the company's strategic focus on innovation to maintain its market leadership. The results are clear: Apple has a 92% retention rate among iPhone users and 84% of iPhone owners plan to purchase another Apple device to replace their current one (Business Dasher, 2024).

Key takeaway: Apple's relentless investment in R&D and user-centric design sets a gold standard for continuous innovation. By anticipating customer needs and integrating technology seamlessly, Apple drives industry change while maintaining market leadership, loyalty and high satisfaction levels.

TESLA – INNOVATING THE AUTOMOTIVE EXPERIENCE

Tesla has redefined the automotive experience by combining continuous innovation in EV technology with a customer-centric approach – leveraging data and software-led enhancements to deliver a seamless, future-focused ownership journey (Renascence, 2024a). With $4.5 billion invested in R&D in 2024, Tesla's agile, innovation-led approach keeps it at the forefront of global automotive progress (Statista, 2025).

Its direct-to-consumer (DTC) sales model also plays a key role in shaping the brand experience. By eliminating traditional dealerships, Tesla delivers a more seamless, transparent purchasing journey, enhancing customer satisfaction while improving supply chain visibility and operational efficiency (DataNext, 2024).

Key takeaway: Tesla blends advanced technology with a customer-first retail model. Its commitment to continuous improvement and direct engagement is redefining expectations across the automotive industry.

NIKE – INNOVATION THROUGH DIGITAL TOOLS AND SUSTAINABLE DESIGN

Nike has reimagined performance and product innovation by combining cutting-edge technology with sustainability. Its Flyknit material, for example, reduces waste by 60% compared to traditional manufacturing, while its Move to Zero initiative continues to push the boundaries of sustainable design (Nike, 2025).

The brand's innovative digital ecosystem – including Nike Training Club, SNKRS and Nike Run Club – drives deeper engagement. Consumers active on two or more platforms have a lifetime value four times higher than average, highlighting the power of digital connection (BrainStation, 2022).

Nike also leverages generative AI through its Athlete Imagined Revolution (A.I.R.) project, using athlete data to rapidly prototype personalised footwear, shortening development time and aligning design with performance needs (AIM Research, 2024).

Key takeaway: Nike shows how sustainable materials, AI and digital tools can work together to drive innovation, loyalty and long-term brand value.

3M – SUSTAINING LONG-TERM INNOVATION

3M is renowned for its diversified portfolio of over 60,000 products, ranging from Post-it® Notes to advanced medical solutions. The company's success is driven by its '15% rule', which encourages employees to dedicate 15% of their time to innovative projects outside their regular duties. This culture of innovation has led to the creation of some of 3M's most successful products such as the Post-It® Note (3M, 2025).

In 2024, 3M invested approximately $1.085 billion in R&D (Macrotrends, 2025). The company's approach demonstrates that fostering an environment where employees are empowered to explore new ideas leads to sustainable business growth and market leadership.

Key takeaway: 3M shows that a culture of innovation begins with employee empowerment. Through structured freedom and consistent R&D investment, the company fosters breakthrough ideas that drive long-term growth, proving innovation doesn't need to be reactive – it can be built into the culture.

WARBY PARKER - REDEFINING RETAIL THROUGH INNOVATION

Warby Parker disrupted the eyewear industry by introducing an online-first model that prioritised affordability and convenience. Their innovative home try-on programme allows customers to try frames at home before purchasing, revolutionising the way people shop for eyewear (Warby Paker, 2025). Warby Parker also leverages technology to enhance the customer experience, including virtual try-on tools powered by augmented reality (AR) (Forbes, 2019).

This innovative approach has contributed to Warby Parker's success, with the company achieving a valuation of over $6 billion at its direct listing on the New York Stock Exchange in September 2021, far surpassing its previous private valuation of $3 billion (Reuters, 2021; Axios, 2020).

Key takeaway: Warby Parker's customer-first innovation – blending digital convenience with tactile experience – revolutionised the eyewear industry. Virtual tools and home try-ons create a seamless journey, proving that reimagining retail through technology can build loyalty and disrupt traditional markets.

SPOTIFY - INNOVATING THE MUSIC EXPERIENCE

Spotify continues to lead the music streaming industry by using data-driven insights to power personalisation and innovation. Algorithm-based playlists like 'Discover Weekly' offer tailored recommendations that deepen user engagement, while regular platform updates keep the experience fresh and relevant (Renascence, 2024b).

A culture of continuous innovation is embedded in Spotify's internal 'hack weeks', where employees explore and prototype new ideas (Spotify Newsroom, 2023). Recent features, such as AI-powered audiobooks and location-based concert alerts, reflect this agility and contribute to the platform's strong momentum. As of Q1 2025, Spotify reached 678 million monthly active users, underscoring the effectiveness of its innovation strategy in driving sustained growth (RouteNote, 2025).

Key takeaway: Spotify's real-time data usage and internal innovation practices fuel a highly personalised and evolving user experience. Its agile approach ensures the platform remains competitive, relevant and deeply engaging for users around the world.

HOW TO MEASURE SUCCESS WITHIN RETURN ON INNOVATION

To ensure innovation delivers real, measurable value, businesses must go beyond anecdotal wins and instinct. A structured measurement framework helps track both the impact and scalability of innovation efforts, providing clarity on what's working, where to iterate and how innovation contributes to business growth. These metrics serve as guideposts for accountability, investment decisions and future innovation strategy.

Revenue growth from new products and services

This metric tracks the proportion of revenue generated from recently launched offerings. It's a leading indicator of whether your innovation efforts are translating into tangible business performance.

- **How to measure:** Analyse financial reports to segment revenue by product age and identify contributions from new offerings (typically within 1–3 years of launch).
- **Insight:** High revenue contribution from new products shows that innovation is driving relevance, differentiation and sustainable growth.

Time-to-market efficiency

Time-to-market measures how quickly your business can move from concept to launch. It reflects the agility of your innovation process and operational effectiveness.

- **How to measure:** Use project management tools to track timelines from idea approval to public release.
- **Insight:** Faster time-to-market indicates a more agile innovation culture – one that can respond quickly to change and reduce missed opportunities.

Customer feedback on new products

This metric captures how customers perceive newly launched offerings, helping validate whether your innovations resonate in the real world.

- **How to measure:** Collect and analyse post-launch feedback via surveys, product reviews and social media sentiment.
- **Insight:** Strong feedback reflects product-market fit and ensures future development stays aligned with actual customer needs.

Employee participation in innovation initiatives

Tracks how involved employees are in contributing ideas and collaborating across innovation projects, regardless of department or role.

- **How to measure:** Monitor participation in idea submissions, hackathons, innovation workshops or internal challenges.
- **Insight:** High involvement shows that innovation is embedded in your culture, not siloed in a single function, which supports broader creativity and engagement.

Number of patents filed

Patents serve as a proxy for originality and defensibility. This metric tracks how much of your innovation is unique, IP-worthy and contributing to your long-term strategic value.

- **How to measure:** Monitor the volume of patent applications and approvals over time, including regional and global filings.

- **Insight:** A growing patent portfolio signals a pipeline of proprietary value that can strengthen your market position and protect competitive advantage.

Experiment success rate

This tracks how many of your innovation tests lead to something viable, whether that's a pilot, new product or implemented solution. It's not about success for its own sake, but about learning and iteration.

- **How to measure:** Compare total experiments run versus those that result in viable outcomes (scaled, launched or implemented).
- **Insight:** A balanced success rate shows you're testing enough, learning often and maintaining a healthy innovation rhythm – not over-indexing on perfection.

Innovation pipeline health

Pipeline health reflects the volume, diversity and progress of ideas in development – not just what's launched, but what's coming next.

- **How to measure:** Track the number of ideas submitted, evaluated, prototyped and advanced across development stages.
- **Insight:** A healthy pipeline shows depth, diversity and consistency – ensuring your innovation strategy isn't reliant on a few big bets, but backed by a flow of future opportunities.

Innovation thrives on experimentation, but it's sustained through insight. By consistently measuring the performance and outcomes of innovation initiatives, organisations can scale what works, pivot when needed and build a culture where innovation is not only encouraged, but strategically guided. These metrics offer more than just numbers, they tell the story of a company's ability to stay relevant, resilient and ahead of the curve.

IMPLEMENTING RETURN ON INNOVATION

Embedding innovation into an organisation requires more than generating ideas, it takes a balance of short-term momentum and long-term systems that support continuous evolution. Quick wins help cultivate an innovation mindset, giving employees space to experiment and contribute creative solutions. Long-term strategies ensure innovation is sustained through leadership, collaboration, investment and a willingness to learn from failure. When every level of the business is engaged in driving innovation, companies become more resilient, adaptable and aligned with future customer needs.

Quick wins

1. **Host focused brainstorming sessions**
   Organise regular brainstorming sessions where employees from different departments come together to explore new ideas and solve challenges creatively. Facilitated to stay productive and inclusive, these sessions generate a pipeline of ideas for evaluation and encourage collaboration, helping to embed innovation as a shared responsibility across teams.

2. **Launch internal innovation challenges**
   Invite employees to participate in company-wide innovation contests focused on solving specific problems or improving internal processes. Winning ideas can be rewarded with recognition or support for development, encouraging creative thinking, friendly competition and greater employee ownership in driving innovation forward.

3. **Establish recognition programmes for innovators**
   Celebrate and reward employees who contribute innovative solutions by creating formal recognition initiatives. Monthly

'Innovation Champion' awards or shout-outs in internal communications foster a culture where creativity is acknowledged, motivating individuals to share and act on new ideas.

4. **Empower teams to run small pilot projects**
   Give employees the autonomy and budget to test small-scale pilot ideas within short time frames. This creates a fast feedback loop, allowing the business to evaluate feasibility with minimal risk. Even unsuccessful pilots provide valuable learning, while successful ones can be scaled and refined.

5. **Implement employee innovation portals**
   Introduce a digital platform where staff can submit, comment on and vote for innovative ideas. A centralised system makes it easier to track, develop and implement ideas while encouraging continuous contribution from across the organisation.

Long-term strategies

1. **Invest in a dedicated R&D function**
   Create a focused research and development team responsible for driving long-term innovation efforts. With clear goals aligned to business strategy, the R&D team can proactively identify opportunities, test solutions and foster a structured approach to innovation beyond day-to-day operations.

2. **Embed innovation in the onboarding process**
   Introduce new hires to the company's innovation mindset from day one. Incorporate workshops, storytelling and early opportunities to contribute ideas so that employees understand their role in shaping the future of the business and feel empowered to challenge the status quo.

3. **Create cross-functional innovation hubs**
   Establish teams composed of employees from different departments to work on high-impact innovation projects. These hubs break down silos, encourage knowledge-sharing and combine diverse expertise to solve complex problems and uncover new business opportunities.

4. **Implement a continuous learning programme**
   Offer ongoing development opportunities focused on innovation, such as online courses, design thinking workshops or access to industry events. Continuous upskilling ensures employees stay informed, adaptable and confident in experimenting with new ideas and approaches.

5. **Foster strategic partnerships for innovation**
   Collaborate with external startups, academic institutions or research bodies to bring fresh thinking and new capabilities into the business. Strategic partnerships help accelerate innovation, expand access to resources and expose the organisation to new technologies and methodologies.

6. **Incorporate innovation metrics into performance reviews**
   Align employee development with the company's innovation goals by including innovation-related KPIs in performance assessments. Tracking contributions to idea generation, pilot projects or creative problem-solving helps reinforce that innovation is a valued part of every role.

7. **Build a fail-fast, learn-fast culture**
   Create an environment where employees are encouraged to take calculated risks and learn from failure. Leaders should role-model this behaviour by sharing their own lessons and

supporting experimentation, reinforcing that failure is part of growth and not a barrier to innovation.

8. **Review and evolve the innovation strategy regularly**
   Schedule periodic reviews, annually or bi-annually, of your innovation approach to assess progress, identify emerging gaps and update initiatives. Keeping your strategy dynamic ensures it remains relevant to changing business needs and external market conditions.

9. **Establish a structured customer feedback loop**
   Collect, analyse and act on customer feedback throughout the innovation process. Feeding real-world insights into product and service development helps ensure ideas are grounded in actual needs, while also building loyalty by demonstrating that customer input shapes company decisions.

10. **Promote internal innovation ambassadors**
    Select and support individuals across departments to champion innovation within their teams. These ambassadors lead workshops, surface ideas and keep momentum going between larger initiatives, making innovation a day-to-day mindset, not just a top-down directive.

Driving engagement at every level

For executives and senior leadership

- **Align innovation with strategic goals and customer needs**: Ensure innovation efforts are tied directly to long-term business objectives and are rooted in solving real customer problems.

- **Foster a culture of experimentation**: Lead by example by supporting calculated risks and celebrating iterative progress. Demonstrating executive commitment empowers teams to explore new ideas without fear of failure.
- **Invest in emerging technologies**: Tools like AI, automation and data analytics can fast-track innovation, enabling responsiveness to market shifts and evolving customer demands.

For managers and operational leaders

- **Facilitate cross-functional collaboration**: Act as a bridge between teams to break silos, share insights and drive integrated innovation initiatives.
- **Monitor progress and adapt quickly**: Implement agile feedback loops, review innovation outcomes regularly and be ready to pivot strategies based on learning and performance data.
- **Support resource allocation and momentum**: Ensure teams have the time, budget and space to experiment while staying aligned with broader business priorities.

For product and R&D teams

- **Prioritise customer-driven development**: Base innovation on customer feedback, usage trends and behavioural insights to ensure new offerings meet real-world needs.
- **Encourage interdisciplinary approaches**: Bring together diverse expertise – technical, design, user experience – to co-create well-rounded solutions.
- **Accelerate go-to-market strategies**: Shorten the path from ideation to launch, using pilots and prototypes to validate quickly and reduce risk.

For marketing and sales teams

- **Leverage customer data to inform innovation**: Use behavioural insights and feedback to shape messaging, features and value propositions that resonate.
- **Use A/B testing for ongoing refinement**: Regularly test content, campaigns and product updates to identify what drives engagement and conversions.

- **Position innovation as a brand advantage**: Storytelling around innovation helps customers understand its value and builds market leadership and trust.

For customer experience and support teams

- **Guide seamless adoption of new innovations**: Equip teams with the tools and knowledge to onboard and support customers through change.
- **Capture feedback and track sentiment**: Monitor customer reactions to innovation rollouts, using data to refine support and flag friction points early.
- **Use innovation to enhance service efficiency**: Implement AI-powered tools, chatbots and personalised support pathways to improve responsiveness and customer satisfaction.

By embedding innovation into every aspect of the business, organisations can remain adaptable, continuously meet customer expectations and secure long-term growth in an evolving market.

THE LASTING IMPACT OF RETURN ON INNOVATION

Return on Innovation is more than a strategic initiative, it's a business imperative. In today's fast-paced, competitive landscape, the companies that thrive are those that embed innovation into their culture, strategy and daily operations. This chapter has shown that innovation isn't reserved for R&D departments or one-off product launches – it's a mindset that drives long-term relevance, adaptability and growth.

Case studies from Apple, Tesla, Nike, 3M, Warby Parker and others illustrate that successful innovators consistently challenge convention, stay close to customer needs and build systems that turn creative ideas into tangible results. From Apple's iterative design to 3M's employee-led breakthroughs and Nike's digital and sustainable innovation, the common thread is clear: innovation flourishes when it's supported by leadership, customer insight and an open culture of experimentation.

To make innovation sustainable, organisations must measure it meaningfully. Tracking metrics like revenue from new products, time to market, customer satisfaction and internal participation helps teams understand what's working and where to go next. These insights not only guide investment but also embed innovation as a measurable, accountable part of business performance.

Leadership plays a vital role in setting the tone. When leaders champion creativity, reward risk-taking and prioritise learning over perfection, innovation becomes a natural part of the company's rhythm. Combined with structures like cross-functional collaboration, training and agile processes, this creates a fertile ground for continuous progress.

Building an innovation-driven business requires both quick wins and long-term commitment. Initiatives like pilot programmes, idea challenges or innovation champions can energise teams immediately. At the same time, investing in R&D, forming strategic partnerships and embedding innovation into onboarding and performance reviews ensures momentum is sustained.

Of course, innovation has obstacles – fear of failure, change resistance and limited resources among them. But these can be overcome with the right culture. A fail-fast mentality, transparent communication and access to new perspectives – whether from customers, employees or partners – can turn barriers into breakthroughs.

Ultimately, Return on Innovation is about creating a continuous cycle of improvement, not just for business outcomes but for the people behind them. Organisations that embrace this approach position themselves as leaders – resilient, future-ready and aligned with evolving customer needs.

In a world that demands reinvention, innovation isn't optional. It's the key to staying relevant, unlocking growth and delivering meaningful value, again and again.

TAKE ACTION

Now that you've explored the principles of Return on Innovation, it's time to translate insight into momentum. Start by identifying one area of your business where innovation feels stalled or where small experiments could unlock new value.

This might mean launching a pilot programme, inviting cross-functional teams to co-create new ideas or carving out time for employees to explore solutions to persistent challenges. Even simple changes – like shifting how you gather feedback or recognising small wins – can spark a culture of innovation from the ground up.

Innovation doesn't require a lab, it requires a mindset. With the right support, structure, and intent, you can turn creativity into action and ideas into impact.

The future belongs to those who build it. Start today.

REFERENCES

3M (2025) '3M's 15% Culture | Cultivate & Pursue Your Innovative Ideas'. Available at: www.3m.co.uk/3M/en_GB/careers/culture/15-percent-culture/ (Accessed: 2 May 2025).

AIM Research (2024) 'How Nike is Using AI to Transform Product Design, Customer Experience, and Operational Efficiency'. Available at: www.aimresearch.co/

market-industry/how-nike-is-using-ai-to-transform-product-design-customer-experience-and-operational-efficiency (Accessed: 2 May 2025).

Axios (2020) 'Scoop: Warby Parker now valued at $3 billion'. Available at: www.axios.com/2020/08/27/warby-parker-3-billion-valuation (Accessed: 2 May 2025).

BrainStation (2022) 'Nike's Digital Ecosystem Paved the Way for D2C Transformation'. Available at: www.brainstation.io/magazine/nikes-digital-ecosystem-paved-the-way-for-d2c-transformation (Accessed: 2 May 2025).

Business Dasher (2024) '9+ Apple brand loyalty statistics: A must-know in 2024'. Available at: www.businessdasher.com/apple-statistics/ (Accessed: 2 May 2025).

DataNext (2024) 'Tesla's Direct Sales Model: Revolutionizing the Car Industry'. Available at: www.datanext.ai/case-study/tesla-direct-sales-model/ (Accessed: 2 May 2025).

Forbes (2019) 'The Fascinating Ways Warby Parker Uses Artificial Intelligence And AR To Change Retail'. Available at: www.forbes.com/sites/bernardmarr/2019/04/18/the-fascinating-ways-warby-parker-uses-artificial-intelligence-and-ar-to-change-retail/ (Accessed: 2 May 2025).

Macrotrends (2025) 'M Research and Development Expenses 2010–2024 | MMM'. Available at: www.macrotrends.net/stocks/charts/MMM/3m/research-development-expenses (Accessed: 2 May 2025).

McKinsey & Company (2024) 'How top performers use innovation to grow within and beyond the core'. Available at: www.mckinsey.com/capabilities/strategy-and-corporate-finance/our-insights/how-top-performers-use-innovation-to-grow-within-and-beyond-the-core (Accessed: 2 May 2025).

Nike (2025) 'Sustainable Materials + Innovation'. Available at: www.nike.com/gb/sustainability/materials (Accessed: 2 May 2025).

Renascence (2024a) 'How Tesla Enhances Customer Experience (CX) Through Innovation and Customer-Centricity'. Available at: www.renascence.io/journal/how-tesla-enhances-customer-experience-cx-through-innovation-and-customer-centricity (Accessed: 2 May 2025).

Renascence (2024b) 'How Spotify Delivers a Unique Customer Experience (CX) with Personalized Music Recommendations'. Available at: www.renascence.io/journal/how-spotify-delivers-a-unique-customer-experience-cx-with-personalized-music-recommendations (Accessed: 2 May 2025).

Reuters (2021) 'Eyewear company Warby Parker valued at over $6 bn after shares climb in debut'. Available at: www.reuters.com/business/retail-consumer/eyewear-company-warby-parker-valued-over-6-bln-after-shares-climb-debut-2021-09-29/ (Accessed: 2 May 2025).

RouteNote (2025) 'Spotify Q1 2025: How many people use and pay for....' Available at: www.routenote.com/blog/spotify-q1-2025/ (Accessed: 2 May 2025).

Spotify Newsroom (2023) 'Tips for Creating a Successful Hack Week'. Available at: www.newsroom.spotify.com/2023-03-16/tips-for-creating-a-successful-hack-week/ (Accessed: 2 May 2025).

Statista (2024a) 'Apple: expenditure on research and development 2007–2024'. Available at: www.statista.com/statistics/273006/apple-expenses-for-research-and-development/ (Accessed: 2 May 2025).

Statista (2025b) 'Tesla's R&D costs 2024'. Available at: www.statista.com/statistics/314863/research-and-development-expenses-of-tesla/ (Accessed: 2 May 2025).

Warby Parker (2025) 'Home Try-On'. Available at: www.warbyparker.com/home-try-on (Accessed: 2 May 2025).

Wikipedia (2025) 'History of Apple Inc'. Available at: www.en.wikipedia.org/wiki/History_of_Apple_Inc (Accessed: 2 May 2025).

CHAPTER 11
RETURN ON INTEGRATION – UNITING TEAMS AROUND ONE CLEAR GOAL

INTRODUCING RETURN ON INTEGRATION

In today's interconnected business landscape, success no longer depends solely on the strength of individual departments – it hinges on how well those departments work together. Customers don't experience a brand in silos. They experience a journey that spans marketing, sales, product, operations and service. If those teams aren't aligned, it shows.

Return on Integration is about the value created when an organisation moves from fragmentation to unity. When people, processes, data and systems are aligned, every part of the business becomes more effective and every customer experience becomes more consistent and seamless. This is no longer a back-office issue. Integration is a competitive differentiator.

Fragmentation slows progress, causes duplicated effort and weakens communication. According to Panopto, the average large U.S. business loses $44 million in productivity annually due to inefficient knowledge sharing, resulting in delayed projects, missed opportunities and significant financial impact (Panopto, 2023). Integration, on the other hand, creates operational efficiency, enhances decision-making and drives more cohesive customer journeys. When teams understand each other's roles, share data and work toward common goals, collaboration becomes the norm, not the exception, and internal trust is cemented.

In a time when customer expectations, data complexity and technological demands continue to rise, the ability to operate as one aligned, collaborative organisation is no longer optional – it's essential. Integration connects the dots between strategy and execution, internal workflows and external experience and cross-functional innovation and scalable success.

This chapter explores why integration is more than just a system fix – it's a cultural and strategic imperative for modern organisations. Through real-world case studies, actionable strategies and practical tools, you'll learn how to create alignment that unlocks long-term growth, resilience and customer value.

LEVERAGING RETURN ON INTEGRATION

True organisational success isn't just about individual teams performing well, it's about how those teams work together. Return on Integration focuses on aligning departments, people and processes around a shared mission to enable seamless collaboration, eliminate silos and deliver strategic growth. In an increasingly complex and fast-paced business landscape, integration has become a powerful differentiator.

By the end of this chapter, you will have a clear understanding of how to implement and sustain Return on Integration across your organisation. You'll gain strategic insights and practical tools to embed collaboration, alignment and efficiency across every level of the business. This chapter will equip you to:

- **Maximise the strategic value of Return on Integration**
  Explore why integration is essential for staying competitive, agile and customer-centric. Learn how aligning teams around shared goals supports innovation, improves customer experiences and enables scalable, sustainable growth – especially in a digitally driven environment.

- **Build the core elements of effective integration**
  Identify the key drivers of integration, from leadership alignment and transparent communication to cross-functional collaboration and enabling technologies. Understand how to create systems and behaviours that allow teams to work in sync while staying focused on a common goal.

- **Implement best practices from leading organisations**
  Learn from real-world examples of companies like Microsoft, Southwest Airlines and Spotify. These case studies showcase how integrated operating models, such as product squads,

shared platforms and cross-team planning, have improved performance, innovation and employee engagement.

- **Measure success using meaningful integration metrics**
  Develop a measurement framework to track the effectiveness of integration initiatives. Key performance indicators include cross-functional project success rates, employee engagement, customer satisfaction (CSAT) and operational efficiency gains – all helping inform what's working and where to improve.

- **Apply practical strategies for immediate and long-term impact**
  Discover both quick wins and strategic plays. Immediate steps include introducing shared OKRs, running cross-departmental workshops and adopting collaborative tech tools. Long-term approaches include process redesign, leadership training and embedding integration into team performance metrics.

- **Align integration efforts across the organisation**
  Explore how every stakeholder – from executives to frontline teams – can contribute to and benefit from integration. This section offers role-specific guidance on building buy-in, driving accountability and creating a culture where integrated ways of working become the norm.

Now let's bring Return on Integration to life.

RETURN ON INTEGRATION IN ACTION

To showcase the power of Return on Integration, you will explore companies that have broken down silos and aligned teams around shared goals. These case studies reveal how cross-functional collaboration, internal alignment and unified customer experiences drive innovation, agility and growth. Whether through integrated digital ecosystems, collaborative squads or omnichannel strategies, each example highlights how cohesion across departments enhances performance and strengthens brand impact.

MICROSOFT – DRIVING A UNIFIED CLOUD STRATEGY

Under CEO Satya Nadella's leadership, Microsoft underwent a strategic transformation that highlighted the importance of Return on Integration. The shift from a traditional software company to a 'cloud-first' organisation required cohesive collaboration across all departments. Teams within engineering, marketing, sales and customer support had to align their efforts to promote and support Microsoft Azure, the company's cloud computing platform. This meant developing cross-functional strategies where communication was streamlined and objectives were shared across different business units (Forbes, 2016).

The 'Microsoft Annual Report 2022' credits this cross-functional integration and shared objectives as key drivers behind Azure's rapid growth and Microsoft's increased market capitalisation (Microsoft, 2022). This example underscores how aligning an organisation around a central objective can accelerate growth and foster resilience.

Key takeaway: Microsoft's transformation into a cloud-first organisation illustrates the power of aligning teams around a shared objective. By integrating departments across engineering, marketing, sales and support, the company accelerated growth, enhanced resilience and drove long-term success through cohesive execution.

SOUTHWEST AIRLINES – A CULTURE OF COLLABORATIVE CUSTOMER SERVICE

Southwest Airlines has long demonstrated the power of Return on Integration by aligning its people, culture and processes around a shared purpose: delivering exceptional customer service. Rather than operating in silos, Southwest fosters a culture where collaboration, communication and cross-functional alignment are embedded into the everyday fabric of the organisation. This cultural cohesion drives leadership, strategy and coordination at every level (Fearless Culture, 2020).

Employees are empowered to speak up, align their work with the company's purpose and actively contribute to a supportive environment that enables fast, effective responses to customer needs. Physical office spaces are also intentionally designed to support this integration – departments are clustered together to promote chance encounters and open communication between teams, reinforcing the collaborative ethos (Human Synergistics, 2022). This cohesive, integrated culture doesn't just feel good, it delivers results. In 2024, J.D. Power ranked Southwest highest in customer satisfaction for the third year in a row, reflecting the tangible impact of its internal alignment on the customer experience (Business, 2025).

Key takeaway: Southwest's integrated approach to customer service demonstrates how a unified internal culture translates into exceptional external experiences. Seamless collaboration across departments ensures responsive, consistent service and has become a cornerstone of the airline's customer satisfaction and brand loyalty.

SPOTIFY – AGILE CROSS-FUNCTIONAL SQUADS

Spotify's success in the streaming industry is supported by its use of cross-functional squads. These autonomous, collaborative teams bring together employees from product development, marketing, engineering and data analytics to focus on specific projects or features. Each squad operates independently but aligns with Spotify's overarching mission of enhancing the audio streaming experience. This model has enabled rapid development cycles and continuous innovation (Atlassian, n.d.).

As of Q1 2025, Spotify had 268 million premium subscribers, reflecting a 12% year-over-year increase, and demonstrating how its integration strategy continues to drive market leadership and customer loyalty (Spotify, 2025).

Key takeaway: Spotify's use of agile, cross-functional squads enables rapid innovation and aligned execution across teams. This decentralised yet integrated model fosters collaboration, speeds up development and ensures that all initiatives are closely tied to the company's core mission of enhancing user experience.

LEGO – A UNIFIED APPROACH TO PRODUCT DEVELOPMENT

LEGO's resurgence from financial difficulties in the early 2000s to becoming one of the most beloved brands globally is attributed to a strong commitment to integration across teams and with its community. The LEGO Ideas platform exemplifies this approach, allowing fans to submit and vote on new product ideas. With over 2.8 million customers contributing more than 135,000 ideas, this open innovation model has generated significant revenue and deepened customer loyalty by integrating external input directly into product development (Sloan Review, 2023).

Internally, LEGO introduced a new leadership strategy under CEO Niels B. Christiansen, forming a non-hierarchical Working Group, with representatives from across the company, to define and embed a unified leadership model. This created stronger alignment with LEGO's values and strategy, integrating leadership comprehensively across all levels, not just top down (IMD, 2023).

Key takeaway: LEGO's collaborative model across design, marketing and engineering, along with community engagement through LEGO Ideas, shows how integration across internal and external stakeholders drives innovation and product-market fit, fuelling sustained brand growth and customer connection.

ATLASSIAN – LEVERAGING COLLABORATION TOOLS FOR INTERNAL INTEGRATION

Atlassian, the company behind tools like Jira, Confluence and Trello, practises what it preaches by using its own software to drive internal integration. Teams across the organisation use these platforms to manage projects, collaborate in real-time and share information transparently. This seamless communication fosters a culture where integration is part of daily operations. As a result, Atlassian has reported increased productivity and shorter project cycles, solidifying its reputation as a leader in software development (Atlassian, 2025).

Key takeaway: Atlassian exemplifies how internal integration can be driven by harnessing the right tools. By using its own platforms to facilitate real-time, transparent collaboration, the company has embedded integration into everyday operations, boosting productivity and organisational agility.

DOMINO'S - INTEGRATING DIGITAL PLATFORMS AND OPERATIONS FOR SEAMLESS SERVICE

Domino's has redefined the customer experience by tightly integrating its digital ordering platforms with in-store operations delivering a seamless, consistent service across all channels. This transformation required close alignment between technology, marketing, logistics and store operations, ensuring that innovations like app ordering, voice-activated purchases and real-time order tracking were backed by efficient, synchronised systems behind the scenes (Pivotize, 2024).

By leveraging data from digital interactions and store activity, Domino's delivers personalised promotions, faster service and a cohesive brand experience. In 2024, the company fulfilled 71.7 million orders – up 1.7% year-over-year – with delivery orders rising 2.4% and average delivery times hitting just 25 minutes, underscoring the effectiveness of its integrated model (Ceres, 2025).

Key takeaway: Domino's demonstrates how aligning technology, marketing, and operations can enhance convenience, streamline service and strengthen customer loyalty across digital and physical touchpoints.

HOW TO MEASURE SUCCESS WITHIN RETURN ON INTEGRATION

Measuring the impact of integration is essential to ensuring cross-functional alignment is driving real business value. By tracking both collaboration health and business performance, organisations can assess how well departments are working together, how integrated their systems and strategies are and how this unity contributes to customer satisfaction, operational efficiency and innovation. These metrics provide a foundation for evaluating progress and identifying areas for deeper alignment.

Cross-departmental collaboration metrics

Captures the frequency, quality and responsiveness of interactions between different departments. It reflects how well silos are being broken down and how effectively teams are working together on shared initiatives.

- **How to measure**: Use collaboration software such as Slack, Microsoft Teams and project management platforms to gather data on communication patterns, joint project completion and cross-team response times.
- **Indicators**: The number of collaborative projects completed, interdepartmental response times and qualitative feedback from cross-functional team members.
- **Insight**: High scores on these metrics often correlate with increased innovation rates, better knowledge-sharing and faster decision-making.

Employee engagement and satisfaction surveys

Measures how connected employees feel to the broader business, and how positively they view their collaboration with other teams. Integration isn't just a structural change, it's a cultural one, and employee sentiment is a critical indicator.

- **How to measure**: Conduct regular pulse surveys and annual engagement questionnaires. Focus on responses related to team cohesion, understanding of company goals and inter-departmental trust.
- **Key metrics**: Engagement levels, collaboration confidence and satisfaction with cross-functional communication.
- **Insight**: A rise in engagement scores typically indicates that employees feel more integrated into the organisation's larger objectives, fostering alignment and motivation.

Customer experience metrics (NPS and CSAT)

Integration should be felt not only inside the organisation, but also by customers. This metric assesses whether internal alignment translates into smoother, more consistent experiences across touchpoints.

- **How to measure**: Regularly collect NPS and CSAT scores and compare trends across functions or channels.
- **Data insights**: Cross-reference customer scores with internal collaboration data to identify links between service quality and team integration.
- **Benefits**: Higher customer scores often point to smoother internal coordination and a more cohesive service delivery – evidence that integration is being felt externally.

Operational efficiency indicators

These metrics track the impact of integration on delivery speed, project execution and overall responsiveness. True integration should eliminate delays and reduce duplication of effort across teams.

- **How to measure**: Use workflow tools to monitor time-to-market, project cycle times and cross-functional process completion.
- **Expected results**: Shorter project durations and reduced delays indicate well-integrated teams and streamlined systems.

- **Long-term value**: Sustained efficiency gains support cost savings, responsiveness and stronger market positioning.

Time-to-resolution for cross-functional challenges

Measures how quickly the organisation can resolve issues spanning multiple departments. A direct indicator of the strength of cross-team communication and alignment under pressure.

- **How to measure**: Implement tracking within project management software to log and analyse resolution times for complex, multi-team challenges.
- **Significance**: Faster issue resolution signals that collaboration structures are working and team alignment is high.
- **Follow-up**: Regular review of these metrics can uncover patterns or bottlenecks and support continuous improvement.

Revenue growth from integrated initiatives

Ties integration to commercial impact by measuring how much revenue is generated through cross-functional efforts. Reflects how well collaboration is being leveraged to deliver market-facing outcomes.

- **How to measure**: Attribute revenue streams to initiatives involving multiple departments, such as product launches, bundled services or sales campaigns. Use revenue tracking dashboards or project-based attribution.
- **KPI examples**: Revenue uplift from joint offerings, increase in customer value from integrated services or growth tied to cross-functional strategic plays.
- **Strategic value**: Demonstrates that Return on Integration contributes not just to alignment, but to measurable business performance and competitive advantage.

Together, these metrics offer a well-rounded picture of integration success – from internal alignment to customer outcomes. Monitoring progress across collaboration, engagement, service consistency and financial performance allows organisations to continuously refine their integration efforts. Over time, these insights ensure that integration isn't a one-off initiative, but an embedded capability that supports agility, resilience and long-term strategic growth.

IMPLEMENTING RETURN ON INTEGRATION

Achieving organisational alignment requires both quick, tactical actions and long-term structural shifts that break down silos and promote shared ownership. Quick wins create momentum by encouraging collaboration, improving communication and fostering cross-functional visibility. Long-term strategies ensure integration is embedded in the company's leadership, systems and culture. When teams are connected through a shared purpose and supported by the right processes, integration becomes a strategic advantage that drives innovation, efficiency and collective success.

Quick wins

1. **Host regular cross-departmental brainstorming sessions**
   Encourage integration and collaboration by organising regular brainstorming sessions that bring together employees from different departments to discuss challenges or new initiatives. These sessions help generate creative solutions, foster inter-team relationships and build momentum toward a more integrated organisational culture.

2. **Introduce a shared collaboration platform**
   Implement a digital collaboration tool like Microsoft Teams, Slack or Asana to centralise communication and project management. When properly introduced and supported with

training, these platforms improve transparency, reduce the need for emails and meetings, and enable teams to collaborate more efficiently and in real time.

3. **Establish short-term cross-functional projects**

   Kickstart integration by launching short-term projects that require input from multiple departments. Select manageable initiatives that can be completed in a few weeks and involve at least two or three teams. Successful execution of these projects can serve as proof of concept for broader integration efforts and build trust across functions.

4. **Implement an open-door policy for interdepartmental queries**

   Encourage transparency and accessibility by allowing employees to bring cross-functional questions or collaboration ideas directly to managers. Establishing regular time slots or open forums for interdepartmental dialogue promotes a culture of openness and helps resolve cross-functional challenges more quickly.

5. **Initiate recognition programmes for collaborative achievements**

   Celebrate effective cross-departmental teamwork by creating a recognition programme that highlights individuals or teams who excel in collaborative efforts. Whether through awards like 'Integration Champion' or public acknowledgment in internal communications, recognising collaborative achievements reinforces the importance of integration and motivates broader participation.

Long-term strategies

1. **Develop a unified knowledge base**
   Create a centralised, easily accessible repository for resources, project templates, success stories and lessons learned from cross-functional collaborations. Using platforms like SharePoint or Confluence, this shared hub reduces duplication, ensures knowledge is retained and enables all teams to build on past initiatives for greater efficiency.

2. **Embed cross-functional collaboration into performance reviews**
   Incorporate metrics related to teamwork and collaboration into employee performance evaluations to encourage active participation in integration efforts. This reinforces the strategic importance of working across departments and helps employees recognise how collaboration contributes to their development and success.

3. **Invest in leadership training focused on integration**
   Provide targeted training to equip leaders with the skills needed to champion cross-departmental collaboration. Whether through in-house workshops or external experts, these programmes ensure leaders can foster integration effectively, set the tone for a collaborative culture and support cross-functional teamwork.

4. **Foster cross-functional rotational programmes**
   Implement rotational programmes that allow employees to work temporarily in different departments. This hands-on exposure helps build empathy, breaks down silos and enhances communication – ultimately creating a more

adaptable, informed and connected workforce aligned around shared goals.

5. **Continuously review and adapt integration processes**
   Establish regular (quarterly or biannual) reviews of your integration efforts to gather feedback from all levels of the organisation. These reviews help assess what's working, identify opportunities for improvement and ensure that integration strategies evolve alongside the organisation's needs and growth trajectory.

Driving engagement at every level

For executives and senior leadership:

- **Leadership alignment**: Executives must ensure that the company's vision, mission and strategic objectives are clearly communicated and embraced across all departments. This crucial alignment helps create a culture where every team understands their role in contributing to the company's overarching goals. Leadership should act as role models, consistently demonstrating a commitment to collaboration and integration.
- **Resource allocation for collaboration**: Prioritise investments in tools, technology and training programmes that foster cross-departmental integration. Executives should consider integration not just as an operational necessity but as a strategic priority that can drive sustainable growth and long-term success.
- **Foster a unified culture**: Develop initiatives that strengthen company culture, promoting values that emphasise teamwork, transparency and collective success. Executives need to champion policies that encourage teams to collaborate, share knowledge and contribute to each other's goals.

For operational managers:

- **Facilitate cross-functional projects**: Managers play a pivotal role in breaking down silos by actively encouraging their teams to engage in projects that require cross-departmental input. This practice helps build familiarity and trust across functions, leading to more effective collaboration.
- **Empower decision-making**: Allow team members more autonomy to collaborate with other departments and make decisions that benefit the organisation. Managers should act as facilitators, removing barriers that hinder team integration.
- **Regular check-ins and feedback loops**: Implement regular cross-departmental meetings or check-ins to assess ongoing projects and alignment. Open communication between teams ensures that everyone stays informed and that any potential issues are addressed proactively.

For employees:

- **Understand your role in the bigger picture**: Employees should be encouraged to see beyond their specific job functions and understand how their work contributes to the organisation's broader goals. This perspective fosters a sense of shared purpose and motivation.
- **Engage in cross-training opportunities**: Take advantage of any cross-training programmes or collaborative projects that offer exposure to other departments. This not only builds new skills but also enhances relationships across the company.
- **Proactive participation**: Employees should be empowered to contribute ideas and provide feedback during collaborative projects. When individuals feel heard and involved, they are more likely to be engaged and motivated.

By embedding integration into every layer of the organisation, businesses can eliminate silos, strengthen collaboration and unlock more efficient, aligned and future-ready operations.

THE LASTING IMPACT OF RETURN ON INTEGRATION

Return on Integration is more than a management philosophy, it's a strategic imperative that drives alignment, agility and sustainable growth. In today's fast-moving business landscape, the ability to unify departments around a common mission enables companies to move faster, collaborate better and deliver a more consistent and impactful customer experience.

This chapter has shown how integration enhances both internal operations and external outcomes. From Microsoft's cloud-first transformation to Spotify's agile squads and LEGO's post-crisis recovery, the companies leading in integration have made it a core part of their business model. They demonstrate that when teams collaborate across silos – with shared goals, open communication and mutual accountability – innovation accelerates, customer experiences improve and the business becomes more resilient.

Integrated organisations are also better equipped to respond to change. Whether navigating economic disruption, evolving customer expectations or technological shifts, teams that are aligned and connected can pivot quickly and act with clarity.

Of course, integration doesn't happen by accident – it requires intention, investment and cultural commitment. Leaders must actively model collaboration, managers must facilitate cross-functional teamwork, and employees must see how their contributions support the bigger picture. Embedding integration into performance reviews, training programmes and shared systems helps make it part of how the organisation operates every day.

Quick wins like cross-departmental brainstorming, knowledge sharing platforms or joint performance goals can spark early momentum. Long-term strategies – such as rotational programmes, leadership development focused on collaboration and regular reviews of integration effectiveness – ensure momentum lasts.

When integration becomes part of the organisational DNA, businesses unlock the full potential of their people, systems and strategy. The result is a company that doesn't just function more efficiently, it thrives through alignment, trust and collective purpose.

TAKE ACTION

Start small: identify one team, project or process where greater collaboration could make an immediate difference. From cross-functional initiatives to shared goals, even small steps can build momentum.

Integration thrives when it's visible, intentional and supported from the top. Lead by example, break down silos and make collaboration part of how your business works – not just a value on paper.

Return on Integration isn't a one-off initiative – it's a mindset that creates stronger teams, smarter decisions and more resilient businesses.

REFERENCES

Atlassian (2025) 'Customer Stories', Atlassian. Available at: www.atlassian.com/customers (Accessed: 3 May 2025).

Atlassian (n.d.) 'The Spotify Model for Scaling Agile', Atlassian Agile Coach. Available at: www.atlassian.com/agile/agile-at-scale/spotify (Accessed: 3 May 2025).

Business.com (2025) 'What Your Business Can Learn From Southwest Airlines', Business.com. Available at: www.business.com/articles/southwest-airlines-great-customer-service/ (Accessed: 3 May 2025).

Ceres (2025) 'Domino's Bets on Expansion Despite Sluggish Start to 2025', Ceres Shop Blog, 2 May. Available at: www.ceres.shop/blog/dominos-bets-on-expansion-despite-sluggish-start-to-2025/ (Accessed: 3 May 2025).

Fearless Culture (2020) 'Southwest Airlines Culture Design Puts Employees First', Fearless Culture, 12 January. Available at: www.fearlessculture.design/blog-posts/southwest-airlines-culture-design-canvas (Accessed: 3 May 2025).

Forbes (2016) 'Microsoft is marching ahead in its cloud-first, mobile-first journey', Forbes, 2 April. Available at: www.forbes.com/sites/janakirammsv/2016/04/02/microsoft-is-marching-ahead-in-its-cloud-first-mobile-first-journey/ (Accessed: 4 May 2025).

Human Synergistics (2022) 'Southwest Airlines Reveals 5 Culture Lessons', Culture University, 24 June. Available at: www.humansynergistics.com/blog/culture-university/2022/06/24/southwest-airlines-reveals-5-culture-lessons/ (Accessed: 3 May 2025).

IMD (2023) 'Building a New Strategy, Top-Down and Middle-Out', IMD Business School, 24 April. Available at: www.imd.org/research-knowledge/leadership/articles/building-a-new-strategy-top-down-and-middle-out/ (Accessed: 3 May 2025).

Microsoft (2022) 'Microsoft Annual Report 2022'. Available at: www.microsoft.com/investor/reports/ar22/index.html (Accessed: 3 May 2025).

Panopto (2023) 'Valuing Workplace Knowledge'. Available at: www.panopto.com/resource/ebook/valuing-workplace-knowledge/ (Accessed: 4 May 2025).

Pivotize (2024) 'Successful Digital Transformation Case Studies: How Domino's Pizza Became a Tech-Driven Leader'. Available at: www.pivotizett.com/blog/successful-digital-transformation-case-studies-how-dominos-pizza-became-a-tech-driven-leader (Accessed: 3 May 2025).

Sloan Review (2023) 'Lego Takes Customers' Innovations Further', MIT Sloan Management Review, 12 September. Available at: www.sloanreview.mit.edu/article/lego-takes-customers-innovations-further/ (Accessed: 3 May 2025).

Spotify (2025) 'Spotify Reports First Quarter 2025 Earnings', Spotify Newsroom, 29 April. Available at: www.newsroom.spotify.com/2025-04-29/spotify-reports-first-quarter-2025-earnings/ (Accessed: 3 May 2025).

CHAPTER 12

RUTHLESS PRIORITISATION – LEVERAGING NEW ROIS FOR STRATEGIC GROWTH

INTRODUCING RUTHLESS PRIORITISATION

In today's fast-paced, opportunity-rich world, businesses are under constant pressure to grow, innovate and respond to change. The challenge isn't a lack of ideas – it's having too many. From launching new products and entering new markets to investing in technology and improving service, leaders face endless competing demands. The real skill lies not in doing more, but in choosing what matters most.

This is where ruthless prioritisation becomes a strategic imperative.

Ruthless prioritisation is the disciplined practise of focusing your resources – time, money and talent – on the initiatives that will deliver the greatest long-term value. It's not about playing it safe or ignoring opportunities. It's about having the clarity and conviction to say no to good ideas so you can say yes to the right ones.

Some of the world's most successful companies, like Apple, Microsoft and Google, are defined not by how much they do, but by how well they focus. They make bold decisions, align their teams and commit to doing fewer things, better.

A powerful example of ruthless prioritisation is Steve Jobs' return to Apple in 1997. At the time, the company was struggling under a bloated product line and declining performance. Jobs implemented a radical focus on core products, cutting Apple's offerings down to just four main products – two desktops and two portables, each tailored for either consumers or professionals. This decisive move helped Apple return to its core mission and recover from significant financial losses. It also set the foundation for Apple's enduring strategy: do fewer things, and do them exceptionally well (Inc, 2023).

Throughout this book, we've introduced 11 new Return on Investment lenses – measures like Return on Innovation, Return on Insight, Return on Inclusion, and more. This penultimate chapter brings these metrics together to form a powerful framework for prioritisation. By using these 11 ROIs as decision-making tools, organisations can evaluate which initiatives are most aligned with their strategy, customer needs and long-term goals.

You'll explore how ruthless prioritisation fuels sustainable growth, sharpens focus, improves cross-functional alignment and protects your most valuable resource: attention.

LEVERAGING RUTHLESS PRIORITISATION

By the end of this chapter, you will have a clear understanding of how to implement and sustain ruthless prioritisation across your organisation. You'll gain strategic clarity, practical tools and a repeatable framework for aligning your decisions with long-term value creation, not just short-term wins. Whether you're choosing between competing initiatives, reallocating resources or refocusing your team, this chapter will equip you to:

- **Maximise the strategic value of ruthless prioritisation**
  Understand how focus becomes a competitive advantage
  in a fast-moving, opportunity-rich environment. Ruthless
  prioritisation allows businesses to cut through noise, eliminate
  distractions and commit to initiatives that drive the most
  meaningful returns – financially, operationally and culturally.
  When done well, it protects organisational energy and directs
  it toward what matters most.

- **Build the core framework for prioritisation**
  Discover the essential components of effective prioritisation:
  a clear North Star objective, transparent decision-making
  criteria, cross-functional alignment and the discipline to say
  no. You'll learn how to build a system that helps your teams
  focus, execute and adapt quickly to evolving business needs –
  without losing sight of long-term strategy.

- **Use the 11 new ROIs as strategic filters**
  Leverage the 11 new metrics introduced in this book
  – Inspiration, Integrity, Inclusion, Image, Interaction,
  Intervention, Involvement, Improvements, Insight,
  Innovation and Integration – as decision-making filters.
  These ROIs allow you to assess which ideas are worth
  pursuing, which need refinement and which should be
  deprioritised, based on how well they support your vision,
  customers and values.

- **Implement best practices from leading organisations**
  Explore how companies like Microsoft and LEGO have
  achieved transformative results by narrowing their focus and
  doubling down on business goals. These examples demonstrate
  that prioritisation isn't about cutting back – it's about moving
  forward with greater intention and alignment.

- **Measure and sustain prioritisation over time**
  Build a measurement framework to assess the impact of
  your prioritisation efforts. Learn how to use prioritisation
  scorecards, ROI alignment tools and regular review cadences
  to keep your strategy agile, transparent and responsive. With
  the right systems in place, ruthless prioritisation becomes a
  cultural habit – not a one-time event.

SUCCESSES AND FAILURES IN PRIORITISATION

Prioritisation isn't just about choosing what to do – it's about having the
discipline to say no to distractions, even profitable ones. The following
case studies show the outcomes when companies get that balance right, or
disastrously wrong.

From Microsoft's bold pivot to cloud to Kodak's failure to act on its own innovation, these case studies reveal a simple truth: what you prioritise determines whether you grow, survive or fall behind.

Each example highlights how the strategic use, or neglect, of key ROIs can make or break a business.

MICROSOFT - PRIORITISING THE FUTURE OVER THE FAMILIAR

When Satya Nadella became CEO in 2014, Microsoft was seen as a fading tech giant. Rather than defending legacy products, he made a bold pivot by prioritising cloud and mobile as Microsoft's future. He dissolved the Windows division, restructured around innovation and scrapped the toxic stack-ranking system that had fostered internal competition.

Nadella fostered a culture of collaboration through initiatives like the Microsoft Hackathon and a partner-positive approach, backing the shift with major acquisitions like LinkedIn. Within five years, Microsoft hit a $1 trillion valuation, yet Nadella warned that complacency, not competition, would be the real threat (NOBL, 2020).

Key takeaway: Ruthless prioritisation demands clarity, cultural change and full alignment around the future.

KODAK - PRIORITISING PROFIT OVER PROGRESS

Kodak's story is a cautionary tale of what happens when short-term gain outranks long-term growth. In 1975, Kodak engineers invented the first digital camera. But the innovation never saw the light of day – not because it didn't work, but because it threatened the company's highly profitable film business (New York Times, 2015).

Leadership failed to prioritise emerging customer needs and instead doubled down on their legacy model. As digital photography transformed the industry, Kodak clung to the past. By the time it attempted to catch up, rivals had already taken the lead (Forbes, 2012).

This wasn't just a technology miss, it was a failure of Return on Insight and Return on Innovation. Kodak had the data and the early warning signs, but ignored them.

Key takeaway: Without customer-centric prioritisation, even the most innovative companies can become obsolete. Kodak chose to protect margins instead of preparing for change and paid the price as a result.

LEGO - REBUILDING A LEGACY WITH STRATEGIC FOCUS

In the early 2000s, LEGO was on the brink of collapse. The company had overextended itself into video games, clothing lines and theme parks, losing sight of its core offering. But a decisive strategy shift turned things around. LEGO made a conscious choice to prioritise fewer, high-impact initiatives, namely by reconnecting with its customers and reinvesting in product innovation. One of its smartest moves was launching LEGO Ideas, a platform inviting fans to submit and vote on new LEGO set concepts. The best creative suggestions are made into real products (The Guardian, 2017).

This focused approach exemplifies Return on Involvement and Return on Innovation. By choosing depth over breadth, LEGO rebuilt trust, regained relevance and returned to profitability. Today, it stands as one of the world's most admired brands, having topped the Global RepTrak®100 ranking for the third year in a row and five times in the past six years (LEGO Group, 2025).

Key takeaway: LEGO's revival wasn't about doing more – it was about doing less, better. Prioritising customer engagement and co-creation helped rebuild a brand once considered outdated.

NOKIA - PARALYSED BY THE FEAR OF CHANGE

Once the global leader in mobile phones, Nokia's fall was swift and dramatic. While rivals were prioritising the smartphone revolution, Nokia stayed committed to its outdated Symbian operating system and a hardware-first approach. Innovation was deprioritised in favour of protecting existing market share. Leadership hesitated to adapt, not because they lacked awareness, but because they lacked the willingness to prioritise transformation over stability. Meanwhile, Apple and Samsung surged ahead with seamless UX, app ecosystems and relentless iteration (NMG International, 2023).

Nokia's resistance to Return on Innovation and its failure to align around a forward-looking strategy – Return on Integration – ultimately led to its exit from the smartphone market it once dominated.

Key takeaway: Being the market leader means nothing if you prioritise preservation over progress. Nokia had the resources, but not the resolve.

USING THE 11 ROIS AS STRATEGIC FILTERS

The 11 new ROIs introduced throughout this book provide a comprehensive lens through which to evaluate and prioritise competing initiatives. These aren't just modern metrics, they're strategic filters that help organisations identify which projects will deliver the most meaningful returns across employee experience, customer trust, operational performance and long-term growth.

By combining strategic reasoning with key questions, organisations can use each ROI to evaluate which initiatives are most aligned with long-term success. Here's how each ROI can be used to guide prioritisation:

People and culture

- **Return on Inspiration:** Prioritise initiatives that inspire and engage employees, as motivated teams are more productive and creative.
  Questions: Will an initiative inspire and engage your employees? Does it create opportunities for growth, creativity or leadership?

- **Return on Integrity:** Focus on projects that reinforce ethical practices and transparency. Building trust with customers and stakeholders drives loyalty and long-term resilience.
  Questions: Does a project reinforce your values and build trust with stakeholders? Will it increase transparency, ethical standards or customer confidence?

- **Return on Inclusion:** Invest in initiatives that promote diversity and inclusivity, both within the workforce and in how you serve your customers.
  Questions: Will this strategy help you become more inclusive and representative? Does it allow you to better reflect and serve a broader community?

Customer experience and brand

- **Return on Image:** Prioritise efforts that align with brand values and demonstrate social responsibility, enhancing reputation and customer relationships.
  Questions: Will this effort strengthen your brand reputation and sense of purpose? Does it align with customer expectations around responsibility and impact?

- **Return on Interaction:** Focus on improving customer touchpoints across all channels to build seamless, intuitive and loyalty-driving experiences.
  Questions: Will this plan improve how customers interact with you across channels? Is the experience more seamless, consistent and intuitive?

- **Return on Intervention:** Implement strategies that address and solve customer pain points quickly and empathetically, improving satisfaction and retention.

Questions: Will this focus solve a customer pain point or address issues early? Are you proactively delivering value and reducing friction?

- **Return on Involvement:** Personalise customer interactions and messaging to foster deeper engagement and emotional connection.
  Questions: Will this change create a more meaningful and personalised engagement? Are you tailoring content, service or communication based on insights?

Operations and strategy

- **Return on Improvements:** Shift focus from one-off transactions to delivering ongoing value that builds long-term customer relationships.
  Questions: Will this change move you from one-off transactions to continuous service? Does it offer long-term value beyond the initial purchase?

- **Return on Insight:** Prioritise initiatives that generate actionable intelligence to support faster, more informed decisions.
  Questions: Are you using this initiative to generate actionable intelligence? Does it support better, faster and more data-informed decision-making?

- **Return on Innovation:** Focus on fostering a culture of continuous improvement and future-focused thinking to stay ahead of the curve.
  Questions: Does this drive help you evolve, differentiate or stay ahead of the curve? Are you fostering new ideas that meet changing customer needs?

- **Return on Integration:** Ensure collaboration across departments to create synergy, reduce silos and enable smoother execution of strategy.
  Questions: Will this alignment improve how teams work together toward shared goals? Does it promote collaboration, and system-wide efficiency?

By asking these questions across each ROI, businesses can apply a structured and consistent lens to decision-making, ensuring they prioritise initiatives that truly move the business forward.

IMPLEMENTING RUTHLESS PRIORITISATION: A FRAMEWORK FOR ACTION

Knowing what matters is just the start. Embedding ruthless prioritisation into everyday operations requires a structured, repeatable process – one that's understood and applied consistently across departments. This section outlines a practical framework to help your team implement, apply and sustain prioritisation at scale.

To embed ruthless prioritisation into your organisation's culture and operations, you need more than just good intentions, you need a clear, consistent framework and a practical set of tools. This section outlines a step-by-step approach to making prioritisation a day-to-day habit, not just a leadership exercise.

The prioritisation framework

1. **Define the North Star objective:** Start by aligning the business around a clear, strategic goal, whether that's improving customer retention, expanding market share or becoming a more purpose-

led brand. This objective becomes the filter through which all initiatives are assessed.

2. **Assess ROI alignment:** Evaluate each proposed initiative through the lens of the 11 strategic ROIs. Consider which returns are most critical to your current strategy and assess how well each initiative delivers against them.

3. **Score and compare initiatives:** Use a prioritisation scorecard (see opposite) to compare options based on impact, resource demand and speed to value. This allows for transparent, objective decision-making.

4. **Allocate resources accordingly:** Direct time, budget and talent toward high-priority initiatives that align with your strategic goal and multiple ROIs. Place lower-ranking ideas on a backlog or deprioritise entirely.

5. **Review and refine regularly:** Set regular checkpoints to reassess priorities as market conditions, customer needs and internal capacity evolve. Prioritisation is not a one-off, it's an ongoing discipline.

6. **Communicate the 'why':** For prioritisation to succeed, teams need to understand the rationale behind what's being prioritised, and what's not. Clearly explaining the 'why' builds alignment, transparency and commitment across the organisation.

The prioritisation scorecard

Once your team has assessed initiatives through the 11 ROIs, the next step is to evaluate and compare them. The prioritisation scorecard is a simple but powerful tool to score each initiative based on ROI alignment, impact, resource requirement and speed to value.

Initiative	Strategic ROIs Aligned	Impact Score (1–5)	Resource Requirement	Speed to Value	Priority Level
Launch Customer App	Innovation, Interaction, Insight	5	Medium	High	High
Expand Product Line	Image, Inclusion	3	High	Medium	Medium
Upgrade CRM	Involvement, Integration, Insight	4	Medium	Medium	High
Sustainability Campaign	Image, Integrity	3	Low	Long-term	Medium

This scorecard helps bring consistency and objectivity to the process, surfacing high-impact initiatives and revealing distractions that can be deprioritised.

Embedding prioritisation across the organisation

For prioritisation to succeed, it must be adopted across the organisation – not just at the top. This section offers role-specific guidance for ensuring every team, from leadership to frontline, plays their part in maintaining clarity, focus and aligned execution.

For executives and senior leadership:

- **Align priorities with strategic objectives:** Leaders must ensure that resources, time and investments are focused on initiatives that deliver the most significant business and customer impact.
- **Foster a culture of ruthless prioritisation:** Encouraging teams to focus on what truly matters prevents inefficiencies and ensures the organisation remains agile and adaptable.
- **Make data-driven decisions:** Using insights and key performance metrics helps leaders evaluate which projects or initiatives should take precedence.

For operational managers:

- **Streamline processes to eliminate inefficiencies:** Identifying and removing bottlenecks ensures that teams are focusing their efforts on high-value activities.
- **Ensure cross-functional alignment:** Departments must collaborate and avoid duplication of effort, ensuring that prioritisation is consistent across the organisation.
- **Continuously assess and adjust priorities:** Business needs evolve and managers must regularly review initiatives to ensure focus remains on what drives the greatest impact.

For marketing and sales teams:

- **Prioritise high-impact customer engagement strategies:** Marketing efforts should focus on the channels, messaging and campaigns that drive the best results.
- **Use customer insights to refine efforts:** Understanding customer preferences and behaviours helps teams focus on initiatives that generate the highest return.
- **Avoid spreading resources too thin:** Focusing on fewer, more impactful marketing and sales initiatives leads to better results than trying to execute too many campaigns at once.

For customer experience and support teams:

- **Focus on resolving the most critical customer issues:** Prioritising common pain points and high-impact service improvements leads to better customer satisfaction.
- **Ensure frontline teams have the right tools and training:** Empowering employees with the knowledge and resources to handle key priorities improves efficiency and service quality.

- **Use feedback loops to refine priorities:** Regularly reviewing customer feedback helps teams adjust their focus to address the most pressing concerns.

Quick wins

- **Pilot programmes:** Start by implementing a small-scale version of a high-priority project to assess feasibility and gather feedback.
- **Employee workshops:** Conduct workshops to foster a shared understanding of the North Star objective and how prioritisation supports it.
- **Customer feedback loops:** Implement systems to gather quick feedback from customers and use it to refine ongoing initiatives.

Long-term strategies

- **Develop a prioritisation framework:** Create a decision-making framework that integrates the 11 ROIs for evaluating future projects.
- **Build cross-departmental teams:** Foster collaboration across departments to ensure integrated efforts toward shared goals.
- **Invest in technology:** Use advanced tools for data analysis and project management that support prioritisation and align with customer-centric goals.
- **Continuous training:** Develop ongoing training programmes to reinforce the importance of prioritisation and equip employees with the skills to contribute effectively. These should protect focus, sharpen strategy and deliver meaningful, measurable outcomes.

When prioritisation becomes part of your organisational DNA, it protects your focus, sharpens your strategy and drives sustained, meaningful success.

MEASURING THE SUCCESS OF RUTHLESS PRIORITISATION

To effectively track whether your prioritisation is delivering strategic value, measure outcomes against the relevant Return on Investment (ROI) metrics introduced in earlier chapters. The following table summarises key high-level metrics for regularly tracking prioritisation effectiveness, directly linking back to the detailed ROI frameworks covered in this book:

Strategic Area	Key Metrics (High-Level)	Related Detailed ROI Metrics (See Chapter)
Customer Impact	Customer Satisfaction (CSAT), Net Promoter Score (NPS), Customer Lifetime Value (CLV)	Return on Interaction, Intervention, Improvements, Involvement (Chapters 5–8)
People & Culture	Employee Engagement Scores, Retention & Promotion Rates	Return on Inspiration, Inclusion, Integrity (Chapters 1–3)
Innovation & Growth	Revenue from New Products, Innovation Pipeline Health	Return on Innovation (Chapter 10)
Brand & Trust	Brand Sentiment, Customer Trust Index, Social Responsibility Scores	Return on Image, Integrity (Chapters 2 and 4)
Operational Efficiency	Process Efficiency, Cross-Functional Project Success Rate	Return on Integration, Insight (Chapters 9 and 11)

Regularly revisit these metrics in leadership and team meetings, referring back to the detailed chapters when deeper measurement analysis or strategic adjustments are necessary.

THE LASTING IMPACT OF RUTHLESS PRIORITISATION

Ruthless prioritisation, when aligned with the 11 new ROIs, can transform an organisation from one that merely survives to one that thrives. By focusing on initiatives that maximise customer lifetime value, improve employee engagement and foster innovation, businesses can ensure they are building a sustainable future. This approach requires disciplined decision-making, clear communication and a willingness to adapt. The long-term rewards are well worth the effort: enhanced customer relationships, stronger brand loyalty and sustainable growth.

But prioritisation doesn't end with a decision, it continues with the impact. The true test of whether your priorities are working lies in what they deliver. Use the 11 ROIs to revisit and reassess regularly. Are you seeing movement where it matters? Whether in customer satisfaction, innovation, inclusion or operational efficiency, these lenses help you track performance with intention, and adjust when needed.

In the end, ruthless prioritisation isn't just about what you start. It's about what you sustain. And when done well, it becomes not only a way to make decisions – but a way to lead.

TAKE ACTION

Now that you've explored ruthless prioritisation and the 11 new ROIs, it's time to put clarity into practice. Start by choosing one initiative that aligns strongly with your strategic goals and promises significant impact.

Engage your team in a prioritisation exercise using these new ROIs as your guide. Openly discuss which initiatives to prioritise, and which to pause or stop, ensuring your resources focus on creating measurable value.

Remember, prioritisation is about choosing what matters most, aligning your teams and committing fully. Start today and lead your organisation toward sustainable growth.

REFERENCES

Forbes (2012) 'How Kodak failed'. Forbes, 18 January. Available at: www.forbes.com/sites/chunkamui/2012/01/18/how-kodak-failed/ (Accessed: 3 May 2025).

Guardian (2017) 'How Lego clicked: the super brand that reinvented itself'. *Guardian*, 4 June. Available at: www.theguardian.com/lifeandstyle/2017/jun/04/how-lego-clicked-the-super-brand-that-reinvented-itself (Accessed: 3 May 2025).

Inc. (2023) '25 years ago, Steve Jobs saved Apple from collapse'. Inc.com. Available at: .inc.com/nick-hobson/25-years-ago-steve-jobs-saved-apple-from-collapse-its-a-lesson-for-every-tech-ceo-today.htm (Accessed: 3 May 2025).

LEGO Group (2025) 'LEGO Group named world's most reputable company in 2025 Global RepTrak®100'. Available at: www.lego.com/zh-cn/aboutus/news/2025/april/reptrak-2025 (Accessed: 3 May 2025).

New York Times (2015) 'Kodak's first digital moment'. *New York Times*, 12 August. Available at: www.archive.nytimes.com/lens.blogs.nytimes.com/2015/08/12/kodaks-first-digital-moment/ (Accessed: 3 May 2025).

NMG International (2023) 'Corporate history: the fall of Nokia'. Available at: www.nmg-international.com/post/corporate-history-the-fall-of-nokia (Accessed: 3 May 2025).

NOBL (2020) 'How Satya Nadella led Microsoft through a corporate turnaround'. Available at: www.nobl.io/changemaker/how-satya-nadella-led-microsoft-through-a-corporate-turnaround/ (Accessed: 3 May 2025).

CHAPTER 13
LEADING THE WAY – THE ROLE OF THE CEO IN REDEFINING SUCCESS

INTRODUCING THE NEW ERA OF LEADERSHIP

What does it take to lead a business when success is no longer defined by profit alone?

This chapter explores the evolving role of leadership in delivering the new ROIs outlined throughout this book. While the CEO role is used as a reference point, this chapter is for anyone in a leadership position – founders, executives, department heads or change agents – who play a role in shaping culture, setting priorities and driving performance. Embedding these new ROIs into the DNA of a business isn't just the responsibility of the person at the top, it's a collective leadership challenge.

In a marketplace shaped by rising customer expectations, empowered employees and growing demands for accountability, leadership must do more than deliver results. It must set the tone for trust, model inclusivity and create space for continuous improvement. Modern leaders are not only responsible for performance – they are responsible for relevance.

The traditional CEO mandate of maximising profit and shareholder value is no longer enough. Today's most impactful leaders foster connection, empower people and align commercial goals with cultural values. They build organisations where people thrive, customers feel seen and innovation becomes a habit, not a project.

This chapter explores the essential skills, behaviours and cultural mindsets needed to bring the new ROIs to life – from Return on Inspiration to Return on Integration. Through case studies and leadership examples from both global brands and mission-led startups, you will explore what it looks like to lead for both today and tomorrow.

Because in the end, these new ways of measuring success are only as powerful as the people willing to lead through them.

LEVERAGING THE NEW ERA OF LEADERSHIP

By the end of this chapter, you'll be equipped to bring the new ROIs to life – not just in strategy decks, but in everyday leadership. You'll explore how to lead with relevance, build trust at scale and create a culture where the values you stand for are measured and delivered in everything you do. This chapter will equip you to:

- **Lead with clarity, courage and vision**
  Understand the essential qualities modern leaders need to navigate complexity, inspire belief and drive long-term impact – from strategic foresight to empathetic communication.

- **Turn cultural values into operational drivers**
  Learn how to embed trust, inclusion, transparency and continuous learning into the way your organisation works, not just what it says.

- **Adopt leadership models that scale impact**
  Discover proven frameworks that help align people, purpose and performance across departments, regions and roles.

- **Learn from those who've led change – and those who didn't**
  Explore real-world case studies of leaders who successfully delivered on the new ROIs, and cautionary tales from those who failed to adapt.

- **Activate leadership at every level**
  Whether you're a CEO, founder or head of function, gain practical, actionable strategies to shape culture, set direction and create alignment around what matters most.

Because success today isn't just about leading from the front – it's about leading the shift.

LEADERSHIP IN ACTION

Essential skills for CEOs to deliver on new ROIs

Leading through the lens of the new ROIs calls for a different kind of leadership – one that's agile, people-focused and purpose-led. In this section, you will explore the key skills modern leaders need to navigate change, build trust and drive meaningful, measurable progress.

- **Strategic vision and adaptability**

   Strategic vision is the ability to anticipate market shifts and adapt company goals to align with new opportunities. CEOs must possess an acute awareness of industry trends, customer behaviour and emerging technologies to stay ahead. This skill enables them to create long-term strategies that incorporate the principles of customer-centric ROIs.

   Adaptability complements strategic vision by allowing CEOs to pivot when market dynamics change. CEOs must be open to experimentation and flexible in their approaches to incorporating new insights and practices. This is especially important in achieving returns, such as Return on Innovation and Return on Insight, where continuous improvement and quick adaptation are critical.

CASE EXAMPLE: SATYA NADELLA - MICROSOFT

Satya Nadella's leadership at Microsoft is a standout example of strategic vision and adaptability. He steered the company from a product-centric legacy to a cloud-first, inclusive organisation – recognising the growing importance of services, customer experience and collaboration. By embedding a culture of continuous learning and embracing changing market dynamics, Nadella positioned Microsoft for sustained relevance and growth in the evolving tech landscape (NOBL, 2020).

- **Empathetic communication and active listening**
  Empathetic communication is essential for building trust,
  both internally and externally. CEOs need to engage in active
  listening – understanding employee concerns, customer
  feedback and stakeholder perspectives – to lead effectively. This
  is particularly relevant to achieving Return on Integrity and
  Return on Inclusion, as it demonstrates that leadership values
  transparency and the voices of all stakeholders.

CASE EXAMPLE: HOWARD SCHULTZ – STARBUCKS

Howard Schultz's return to Starbucks as CEO was marked by his
commitment to revitalising the company culture and reconnecting with
both employees and customers. By listening to baristas and gathering
feedback from loyal customers, Schultz reinstated Starbucks' focus on
customer experience and employee satisfaction, ultimately revitalising
the company's brand and financial performance (Schultz, 2011).

- **Decision-making rooted in data and intuition**
  Effective CEOs combine data-driven decision-making with
  intuitive leadership. This hybrid approach allows them to
  evaluate customer insights, market analytics and operational
  data while trusting their instincts to make bold moves when
  needed. For example, delivering a strong Return on Insight
  requires not only having the data but also acting on it to
  improve offerings and strategies.

CASE EXAMPLE: REED HASTINGS – NETFLIX

Reed Hastings leveraged data to predict viewing habits and create
original content that resonated with audiences. However, Hastings'
intuitive understanding of shifting viewer preferences and the importance

of streaming led Netflix to pivot from being a DVD rental service to a streaming giant, positioning the company for sustained growth and customer loyalty (Quartr, 2024).

What smaller business leaders teach us about redefining success

In addition to the high-profile examples of leadership from multinational corporations, smaller businesses often provide compelling insights into how the right leadership skills, cultural values and approaches can foster a significant impact. Below are expanded case studies featuring CEOs from smaller businesses who have successfully leveraged customer-centric strategies and strong cultural leadership to drive their companies forward.

CHIEH HUANG - BOXED (US)

Boxed is an e-commerce company that specialises in delivering bulk goods directly to consumers, often dubbed the 'Costco for millennials.' Founded in 2013, the company has gained a reputation for its innovative business model and commitment to customer-centric values (Forbes, 2016).

Leadership and values: CEO Chieh Huang has consistently prioritised employee well-being and ethical leadership. His leadership reflects a strong commitment to Return on Integrity and Return on Inspiration by offering employees benefits, such as paying for weddings and free college tuition for their children – initiatives rooted in Huang's belief that investing in employees' futures results in a more dedicated and motivated workforce (Entrepreneur, 2022).

Impact on the business: Under Huang's leadership, Boxed has maintained low employee turnover and high staff loyalty, thanks to its generous employee benefits and a people-first culture. The company's ethical approach also generated positive media coverage and strong brand sentiment, reinforcing its reputation as a trusted name in the e-commerce space. Huang credits these investments in people as a key factor in Boxed's ability to scale and eventually go public (Entrepreneur, 2022).

Key takeaway: CEOs of smaller businesses can learn from Huang's example by recognising that investing in employee well-being and education is not just an expense, but an investment in long-term company success.

TRISTAN WALKER - WALKER & COMPANY

Walker & Company, founded by Tristan Walker in 2013, creates beauty and personal care products tailored to the unique needs of people of colour. The company's flagship product, Bevel, is a shaving system designed for coarse and curly hair, addressing an often-overlooked segment of the market
(NYLON, 2017).

Leadership and values: Walker's leadership exemplifies Return on Inclusion and Return on Innovation. He recognised a gap in the market where traditional personal care companies failed to serve the diverse needs of their customers. By focusing on inclusivity and product innovation, Walker & Company created a loyal customer base that resonated with the brand's mission.

Impact on the business: The focus on inclusivity and customer-centric innovation positioned Walker & Company as a leader in its niche market. This customer focus attracted the attention of major players, leading to its acquisition by Procter & Gamble in 2018. The acquisition allowed Walker & Company to maintain its cultural identity while expanding its reach, demonstrating that a strong commitment to values can pave the way for growth and success (Marketing Dive, 2018).

Key takeaway: Smaller business leaders can emulate Walker's approach by identifying unmet needs within their target market and focusing on authentic customer engagement and inclusivity.

ARI WEINZWEIG - ZINGERMAN'S COMMUNITY OF BUSINESSES

Zingerman's is a small business based in Ann Arbor, Michigan, known for its deli and expansion into a community of food-related businesses.

Under the leadership of Ari Weinzweig, Zingerman's has become a model for how small businesses can scale while maintaining their core values and culture (Zingerman's Deli, 2025).

Leadership and values: Weinzweig's approach to leadership is rooted in servant leadership, transparency and fostering a supportive work environment. His dedication to Return on Integrity and Return on Inspiration is evident in Zingerman's open-book management system, where employees are educated about the company's financials and involved in decision-making processes. This transparency not only builds trust but also inspires employees to take ownership of their work (ZingTrain, 2023).

Impact on the business: Zingerman's growth from a single deli into a $50 million ecosystem of nine businesses and 650 employees is a testament to its values-driven leadership. Its commitment to open-book management, entrepreneurial thinking and a culture of trust has resulted in high productivity, strong employee retention and a loyal customer base. These principles have not only fuelled long-term growth, but also positioned Zingerman's as a benchmark for sustainable success in the small business landscape (Korn Ferry, 2014).

Key takeaway: Smaller businesses can benefit from adopting open-book management and transparent leadership, as it fosters employee trust and engagement, leading to better customer service and long-term success.

KIM MALEK - SALT & STRAW

Salt & Straw is an artisanal ice cream company founded by Kim Malek in 2011. With a focus on creativity and community involvement, the company has grown from a single ice cream cart in Portland, Oregon, to multiple locations across the United States (Salt & Straw, 2025).

Leadership and values: Malek's leadership emphasises Return on Inspiration and Return on Community Involvement. Inspired by her time at Starbucks, she envisioned the company as a 'third place' that brings people together. With 90% of management promoted internally, Malek fosters a culture of kindness, transparency and growth. Social impact is central – from supporting local producers to making conscious, values-led decisions (QSR Magazine, 2024). Each new store launch includes collaborations with local artisans to create regionally inspired flavours, deepening community ties (Salt & Straw, 2025). This values-driven approach fuels employee engagement and strengthens the brand's community-focused reputation.

Impact on the business: Salt & Straw's business success is rooted in its innovative approach to flavour, deep community engagement and strong internal culture. Since starting as a single pushcart in 2011, the brand has expanded to over 40 locations nationwide, including high-profile sites like Disneyland, while staying true to its identity and values (Guidant Financial, 2024).

Key takeaway: Leaders of small businesses can learn from Malek's example by integrating community-focused practices and employee empowerment into their growth strategies, resulting in stronger customer relationships and a distinct brand identity.

BLAKE MYCOSKIE - TOMS SHOES

TOMS Shoes is a footwear company founded by Blake Mycoskie in 2006, known for its 'One for One' business model. For every pair of shoes purchased, TOMS donates a pair to a child in need. This approach positioned the company as a pioneer in social entrepreneurship and helped define a generation of mission-driven brands (TOMS, 2025).

Leadership and values: Mycoskie's leadership reflects Return on Integrity. His mission-driven approach embedded philanthropy into the DNA of the company, appealing to consumers who wanted their purchases to contribute to a greater cause. By prioritising ethical practices and social impact, Mycoskie established a brand that customers trust and feel good supporting.

Impact on the business: TOMS' unique business model resonated with consumers worldwide, leading to rapid growth and significant brand recognition. The brand expanded into eyewear, coffee and other categories, all tied to a give-back model. Although the company has faced challenges in recent years due to increased competition and the evolving retail landscape, its commitment to social responsibility remains a strong differentiator (Forbes, 2021).

Key takeaway: CEOs of smaller businesses can draw inspiration from Mycoskie's approach by finding meaningful ways to integrate social impact into their business models. This not only builds customer loyalty, but also differentiates the brand in a competitive landscape.

YVON CHOUINARD - PATAGONIA

While Patagonia has become a globally recognised brand, it began as a small business focused on outdoor apparel. Founded by Yvon Chouinard in 1973, Patagonia has remained committed to its environmental roots and sustainability-focused mission (Patagonia, 2025).

Leadership and values: Chouinard's leadership exemplifies Return on Integrity, Return on Image, and Return on Inclusion, pioneered initiatives such as donating 1% of sales to environmental causes, producing goods with recycled or organic materials and encouraging customers to repair rather than replace their gear. His transparency about Patagonia's environmental impact, both good and bad, set a new benchmark for corporate accountability (Patagonia, 2025).

Impact on the business: Patagonia's ethical supply chains, purpose-led marketing and environmental activism have generated exceptional customer loyalty and industry recognition (Forbes, 2025). In 2022, Chouinard and his family transferred ownership of the company to a trust and non-profit to ensure that all future profits are used to protect the planet – cementing Patagonia's role as a model of responsible capitalism (New York Times, 2022).

Key takeaway: Small businesses aiming to grow sustainably can take cues from Chouinard's steadfast dedication to purpose and transparency. Integrating environmental or social missions into the core of a company's operations builds trust, deepens customer loyalty and helps create long-term impact.

These examples demonstrate that impactful leadership isn't limited to the Fortune 500. CEOs of smaller businesses can make significant strides by prioritising integrity, inclusivity and community engagement.

Successful leaders show that cultivating a company culture centred on ethical practices, customer-centric innovation and transparency not only resonates with consumers but also creates a sustainable business model. By leveraging these lessons, smaller business leaders can establish strong foundations that support long-term growth, customer loyalty and resilience in an ever-changing market.

IMPLEMENTING THE NEW ROIS THROUGH LEADERSHIP

To embed the new ROIs into the fabric of an organisation, leaders must go beyond vision-setting. They must actively model the values, adopt leadership frameworks and apply both quick wins and long-term strategies that turn principles into practice. This section explores how CEOs and senior leaders can create environments where culture, behaviour and performance are aligned – consistently and sustainably.

CULTURAL VALUES THAT CEOS MUST CHAMPION

Integrity and transparency

Building trust starts with integrity and transparency. CEOs must set the tone for ethical behaviour and ensure that the organisation's values align with these principles. This alignment is crucial for delivering a Return on Integrity and fostering a culture where employees feel safe and motivated to act in the best interest of the customer.

- **Practical strategy:** Create open channels for communication where employees can report ethical concerns without fear of retaliation. Lead by example by being transparent in decision-making processes and public communications.

Inclusivity and diversity

Promoting inclusivity is vital for reflecting the diversity of the customer base and fostering a variety of perspectives within the company. CEOs who prioritise diversity create an environment where all employees feel valued and empowered to contribute, which is key to achieving a Return on Inclusion.

- **Practical strategy:** Build a culture of inclusion by embedding DEI into day-to-day team rituals, decision-making norms and leadership expectations – not just HR initiatives. Support underrepresented employees through ERGs, mentorship and pathways to leadership.

Innovation and continuous learning

A culture that embraces continuous learning and innovation ensures that a company remains competitive and relevant. CEOs must encourage teams to take calculated risks and view failures as opportunities for growth. This approach supports a Return on Innovation by fostering an environment where creative thinking is rewarded.

- **Practical strategy**: Implement professional development programmes that focus on both technical and soft skills. Promote cross-departmental projects to break silos and stimulate collaborative problem-solving.

LEADERSHIP FRAMEWORKS FOR ROI SUCCESS

Servant leadership

Servant leadership places the needs of employees and customers above those of the organisation's leaders. By prioritising the well-being and development of their teams, CEOs can create a culture where employees feel inspired and supported, resulting in a strong Return on Inspiration.

- **Practical strategy:** Practise servant leadership by conducting regular one-on-ones that focus on personal growth as much as performance. Encourage feedback loops where employees feel safe sharing ideas and concerns, and build a culture of recognition that rewards empathy, collaboration and acts of service.

Transformational leadership

Transformational leadership involves inspiring and motivating teams to exceed expectations by fostering an environment of trust and innovation. This approach encourages employees to align their goals with those of the organisation and contribute beyond their job descriptions.

- **Practical strategy:** Support transformational leadership by clearly communicating a compelling vision that teams can rally behind. Set ambitious, values-aligned goals that stretch capabilities and empower employees with the autonomy to lead initiatives, innovate and take ownership of outcomes.

Quick wins

1. **Host town halls and Q&A sessions**: Foster open communication by holding regular meetings where employees can ask questions and hear directly from leadership.

2. **Launch employee feedback platforms**: Implement tools that allow employees to share feedback on leadership and company practices, showing that their voices matter.

3. **Highlight ethical wins**: Publicly celebrate moments when the company acts with integrity, reinforcing the importance of transparency and trust.

Long-term strategies

1. **Develop leadership training programmes**: Establish training programmes for all leadership levels focused on empathy, communication and strategic thinking.

2. **Create a cross-departmental innovation lab:** Encourage collaboration by setting up a lab where employees from different departments can work on innovative projects.

3. **Commit to diversity and inclusion goals**: Set measurable targets for improving diversity within the company and regularly review progress to ensure accountability.

Key takeaways for CEOs

- **Adopt a holistic leadership style:** CEOs should blend servant and transformational leadership approaches to inspire employees, foster inclusivity and champion customer-centric values.
- **Be data-driven but trust your instincts**: While data is essential for informed decision-making, CEOs must also rely on intuition to make bold, innovative moves that resonate with customers.
- **Lead with empathy and transparency:** Building trust starts with integrity and clear communication. CEOs must model these values to create an organisation that reflects them at every level.
- **Prioritise continuous learning**: Encourage a culture that embraces failure as a learning opportunity and continuously seeks innovation to stay ahead in the market.

Embedding new ways of measuring success isn't a one-off initiative – it's a leadership commitment. By modelling the right values, applying people-first frameworks, and taking intentional action both now and over time, leaders at every level can turn the ROIs from ideas into everyday impact. This is how meaningful change takes root and how modern businesses build cultures that last.

LEADING WITH PURPOSE: TURNING VISION INTO ACTION

The true test of leadership lies not in what's promised, but in what's practised. For CEOs, it's not enough to set a compelling vision – they must bring it to life through the culture they shape, the values they embody and the commitments they honour. In this final section, you will explore how CEOs can translate purpose into impact, aligning leadership with long-term success.

The role of the CEO in driving sustainable success

In a business environment where customer trust, employee engagement and adaptability are paramount, the role of the CEO has never been more critical. More than ever, the success of an organisation hinges on its ability to move beyond traditional financial metrics and embrace a holistic, customer-centric approach that balances profitability with purpose.

The modern CEO is not just a decision-maker; they are a cultural architect, a visionary leader and a catalyst for change. By embodying the skills, cultural values and leadership qualities outlined in this chapter, CEOs can drive their organisations to deliver on the new ROIs, ensuring long-term resilience, adaptability and sustainable success.

Reframing leadership for the future

Traditional leadership models focused on hierarchical decision-making, cost control and operational efficiency are no longer sufficient in a landscape where customer expectations, technological advancements and market disruptions continue to evolve at an unprecedented pace. The modern CEO must lead with purpose, ensuring that their organisation is not only financially viable but also ethically responsible, deeply customer-focused and agile in responding to change.

The shift from short-term shareholder value to long-term stakeholder value means that CEOs must proactively redefine their organisation's measures of success. This requires:

- Embedding customer-centricity at the core of decision-making.
- Fostering a high-performance culture based on trust, inclusion and innovation.
- Ensuring that sustainability and ethical leadership are non-negotiable pillars of business strategy.
- Encouraging a culture of continuous learning and adaptability.

Delivering the new ROIs: a CEO's playbook

To truly drive transformation, CEOs must evaluate their leadership impact across the 11 new ROIs that redefine business success:

1. **Return on Inspiration** – Are you inspiring your employees and customers to engage with your vision?
2. **Return on Integrity** – Is your organisation trusted and respected for its ethical approach?
3. **Return on Inclusion** – Does your leadership foster a diverse and inclusive environment that mirrors the world your customers live in?
4. **Return on Image** – How does your brand's reputation reflect its social and environmental commitments?
5. **Return on Intervention** – Are you removing friction for customers and employees, ensuring swift problem resolution?
6. **Return on Interaction** – Are you engaging with customers across all touchpoints to deliver a seamless experience?
7. **Return on Improvements** – How effectively are you shifting from transactions to building long-term service-driven relationships?
8. **Return on Involvement** – Are you fostering customer and employee advocacy, making them feel truly connected to your brand?
9. **Return on Insight** – How well are you leveraging data and insights to make informed strategic decisions?

10. **Return on Innovation** – Is your organisation evolving, experimenting and adapting fast enough to stay ahead?
11. **Return on Integration** – Are all functions within the business aligned to support a unified vision and seamless execution?

A CEO's commitment to long-term success

The journey requires an unwavering commitment to integrity, inclusivity and innovation, but the payoff is a resilient, customer-centric organisation that not only withstands disruption but thrives in an ever-changing world. By embracing these new ROIs, CEOs can shift from reactive, short-term decision-making to proactive, long-term leadership, ensuring that their organisation remains relevant, competitive and impactful in the years to come. The future belongs to the leaders who dare to redefine success – not just in financial terms, but in the lasting impact they create for their employees, customers and society at large.

Take action: your leadership impact assessment

Bringing the new ROIs to life starts with honest reflection. Use the table below to assess how effectively your organisation is delivering across each of the 11 ROIs. Score each area out of 10, identify strengths and weaknesses and capture one clear improvement you can lead or influence.

Prompts

- Where are you already delivering meaningful impact?
- Where do you need to step up or lead differently?
- Which 1–2 ROIs will you prioritise over the next 90 days?
- How will you hold yourself – and your team – accountable for progress?

ROI Assessment Table

ROI	Score (out of 10)	Strength / Weakness?	Improvement Opportunity
Return on Inspiration			
Return on Integrity			
Return on Inclusion			
Return on Image			
Return on Intervention			
Return on Interaction			
Return on Improvements			
Return on Involvement			
Return on Insight			
Return on Innovation			
Return on Integration			

REFERENCES

Entrepreneur (2022) 'He took a $900 million company public while paying for his workers' college degrees and weddings', Entrepreneur, 4 January. Available at: www.entrepreneur.com/growing-a-business/he-took-a-900-million-company-public-while-paying-for-his/404064 (Accessed: 3 May 2025).

Forbes (2016) 'Costco for millennials: How Chieh Huang built Boxed, a mobile juggernaut with $100M+ in revenue', Forbes, 19 October. Available at: www.forbes.com/sites/forbestreptalks/2016/10/19/costco-for-millennials-how-chieh-huang-built-boxed-a-mobile-juggernaut-with-100m-in-revenue/ (Accessed: 3 May 2025).

Forbes (2021) 'The Rise And Fall Of The Buy-One-Give-One Model At TOMS', Forbes, 28 April. Available at: www.forbes.com/sites/davidhessekiel/2021/04/28/the-rise-and-fall-of-the-buy-one-give-one-model-at-toms (Accessed: 4 May 2025).

Forbes (2025) 'Why Customers Pay More For Brands With Purpose: The Patagonia Model', Forbes, 16 March. Available at: www.forbes.com/sites/shephyken/2025/03/16/why-customers-pay-more-for-brands-with-purpose-the-patagonia-model/ (Accessed: 4 May 2025).

Guidant Financial (2024) 'From 401(k) to Ice Cream Empire: The Rise of Salt & Straw', Guidant Financial Blog, 29 April. Available at: www.guidantfinancial.com/blog/salt-straw/ (Accessed: 3 May 2025).

Korn Ferry (2014) 'Happy People Spark Serious Productivity', Korn Ferry Briefings Magazine, 10 August. Available at: www.kornferry.com/insights/briefings-magazine/issue-20/happy-people-spark-serious-productivity (Accessed: 3 May 2025).

Marketing Dive (2018) 'P&G buys Walker & Company, a disruptor marketer catering to consumers of color', Marketing Dive, 13 December. Available at: www.marketingdive.com/news/pg-purchases-walker-company-a-disruptor-marketer-catering-to-consumers/544213/ (Accessed: 3 May 2025).

New York Times (2022) 'Billionaire No More: Patagonia Founder Gives Away the Company', *New York Times*, 14 September. Available at: www.nytimes.com/2022/09/14/climate/patagonia-climate-philanthropy-chouinard.html (Accessed: 4 May 2025).

NOBL (2020) 'How Satya Nadella led Microsoft through a corporate turnaround'. Available at: www.nobl.io/changemaker/how-satya-nadella-led-microsoft-through-a-corporate-turnaround/ (Accessed: 3 May 2025).

NYLON (2017) 'How Bevel is diversifying the shaving experience', NYLON, 28 February. Available at: www.nylon.com/articles/bevel-razor-product-review (Accessed: 3 May 2025).

Patagonia (2025) 'Company History'. Available at: www.eu.patagonia.com/gb/en/company-history/ (Accessed: 4 May 2025).

QSR Magazine (2024) 'How Kim Malek Built the Ice Cream American Dream', QSR Magazine, 22 April. Available at: www.qsrmagazine.com/growth/how-kim-malek-built-the-ice-cream-american-dream/ (Accessed: 3 May 2025).

Quartr (2024) 'Reed Hastings: The Architect of Netflix's Rise'. Quartr. Available at: www.quartr.com/insights/business-philosophy/reed-hastings-the-architect-of-netflixs-rise (Accessed: 3 May 2025).

Salt & Straw (2025) 'Our Story'. Available at: www.saltandstraw.com/pages/our-story (Accessed: 20 April 2025).

Schultz, H. (2011) *Onward: How Starbucks Fought for Its Life without Losing Its Soul.* New York: Rodale.

TOMS (2025) 'Our Story'. Available at: www.toms.com/our-story (Accessed: 4 May 2025).

Zingerman's Deli (2025) 'The Story of Our Deli'. Available at: www.zingermansdeli.com/about-us/story-of-our-deli/ (Accessed: 4 May 2025).

ZingTrain (2023) 'What is Open Book Management?', ZingTrain Blog. Available at: www.zingtrain.com/blog/what-is-open-book-management/ (Accessed: 3 May 2025).

FINAL WORD
A NEW STANDARD FOR SUCCESS

I n a world where customer expectations evolve by the day, businesses that cling to outdated metrics will struggle to stay relevant. Traditional ROI may have once captured success, but it no longer tells the full story.

The 11 new ROIs introduced in this book offer a new standard – one that reflects what modern success truly looks like: trust, purpose, innovation, inclusion and connection. They invite you to measure more than money. They challenge you to build businesses that prioritise people, planet and long-term impact alongside profit.

Too many organisations still chase quarterly wins at the expense of long-term growth. But the cost of short-termism is high: burnout, disengaged teams, customer churn, reputational risk and missed opportunities for innovation.

This book has shown that:

- An inspired workforce drives creativity, loyalty and performance.
- Trust and transparency build long-term relationships.
- Inclusion isn't a nice-to-have – it's essential for relevance and resilience.
- Insight and innovation are key to keeping pace with constant change.

The businesses that thrive will be those that focus on customer experience, nurture internal culture and make purpose part of their business model – not just their marketing.

Companies that adopt this new model of success will not only outperform their competitors, they'll create stronger relationships with customers, employees and stakeholders, ensuring sustained growth and meaningful impact in an ever-evolving world.

Implementing the 11 ROIs is not just about tracking new metrics. It requires a shift in how you think, operate and lead. It asks you to rethink success from the inside out.

To make the shift:

- **Identify where you're falling short:** Use the assessment tools and reflection prompts to evaluate your organisation's gaps across the 11 ROIs.
- **Set goals that matter:** Define KPIs based on what truly drives sustainable success for your customers, employees and stakeholders.
- **Lead from the top:** Customer-centricity must be embedded at the highest levels of leadership.
- **Break down silos:** Collaboration across teams is essential to delivering the consistency and alignment these ROIs require.
- **Measure, review and refine:** Make ROI reflection part of your business rhythm.

This is not a one-off initiative. It's a leadership commitment.

These 11 ROIs aren't a checklist – they're a mindset.

Adopt them, adapt them and lead with them. You'll stay relevant and you'll become the kind of business the future demands.

ACKNOWLEDGEMENTS

There are several people whom I want to call out for their support during process of writing this book. My wife Laura and my daughters Antonia and Saskia are always supportive of my exploits.

I will always be indebted to my former Executive Assistant, Tiffiny, without whose support, I would never have come close to completing the book in the time allotted. She has provided so much help with sources, editing and with formatting the manuscript. Thank you, Tiff.

Finally, I want to thank my colleagues from The Customer First Group. Both for their support during this process as well as for the support they provide our clients in helping them to continually improve the levels of service they deliver for consumers.

ABOUT MARTIN NEWMAN

Martin Newman is a globally recognised authority on customer-centric business strategies, known for his pioneering, innovative practices that drive customer loyalty and business growth. With over 40 years of experience, Martin has worked extensively with leading international brands, influencing boardrooms and guiding strategic transformations across diverse sectors, including retail, automotive, hospitality and financial services.

His impressive career includes pivotal positions at iconic brands, such as Burberry, Ted Baker, Harrods and Intersport, where he led projects aligning business strategies closely with customer needs and expectations. Martin's holistic understanding of consumer-facing businesses provides him with a unique ability to bridge strategic insights and practical, actionable advice – a rare combination that makes him exceptionally credible to both executives and operational leaders.

Martin's entrepreneurial spirit led him to establish Practicology, a strategic digital consultancy. Martin successfully scaled Practicology into a global firm dedicated to solving omnichannel and digital challenges for retail and consumer brands across the UK, UAE, China, Hong Kong and Australia. Pattern acquired Practicology in 2018 and is a global leader in e-commerce growth intelligence, ranking among the top 10 Amazon sellers worldwide. Martin has since founded The Customer First Group, a consultancy helping brands across sectors to adopt customer-centric cultures and enhance customer experience.

A celebrated author, Martin has written two influential books: *100 Practical Ways to Improve Customer Experience*, a finalist in the 2019 Business Book of the Year Awards, and *The Power of Customer Experience*. His commitment to customer-focused innovation is also evident in his educational initiatives, including the Mini MBA in Customer Centricity, developed with the Oxford College of Professional Education, attracting global brands, such as British Airways, Schuh, Haleon, Sodastream and Hunkemöller. Additionally, Martin's 'MBA in a Day' workshop has been successfully delivered to esteemed and diverse organisations like Toyota, Verisure, the Tate and The Fragrance Shop, highlighting his practical impact on businesses worldwide.

As a globally recognised keynote speaker and respected judge for numerous industry awards – including the World Retail Awards, UK Customer Experience Awards, Drapers Digital Awards, the People In Retail Awards (PIRA), the Ecommerce Awards, the Enterprise Vision Awards (EVAs), and the Great British Entrepreneur Awards – Martin's insights shape the conversation around customer-centric innovation internationally.

Martin also holds positions as non-executive chairman of the Scout Store, chair of the Customer Xperience Alliance and Board Adviser to consumer-focused businesses, including Neve Jewels Group and Clearpay. His advisory roles underscore his commitment to fostering sustainable growth, operational excellence and customer-focused strategies.

Martin Newman is uniquely positioned to author this book because of his unrivalled expertise in developing customer-centric strategies and his consistent advocacy for metrics that genuinely reflect long-term business success. Martin's practical insights into customer engagement, innovative thinking and sustainability have directly informed the 11 new Returns on Investment (ROIs) presented in this book. Martin's ability to distil complex strategic principles into clear, actionable guidance makes him an indispensable resource for leaders, strategists and practitioners seeking to transform their organisations by measuring what truly matters.

Discover more about Martin Newman at www.martinnewman.co.uk
Follow Martin @martinnewmancc 🔗 ✖ 🔵 ⭕ ▶

www.ingramcontent.com/pod-product-compliance
Lightning Source LLC
Chambersburg PA
CBHW030454210326
41597CB00013B/663